BARTLETT'S
UNFAMILIAR
QUOTATIONS

BARTLETT'S
UNFAMILIAR
QUOTATIONS

LEONARD LOUIS LEVINSON

COWLES BOOK COMPANY, INC.

A Subsidiary of Henry Regnery Company

For My Daughter
Robin Sokal

If you believe everything you read, better not read.
Japanese proverb

PREFACE

The last thing one knows when writing a book is what to put first.

Blaise Pascal

Always read the preface of a book. It enables you to survey more completely the book itself. You frequently also discover the character of the author from the preface.

B. W. Procter

Prefaces are like speeches before the curtain; they make even the most self-forgetful performers self-conscious.

Charles Neilson

Proverbs. Few words, right sense, fine image.

Moses ibn Ezra

Patch grief with proverbs.

William Shakespeare

Shakespeare was a dramatist of note
Who lived by writing things to quote.

H. C. Bunner

Now we sit through Shakespeare in order to recognize the quotations.

Orson Welles

There is nothing so absurd but some philosopher has said it.

Cicero

Quotation is the highest compliment you can pay to an author.

Dr. Sam'l Johnson

He who never quotes is never quoted.

Charles Haddon Spurgeon

I quote others only the better to express myself.

Michel de Montaigne

With just enough of learning to misquote.

Lord Byron

Despise not the discourse of the wise, but acquaint thyself with their proverbs.

Ecclesiasticus

All the world loves a proverb.

Henry Fielding

Nothing is so useless as a general maxim.

Thomas Babington, Lord Macaulay

Constant popping off of proverbs will make thee a byword thyself.

Dr. Thomas Fuller

Some for renown, on scraps of learning dote,
And think they grow immortal as they quote.

Edward Young

Quotation: Something that somebody said that seemed to make sense at the time.

LLL

INTRODUCTION

If you find more than a few quotations herein familiar, I congratulate you! You are extremely erudite, wonderfully equipped with a remarkably retentive memory and possess the most discriminating of literary tastes.

However, if a quote seems *very* familiar, look again; it probably has been altered by a letter or a word or two, and that is why it is included. Some quotations may seem a bit familiar because while a fragment or phrase may be well known, the full text is not.

The approximately five thousand quotations in this book have been selected from years of reading and writing. Some of the quotes are so old they are new again; a few are so pompous they are amusing for that reason.

But you will also find much of the accumulated wisdom and wit of such men as Will Shakespeare, George Bernard Shaw, Mark Twain, Josh Billings, Jules Renard, Stanislaw Lec, James Whistler, the Hubbards—Kin and Elbert—the Samuel Butlers (I) and (II), the Wilsons, Woodrow and Earl, and a few quotes from my departed friends, Fred Allen, Frank Scully, and Don Quinn, as well as many by that most prolific author, Anon.

The frequent appearance of Anon in this book is explained by the author's inability to find the true name of the source. The author refuses to acknowledge, and therefore does not credit, any newspaper, magazine, or corporate entity with the creation of thoughts or sayings. It takes a person, and I mourn that he must remain Anon.

Readers are warned not to form the conclusion that all the opinions expressed herein by authors (some taken out of context) are the authors' own beliefs. Many novelists and playwrights, even poets, put into the mouths of characters thoughts and sentiments different, even contrary, from their own. It would be quite wrong, for instance, to ascribe to Shakespeare himself many of the speeches he wrote for his dramatis personae to say.

Shaw is a different story. He was by far the most memorable of all the characters he created, and his many startling, heretical, and contrary utterances, which found their way into the world press, comprise a one-man comedy which could be titled: "Taken Seriously by the World," a joke Shaw enjoyed the better part of his life.

LLL

ABILITY

No one knows what he can't do until he tries.

Anon

ABSENCE

Destroys small passions, and increases great ones.
The wind extinguishes tapers, but kindles fires.

François, Duc de la Rochefoucauld

The most cruel absence is one which can be touched with the hand.

Paul-Jean Toulet

Those who are absent are always wrong to return.

Jules Renard

ABSENT-MINDED

The butcher looked for his knife, when he had it in his mouth.

German proverb

ABUSE

I can understand anyone's allowing himself to be bullied by the living, but not, if he can help it, by the dead.

Samuel Butler (II)

One can only abuse the things which are good.

Montaigne

The older the abuse is, the more it is sacred.

Voltaire

ACCOMPLISHMENT

If you want a thing done, go; if not, send.

Anon

To accomplish great things, we must live as if we were never going to die.

Luc de Clapiers, Marquis de Vauvenargues

You can get almost everything accomplished if you don't care who gets the credit.

Ned Hay

The surest way to get a thing done is to give it to the busiest man you know, and he'll have his secretary do it.

Anon

ACCUSATION

Point not at other's spots with a foul finger.

Proverb

ACKNOWLEDGMENT

Everything I owe, I owe because of my wife.

Anon husband

ACQUAINTANCES

Buy visiting cards for the cat; she knows a lot more cats than we know people.

Barry Pain

ACTING

I am not sure acting is a thing for a grown man.

Steve McQueen

ACTIONS

Actions speak louder than words—but not as often.

LLL

When, against one's will, one is high-pressured into making a hurried decision the best answer is always "No" because "No" is more easily changed to "Yes" than "Yes" is changed to "No."

Charles E. Nielson

ACTORS

Are the opposite of people.

Tom Stoppard

All men are comedians, except perhaps some actors.

Sacha Guitry

That incorrigible peerage against which, along with gypsies and vagabonds, laws once were made lest they cause living to be attractive, fear unthinkable, and death dignified, thereby robbing church and state of their taxes on unhappiness.

John Steinbeck

ADAGES

Two heads are gaudier than one.

LLL

Many a true word is spoken by Jessel.

LLL

ADAM

Adam was but human—this explains it all. He did not want the apple for the apple's sake, he wanted it only because it was forbidden. The mistake was in not forbidding the serpent; then he would have eaten the serpent.

Mark Twain

ADAM AND EVE

It is not true that woman was made from man's rib; she was really made from his funny bone.

Sir James Barrie

God created Adam out of dust and then made Eve to dampen him down.

LLL

ADDLED AXIOMS

A biting dog seldom barks.

LLL

All work and no play makes jack.

Anon

New grooms sleep keen.

LLL

ADMONITION

Trust me, but look to thyself.

Irish proverb

Thou shalt not bare false bosoms against thy neighbor.

LLL

ADULTERY

. . . one of the most frequent causes of adultery: the longing a transparent man feels to become opaque. He suddenly finds himself wrapped in mystery, as if he had bought a new suit. This mystery is most becoming; it conceals the fact that the left shoulder is lower than the right, it nips in the waist, it makes the leg more slender. Oh, it's a marvelous tailor! The unexpected new suit makes you look fifteen years younger.

Jean Dutourd

What men call gallantry, and gods adultery,
Is much more common when the climate's sultry.

Lord Byron

A man does not look in the closet unless he has stood there himself.

LLL

Even a rat likes to go into a different hole once in a while.

Old Bohemian saying

ADULTS

Are obsolete children.

Dr. Suess

ADVANTAGE

One of the advantages of marriage is that you can't do something stupid without hearing about it.

Anon

ADVENTURER

An adventurer is always of low status. If he was of high status, he would be a businessman.

Auguste Detoeuf

ADVERTISING

TV announcer: "We have just received a bulletin about a catastrophe, the like of which has never been known to mankind—but, first, a word from our sponsor."

When a man throws an empty cigaret package from an automobile, he is liable to a fine of $50; when a man throws a billboard across a view, he is liable to be richly rewarded.

Governor Edmund Brown

Advertising has annihilated the power of the most powerful adjectives.

Paul Valéry

Advertising has given American thinking the worst case of mental constipation it has ever experienced.

LLL

If you think advertising doesn't pay, we understand there are twenty-five mountains in Colorado higher than Pike's Peak. Can you name one?

Anon

Don't advertise; tell it to a gossip.

Anon

ADVICE

We all admire the wisdom of people who come to us for advice.

Jack Herbert

In many cases the person who gives another advice hasn't tried it himself and wishes to see it tested to see if it really works.

Anon Englishman

We ask advice but seek corroboration.

LLL

Counsel is to be given by the wise, the remedy by the rich.

British saying

In those days he was wiser than he is now; he used frequently to take my advice.

Winston Churchill

Every fool wants to give advice.

Italian proverb

ADVICE TO DAUGHTERS

Don't love everybody—specialize.

Anon parent

ADVICE FROM SOCRATES

By all means marry; if you get a good wife, you'll become happy; if you get a bad one, you'll become a philosopher.

ADVICE TO MOTHERS

Simply imagine that it's not your child, but someone else's. Everybody knows how to bring up other people's children.

Anon Russian

AFFAIRS

Affairs are not really tiring except when one doesn't have them.

Pierre Veron

AFRICAN ADAGE

Both Lively-Stepper and Habitual-Recliner want food, but Lively-Stepper is the one who gets it.

AFTER-DINNER SPEECHES

A dreadful experience is to ask an innocent question at 8 P.M. following dinner, and get an answer that ties you to an uncomfortable chair until 11:02.

William Feather

AGE

The older you are the more slowly you read a contract.

LLL

You are old when you do more and more for the last time and less and less for the first time.

Dr. Martin Gumpert

If you want to know how old a woman is, ask her sister-in-law.

E. W. Howe

The principal objection to old age is that there's no future in it.

Anon

By the time a man's wise enough to watch his step he's too old to go anywhere.

Earl Wilson

You are getting old when the gleam in your eyes is from the sun hitting your bifocals.

Anon

AGE FORTY-FIVE

Any man worth his salt has by the time he is forty-five accumulated a crown of thorns, and the problem is to learn to wear it over one ear.

Christopher Morley

Never let the foolishness of age be tempted by the cynicism of youth.

LLL

AGING

It's a sign of age if you feel like the day after the night before and you haven't been anywhere.

Anon

I do wish I could tell you my age, but it is impossible. It keeps changing all the time.

Greer Garson

There are people whose watch stops at a certain hour and who remain permanently at that age.

Charles Augustin Sainte-Beuve

The people who will always seem young are those who never reveal their rage.

Anon

One compensation of old age is that it excuses you from picnics.

William Feather

About the best way to grow old is not to be in so much of a hurry about it.

Anon

A student of twenty who has a bad memory is likely to rate a D in his course, but if a man over sixty-five forgets something he may be suspected of senility.

George Soule

It may be true that *life* begins at forty, but everything else starts to wear out, fall out, or spread out.

Beryl Pfizer

Almost the only consolation for growing old is knowing that your friends haven't been standing still.

LLL

One of the delights known to age, and beyond the grasp of youth, is that of Not Going.

J. B. Priestley

A man of forty today has nothing to worry him but falling hair, inability to button the top button, failing vision, shortness of breath, a tendency of the collar to shut off all breathing, trembling of the kidneys to whatever tune the orchestra is playing, and a general sense of giddiness when the matter of rent is brought up. Forty is Life's Golden Age.

Robert Benchley

It is only in going uphill that one realizes how fast one is going downhill.

George Du Maurier at 62

AGITATED ADAGES

I felt bad because I had no shoes until I met a man who had no laces.

LLL

Familiarity breeds attempt.

Anon

7

AGNEW

I always consider it a small badge of honor to be attacked by this impossible demagog. If he ever said anything good about me, I would know I was off the track.

Sen. George McGovern (D-S.D.)

AH, THERE, DR. SPOCK!

We spared the rod and wound up with the beat generation.

L. J. Wolf

AIM

To become what we are capable of becoming is the only end in life.

Robert Louis Stevenson

It is a funny thing—you work all your life toward a certain goal and then somebody moves the posts on you.

Herb Caen

Some people reach the top of the ladder only to find it is leaning against the wrong wall.

Anon

AIR POLLUTION

The haze on the distant hills used to be one of autumn's loveliest attractions, but nowadays the air is so hazy you can't see the haze.

Burton Hillis

Is turning Mother Nature prematurely gray.

Irv Kupcinet

AIR TRAVEL

They may kill you, but they ain't likely to hurt you.

Sachel Paige

ALIMONY

You never realize how short a month is until you pay alimony.

John Barrymore

ALLERGIES

Hay fever is the real Flower Power.

LLL

ALL RIGHT

We shouldn't use the word Alright, but if you write like "all right," then it's perfectly alright.

Anon, Jr.

ALONE

Many people live alone and like it, but most of them live alone and look it.

Gelett Burgess

ALTERATION

Alteration is not always improvement, as the pigeon said when it got out of the net and into the pie.

Charles Spurgeon

ALTRUISM

Is the art of using others with the air of loving them.

Rene Dubreuil

AMATEUR

There are two businesses in the world where amateurs are better than professionals: strategy and prostitution.

General Carl Spaatz

AMBIDEXTROUS

Means being clumsy with both hands.

Gene Hardison

AMBITION

Nothing arouses ambition so much . . . as the trumpet clang of another's fame.

Gracián

I maintain what I have said: If Bonaparte remained an artillery lieutenant, he would still be on the throne.

Henri Monnier

Every scarecrow has a secret ambition to terrorize.

Stanislaus J. Lec

You aim for the palace and get drowned in the sewer.

Mark Twain

AMERICA

Someone has suggested that America's greatest gifts to civilization are three: cornflakes, Kleenex, and credit.

Louis T. Benezet

If Karl Marx were alive today, his problem would be to find parking spaces for the American proletariat rather than break their chains of economic slavery.

G. K. Reddy

American economy is state socialism for the rich.

quoted by "Adam Smith"

AMERICAN CITIES

Writing about most American cities is like writing a life of Chester A. Arthur. It can be done, but why do it?

Clifton Fadiman

AMERICA/ENGLAND

An English motorcar comes knocked-down in a kit so it can be assembled by the owner. The American way is to get the auto in one part and then let the wife, children, and parking-lot attendant gradually take it apart.

Senator Soaper

AMERICANISM

The American system of ours, call it Americanism, call it Capitalism, call it what you like, gives each and every one of us a great opportunity if we only seize it with both hands and make the most of it.

Al Capone

AMERICANS

Americans have a disease which has led them to believe that all they need is their father's money and their mother's charm.

Alexander King

The beauty of America is that the average man always thinks he is above average.

Sam Levenson

AMERICAN WOMEN

The American woman's ambitions are too high. In Europe a woman decides early what type she will be—mother, cook, or siren. Women here want to be all of these and also run Wall Street.

Alistair Cooke

AMOUR

The ability to make love frivolously is the chief characteristic which distinguishes human beings from beasts.

Heywood Broun

ANCESTRY

Because you are an aristocrat, you think you are a great genius. What have you done for all your money? You went to some pains in choosing your parents, that's all.

Pierre de Beaumarchais (The Marriage of Figaro)

ANECDOTAGE

No one ever told a story well standing up, or fasting.

Honoré de Balzac

ANGER

Don't look back in anger, look forward in fury.

LLL

An angry man opens his mouth and shuts his eyes.

Cato

ANIMALS

We can divide animals into people with intelligence and people with talent. The dog and the elephant are people with intelligence; the nightingale and the silkworm, people of talent.

Antoine de Rivarol

Every youngster should be taught to handle animals with the utmost care. For he who pulls a rabbit out of a hat is hailed as a magician, while he who lets the cat out of the bag is denounced as a fool.

Anon

Apes are never more beasts than when they wear men's clothes.

English proverb

Monkeys very sensibly refrain from speech, lest they should be set to earn their livings.

Kenneth Grahame

The great pleasure of a dog is that you may make a fool of yourself with him and not only will he not scold you, but he will make a fool of himself, too.

Samuel Butler (II)

When I play with my cat, who knows but that she regards me more as a plaything than I do her?

Montaigne

Every dog is valiant at his own door.

Anon

Every dog is a lion at home.

Anon

A lean dog gets nothing but fleas.

Spanish proverb

You can't keep a good man down—or an overaffectionate dog.

Anon

The Llama is a wooly sort of fleecy hairy goat
With an indolent expression and an undulating throat.
Like an unsuccessful literary man.

Hilaire Belloc

The mouse that always trusts to one poor hole,
Can never be a mouse of any soul.

Alexander Pope

A mouse does not leave the cathouse with a full belly.

LLL

Feed a pig and you'll have a hog.

British saying

Among the snakes there is a legend that there were a mama and a papa snake in the Garden of Eden and they were corrupted by humans.

LLL

Neither cast ye your pearls before swine, lest they eat them for tapioca.

LLL

ANNOYANCE

It's easy to be an angel when nobody ruffles your feathers.

Anon

ANONYMOUS

After Shakespeare, the world's most prolific writer of quotations was Anon.

ANSWER

It's a good answer which knows when to stop.

Italian proverb

APE

If then the question is put to me, would I rather have a miserable ape for a grandfather or a man highly endowed by nature and possessing great means and influence and yet who employs those faculties and that influence for the mere purpose of introducing ridicule into grave scientific discussion—I unhesitatingly affirm my preference for the ape.

Thomas H. Huxley

APING PEOPLE

We once had a chimp who could sort photographs of apes and human beings into two piles. Apes on one pile, humans on the other. The only trouble was, every time she got to her own picture, she put it on the pile with the human beings.

Dr. Geoffrey H. Bourne, Yerkes Primate Research Center

APPEARANCE

All that glitters isn't gold.
All that doesn't glitter isn't either.

Louis Scutenaire

APPETIZERS

Are little things you keep eating until you lose your appetite.

Richard Armour

APPRECIATION

If you wish to have it good, you must never take anything for granted. . . .

Shirley M. Dever

APPRENTICE

To blow in a flute is not to play it.
It is necessary to move the fingers.

Goethe

ARBITRATION

The go-between wears out a thousand sandals.

Japanese proverb

ARCHAEOLOGY

An archaeologist is a historian with the mind of a policeman—he has to see the corpus delicti before he can believe in the past.

Melvin Maddocks

ARCHITECTURE

The slum was the main contribution of the Victorian Age to architecture.

Robert Furneaux Jordan

ARGUMENT

You have not converted a man because you have silenced him.

Christopher Morley

In any argument the man with the greater intelligence is always wrong, because he did not use his intelligence to avoid the argument in the first place.

Anon

ARISTOCRACY

Send your noble blood to market and see what it will buy.

International proverb

ARMADILLO

What Spain sent against England in 1588.

Anon, Jr.

ARMY

A pentagon is an eight-sided general.

Anon, Jr.

ART

Pop Artist's Credo: Be big as a building, obvious as a billboard, garish as a neon sign.

Reported by Emily Genaur

Art is the Science of Beauty.

James Abbott McNeill Whistler

Anyone can judge of a picture who has not been connoisseured out of existence.

William Blake

The artist must know how far to go too far.

Jean Cocteau

Whatever happens, my audience mustn't know whether I'm spoofing or being serious; and likewise I mustn't know either. I'm in a constant interrogation: when does the deep and philosophically valid Dali begin, and where does the looney and preposterous Dali end?

Salvadore Dali

All my life I've painted pictures so that certain people would drop dead when they looked at them, but I haven't succeeded yet. The worst painting can't hurt you, but a bad driver can kill you, a bad judge can send you to the chair, and a bad politician can ruin an entire country. That is why even a bad painting is sacred.

Man Ray

To say to the painter that Nature is to be taken as she is, is to say to the player that he may sit on the piano.

Whistler

Any fool can paint a picture, but it takes a wise man to be able to sell it.

Samuel Butler (II)

ART/POLITICS

The news that Nikita Khrushchev has taken up painting brings a small glimmer to an otherwise darkish international outlook. It's always better to have dictators ending up as painters than to have painters ending up as dictators.

Alan Coren

ART/SCIENCE

There is no science without fancy, and no art without facts.

Vladimir Nabokov

ARTILLERY

When a gun is fired, if you don't see the smoke before you hear the noise, you're dead.

Anon, Jr.

ASPIRATION

The Shades of Night were falling fast,
As through an Alpine village passed
A youth who bore, 'mid snow and ice,
A banner with the strange device,
"Down With Up!"

After Longfellow

Herodotus claimed that the bitterest sorrow a man can know is to aspire to do much and to achieve nothing. Not so: the bitterest sorrow is to aspire to do much and to do it, and then to discover it was not worth the doing.

Carlyle Marney

ASSES

With all its wonders, Science has found no medicine that cures stupidity.

LLL

ASSOCIATION

Who keeps company with a wolf will learn to howl.

English proverb

ASTRONOMY/ASTROLOGY

Astronomy is to look in the sky and see stars, while astrology is to look up and see lions and virgins and other spooky creatures.

Anon, Jr.

ATHEISM

The least one can ask atheists is to not make their atheism an article of faith.

Aurelien Scholl

ATOMIC AGE

The public is not really concerned over atomic fallout, because so far it has not affected television reception.

Anon

ATTORNEYS

The first thing we do, let's kill all the lawyers.

William Shakespeare

AUTHOR, AUTHOR!

Oh . . . that mine adversary had written a book!

Book of Job

AUTHORS

Like coins, grow dear as they grow old.
It is the rust we value, not the gold.

Alexander Pope

Another damned, thick, square book! Always scribble, scribble, scribble! eh, Mr. Gibbon?

Duke of Gloucester, when another volume of The Decline and Fall of the Roman Empire *appeared*

AUTHORSHIP

Royalties are nice and all that but shaking the beads brings in money quicker.

Gypsy Rose Lee

AUTOGRAPHS

When I see a person's name,
Scratched upon a glass,
I know he had a diamond,
And his father had an ass.

Anon

AUTOMATION

Our great-grandfathers were certainly not horrified by automation. After all, they did provide the ribbed washboard, the crossbuck saw, the spinning wheel, and other labor-saving devices in order to enable great-grandma to do the work of three hired girls.

Anon

AUTOMOBILE

These are difficult days for automobile manufacturers; they're thinking up ways to make their products safer and new names to make them sound more dangerous.

Thomas LaMance

An automobile is a machine with four wheels, a motor, and not quite enough seats, which enables people to get about with great rapidity and ease to places they never bothered going to before and where they'd just as soon not be now, because now that they're there, there is no place to park.

Elinor Goulding Smith

It's not a cheaper car that people want. It's an expensive car that costs less.

Anon buyer

The trouble is that the car of tomorrow is being driven on the highway of yesterday by the driver of today.

Rolfe Arrow

AWAKE-ASLEEP

All men whilst they are awake are in one common world; but each of them, when he is asleep, is in a world of his own.

Plutarch

AWKWARD AGE

A child has reached the awkward age when he begins to ask questions that have answers.

John Carpenter

AXED AXIOMS

Familiarity breeds.

LLL

AXIOM

The narrower the mind, the broader the statement.

Anon

He blows his horn the loudest who is in the greatest fog.

LLL

BABY

A baby is an angel whose wings get smaller as its legs get taller.

Anon

BACHELOR

A bachelor gets tangled up with a lot of women in order to avoid getting tied up to one.

Helen Rowland

When a guy likes to have a ball without the chain, that's a bachelor.

Anon

BACK TO SECAUCUS

At two in the morning the huge, roaring greasy trucks from Jersey rumble into New York and pick up the scraps from the restaurants and delicatessens and haul them over to the pig farms at smelly Secaucus. There they feed the stuff to the pigs, which grow up and are brought to the New York slaughter houses where they are processed into ham and bacon and chops and roasts and sold to the restaurants and delicatessens of New York, where they are fed to the customers. And the resulting scraps are picked up by the trucks. Then, it's back to Secaucus and all over again!

LLL

BAD

The worst is not
So long as we can say "This is the worst."

(King Lear)

BAD LUCK

I'll say this for adversity: people seem to be able to stand it,
and that's more than I can say for prosperity.

Kin Hubbard

BANISHMENT

Is the clemency of tyrants.

André Maurios

BARGAIN

It makes no difference what it is, a woman will buy anything
she thinks a store is losing money on.

Kin Hubbard

BASKETBALL

The basketball season is well underway now. Our favorite basketball conference is the Lutheran league, in which St. Martini recently defeated Mt. Olive.

Anon

BEARDS

An old goat is never the more revered
For his beard

English saying

The brains don't lie in the beard.

Proverb

If the beard were all, a goat might preach.

not by G.B.S.

BEAUTIFUL WOMEN

If you have a great love for beautiful women, then beautiful women will know it and they will be attracted to you. All
women are a little crazy. Cultivate their craziness. . . . They
love a man who encourages them to be crazy.

Roger Vadim

BEAUTY

Beauty will buy no beef.

English saying

The saying that beauty is but skin-deep is but a skin-deep
saying.

Herbert Spencer

Too many people say "beautiful" when they really mean "pretty." To me, a hippopotamus is beautiful. I much prefer them to swans!

Henry Moore

It is not easy to be a pretty woman without causing mischief.

Anatole France

The beautiful woman can destroy surely as the ax.

Japanese proverb

A fair skin often covers a cloudy mind.

LLL

Beauty that don't make a woman vain makes her very beautiful.

Josh Billings

She who is born a beauty is half married.

Don Quinn

Who hath a fair wife, needs more than two eyes.

Proverb

She just missed being a beauty by a nose.

LLL

A soap bubble is the most beautiful thing, and the most exquisite, in nature.

Mark Twain

BEAUTY AND TRUTH

Beauty may be truth and truth beauty, but recall all the beautiful liars you've known.

LLL

BED

Whoever thinks of going to bed before twelve o'clock is a scoundrel.

Samuel Johnson

'Tis very warm weather when one's in bed.

Jonathan Swift

Oh, it's nice to get up in the mornin'
But it's nicer to lie in bed.

Harry Lauder

BED HABITS

Bad habits are like a comfortable bed; easy to get into, but hard to get out of.

Rev. Watson C. Black

BEDFELLOW
Except I be by Silvia in the night,
There is no music in the nightingale.

Shakespeare

BEDLOCK

More belongs to marriage than four bare legs in a bed.

Proverb

BEGGARS

Beggars mounted run their horses to death.

British saying

Better die a beggar than live a beggar.

English proverb

BEGGING

The beggar's work is pure profit.

Japanese proverb

BEHAVIOR

Be plain in dress, and sober in your diet;
In short, my deary! kiss me, and be quiet.

Lady Mary Wortley Montagu

Act like a lamb and the wolves will eat you.

Anon femme

I don't say we all ought to misbehave, but we ought to look as
if we could.

Orson Welles

Blowing out the other fellow's candle won't make yours shine
any brighter.

Anon

BEING

I think, therefore I am—I think.

Professor Wizdumb, by Howard Schneider

BELIEF

Of money, wit, and virtue, believe one-fourth of what you hear.

Proverb

With most men, unbelief in one thing springs from blind belief
in another.

Georg Christoph Lichtenberg

He who believes in nothing still needs a girl to believe in him.

Eugen Rosenstock-Huessy

BENEVOLENCE

Much benevolence of the passive order may be traced to a disinclination to inflict pain upon oneself.

George Meredith

BEQUESTS

There are only two lasting bequests we can give our children. One is roots, the other, wings.

Hodding Carter

BEST THINGS

He who hath good health is young; and he is rich who owes nothing.

Proverb

BEST AND WORST

The best metal is iron, the best vegetable wheat, and the worst animal man.

English proverb

BETRAYAL

We are much harder on people who betray us in small ways than on people who betray others in great ones.

François, Duc de La Rochefoucauld

BETTING

A wager is a fool's argument.

English saying

BEWARE!

Beware of the forepart of a woman, the hind part of a mule, and all sides of a priest.

English proverb

Never Trust the Man who hath reason to suspect that you know he hath injured you.

Henry Fielding

BEYOND BELIEF

Not only should you believe in what you're doing, but you should know what you're doing.

Mason Williams

THE BIBLE

The Bible tells us to love our neighbors, and also to love our enemies; probably because they are generally the same people.

G. K. Chesterton

To prove the Gospels by a miracle is to prove an absurdity by something contrary to nature.

Denis Diderot

Often it does seem such a pity that Noah and his party did not miss the boat.

Mark Twain

A lady from Boston was explaining how she read the *Atlantic Monthly*. She said, "I just skim through it, like the Bible."

Halford E. Luccock

AMBROSE BIERCE

Born in a log cabin, Ambrose Bierce defied Alger's Law and did not become President.

Clifton Fadiman

BIGOTRY

The mind of a bigot is like the pupil of the eye; the more light you pour upon it, the more it will contract.

Oliver Wendell Holmes, Jr.

BILLBOARDS

Five years after enactment, the Highway Beautification Act, which made many road-side billboards illegal, remains paper legislation. Of some 800,000 billboards, only 334 have come down since '65. At that rate, the U.S. will be in the billboard removal business for 11,000 years.

John Deedy

BIOGRAPHY. About chaps.

GEOGRAPHY. About maps.

E. C. Bentley

When you read a biography remember that the truth is never fit for publication.

Shaw

BIRDS

A wild goose never laid a tame egg.

English saying

I like the parrot. It is the only creature gifted with the power of speech that is content to repeat just what it hears without trying to make a good story out of it.

Anon

It will be wonderful when we stop worrying about the hawks and doves and get back to doing something about the starlings.

Bill Vaughan

A bird in the hand is worse than two in the bush.

LLL

A bird in the hand makes a bit of a mess.

Anon birdcatcher

A robin redbreast in a cage
Sets all Heaven in a rage.

William Blake

In and around Boston the only birds to be seen are the Spotted Chevrolet and the Greater and Lesser Buick.

Henry Beston

The bluebird is a bird that carries the sky on his back.

Thoreau

BIRTH

He was not brought by the stork; he was delivered by a man from the Audubon Society, personally.

Fred Allen

Nothing begins, and nothing ends,
That is not paid with moan;
For we are born in other's pain,
And perish in our own.

Francis Thompson

The first breath is the beginning of death.

Proverb

"Never had any mother?"
"What do you mean? Where were you born?"
"Never was born!" persisted Topsy; "never had no father, nor mother, nor nothin'. I was raised by a speculator."

Harriet Beecher Stowe

He that has no fools, knaves, or beggars in his family, was begot by a flash of lightning.

English proverb

BIRTH CONTROL

The best, cheapest oral contraceptive: No!

Anon

BIRTH-DEATH

A man should not be mourned at his death, but at his birth.

Baron de la Brède et de Montesquieu

Everyone is born a king, and most people die in exile.

Wilde

24

BLESSED

Is the man who is too busy to worry in the daytime and too sleepy to worry at night.

Leo Aikman

BLESSING

God defend you from the devil, the eye of a harlot, and the turn of a die.

Spanish proverb

May you live all the days of your life.

Jonathan Swift

BLINDNESS

Love may not be altogether blind. Perhaps there are times when it cannot bear to look.

Anon

BLISS

If ignorance is bliss, why aren't more people happy?

Anon

BLONDES

She was a brunette by birth but a blonde by habit.

Arthur "Bugs" Baer

BLOWING

Puff not against the wind.

Proverb

BOASTING

The advantage of doing one's praising for oneself is that one can lay it on so thick and exactly in the right places.

Samuel Butler (II)

THE BODY

You are not crippled at all unless your mind is in a splint.

Frank Scully

The belly is the coward of the body.

Victor Hugo

The body is but a pair of pincers set over a bellows and a stewpan, and the whole fixed on stilts.

Samuel Butler (II)

Trunks are for storing valuables in, so the human trunk contains such valuables as stomachs, hearts, and a lot of other stuff.

Anon, Jr.

I have finally come to the conclusion that a good reliable set of bowels is worth more to a man than any quantity of brains.

Josh Billings

BODY/SOUL

As for me, I will tell you that I cannot see my soul, that I know and feel only my body, that it is the body that thinks, judges, feels pleasure and pain.

Baron Paul d'Holbach

BOLSHEVISM

Bolshevism is knocking at our gates. We can't afford to let it in. We have got to organize ourselves against it, and put our shoulders together and hold fast. We must keep America whole and safe and unspoiled. We must keep the worker away from red literature and red ruses; we must see that his mind remains healthy.

Al Capone

Christian theology is the grandmother of Bolshevism.

Oswald Spengler

BOOK AND AUTHOR

Novels by women are always "intimate" and "daring." Avant-garde novels are seldom anything but "brilliant." Sports stories customarily are "inside" and "behind the scenes." You can count on a historical novel to be a "magnificent saga." Works on current events must necessarily be "distinguished," "authoritative," "penetrating."

Authors themselves are "best-selling" and "Pulitzer prize winning" (if it happens to be the fact), "distinguished" (if they are more than fifty years old) or "controversial" (if they've had one bad review), in addition, of course to being "daring," "authoritative," and "penetrating." If the author hasn't written a book in the last three years, his new work is "long-awaited."

Charles Peterson

BOOKS

The multitude of books is making us ignorant.

Voltaire

If good books did good, the world would have been converted long ago.

George Moore

It was a book to kill time for those who liked it better dead.

Rose Macaulay

Books are often wiser than their readers.

Russian proverb

No furniture is so charming as books, even if you never open
them or read a single word.

Sydney Smith

Some men borrow books; some men steal books; and others beg
presentation copies from the author.

James Roche

BOOK BORROWERS

I am known as Dr. Jekyll, but I have a darker side,
As the kleptomaniac, bibliomaniac, book-purloining Hyde.
My better self, as Jekyll, is professionally chaste—
You'd never think, to look at me, that I was double-faced;
But when I get the urge to handle other people's books
The fingers of the surgeon change to predatory hooks!
As the kindly Dr. Jekyll I am often asked to pick
A volume that I fancy from the bookshelves of the sick;
But once within my bookcase, it is fated to reside
As a permanent addition to the library of Hyde.
It isn't that I can't afford to buy the books I read,
As the wealthy Dr. Jekyll I can purchase all I need;
But I gaze at my collection—and the devil's half of me
Whispers . . . "Such a lot of literature—and all acquired free!"

P. Nicholson

THE BOONDOCKS

In the provinces, rain is a diversion.

Edmond and Jules de Goncourt

THE BORE

The bore is the same eating dates under the cedars of Lebanon
as over baked beans in Boston.

Oliver Wendell Holmes

Some people are so boring that they make you waste an entire
day in five minutes.

Jules Renard

He has returned from Italy a greater bore than ever; now he
bores on architecture, painting, statuary, and music.

Sydney Smith

If you are a bore, strive to be a rascal also so that you may not
discredit virtue.

Shaw

BOREDOM

Art is long and time is fleeting
Except when you're at a PTA meeting.

LLL

Only the finest and most active animals are capable of boredom. A subject for a great poet—God's boredom on the seventh day of creation.

Nietzsche

The best way to be boring is to leave nothing out.

Voltaire

We often forgive those who bore us, but never those whom we bore.

La Rochefoucauld

BORROWING

A moneylender serves you in the present tense, lends you in the conditional mood, keeps you in the subjunctive, and ruins you in the future.

Joseph Addison

The man who won't loan money isn't going to have many friends—or need them.

Wilson Mizner

THE BOSS

One eye of the master sees more than four of the servants.

Proverb

BOTANY

If you eat a toadstool and don't die, it's a mushroom.

Anon, Jr.

BOY

One of the best things in the world is to be a boy; it requires no experience, but needs some practice to be a good one.

Charles Warner

BOYHOOD

There comes a time in every rightly constructed boy's life when he has a raging desire to go somewhere and dig for hidden treasure.

Mark Twain

BOYS-GIRLS

Nature makes boys and girls lovely to look upon so they can be tolerated until they acquire some sense.

William Lyon Phelps

BRAGGART

A boaster is a man who tries to push himself ahead by patting himself on the back.

LLL

BRAIN

Not only the greatest computer ever devised, but the only one produced by unskilled labor.

Bob Considine

BRAINS

One great mistake made by intelligent persons is to refuse to believe that people are as stupid as they are.

Marquise de Tencin

BRAKES

There are two kinds of brakes: lucky and unlucky ones. I'm not sure about the difference but my daddy has one kind and my mother has the other.

Anon, Jr.

BRANDY

A mixture of brandy and water spoils two good things.

Charles Lamb

BRAVE NEW WORLD

With satellites and rockets hurled
About us willy-nilly,
The trouble with our Brave New World
Is that it scares us silly!

George Starbuck Galbraith

BRAVERY

Only the brave dare ask the fare.

Mrs. J. Hobday

Some have been thought brave because they were afraid to run away.

Russian proverb

BREAD

When man lives by bread alone, he lives alone.

LLL

Today man doth not live by bread at all.

LLL

If you can't get half a loaf, take a whole one—a whole loaf is better than no bread.

Josh Billings

BREATHING

The brain (usually located in the head) does not tell us to breathe. What tells us is the Instinct, which nobody knows where it is located.

Anon, Jr.

BRIBERY

A silver key can open an iron lock.

English saying

Bribes will enter without knocking.

British proverb

A greased mouth cannot say no.

Italian proverb

BRIDEGROOM

An improvident husband is one who gets married without finding a job for his wife.

Mrs. Meade T. Spicer, Jr.

BRIDGE

Bridge, because of its tendency to encourage prolonged smoking and its deadly immobility, is probably the most dangerous game played in England now.

English doctor

BRIEF GLORY

Laurel is green for a season, and love is sweet for a day;
But love grows bitter with treason, and laurel outlives not May.

Algernon Charles Swinburne

THE BRITISH ARISTOCRATIC LOOK

Is either that of an elegant and etiolated horse or of a beery, red-faced workman.

Patrick O'Donovan

BROCCOLI

Is something that's difficult to say anything nice about except that it has no bones.

Johnny Martin

BULLFIGHTS

Every fifth bull is suffering with a nervous disorder, and every fifteenth is completely wrecked. The toreros are in even worse condition.

Dr. Carlos Mendoza

BURDEN

The least boy always carries the greatest fiddle.

Proverb

BUREAUCRACY

The rule of no one has become the modern form of despotism.

Mary McCarthy

BUSINESS

It's a tough world for the American businessman. Every time he comes up with something new the Russians invent it a week later and the Japanese make it cheaper.

Anon

The notion that a business is clothed with a public interest and has been devoted to the public use is little more than a fiction intended to beautify what is disagreeable to the sufferers.

Justice Oliver Wendell Holmes, 1927

The economy may suffer if auto sales drop—but that's the American way; we have to buy more cars than we need or we'll never be able to afford them.

Jack Wilson

Management consultants are people who borrow your watch to tell you what time it is and then walk off with it.

Robert Townsend

A board of directors is supposed to be a tree full of owls— hooting when management heads into the wrong part of the forest. I am still unpersuaded they even know where the forest is.

Robert Townsend

Advertising is a valuable economic factor because it is the cheapest way of selling goods, especially if the goods are worthless.

Sinclair Lewis

They say if you build a better mousetrap than your neighbor, people are going to come running. They are like hell. It's the marketing that makes the difference.

Ed Johnson

Everyone lives by selling something.

Robert Louis Stevenson

He buys honey dear who has to lick it off bees.

LLL

Last week is the time you should have either bought or sold, depending on which you didn't do.

LLL

Dispute the price but don't dispute the weight; you *both* know that is false.

LLL

Don't steal; thou'll never thus compete successfully in business. Cheat.

Ambrose Bierce

A consumer is a shopper who is sore about something.

Harold Coffin

For the merchant, even honesty is a financial speculation.

Charles Baudelaire

Whatever is not nailed down is mine.
Whatever I can pry loose is not nailed down.

Ascribed to Collis P. Huntington

Do other men, for they would do you; that's the true business precept.

Charles Dickens

The nature of business is swindling.

August Bebel

A man is known by the company he merges.

LLL

BUSINESSMEN

A businessman is a hybrid of a dancer and a calculator.

Paul Valery

BUSINESS SCHOOLS

The business schools in the United States universities, set up less than a century ago, have been preparing well-trained clerks.

Peter F. Drucker

SAMUEL BUTLER (I)

1612–80, British poet

SAMUEL BUTLER (II)

1835–1902, British writer

American College Dictionary

BUTTONS

Attend Church Now and Avoid the Easter Rush.
Howard Johnson Serves Pheasant Under Plastic.
My Button Loves Your Button.
It's Bad Luck To Be Superstitous.
Fite Iliterracy.
Sex Trainee

32

BUTTS

Women's rear ends just weren't made for pants.

Coco Chanel

BUYING FOOD

No butcher ever sold my mother a piece of meat without holding it up high and twisting it so she could see how fat it was. You take the meat as it comes today, wrapped in plastic and half-hidden by cardboard trays out of those refrigerated boxes in the supermarket. If babies came in plastic the way our food does, the world would be filled with waifs.

Harry Golden

BUYING AND SELLING

To sell something, tell a woman it's a bargain; tell a man it's deductible.

Earl Wilson

Isn't it frightening how soon later comes, after you buy now?

Quoted by Earl Wilson

If the customers don't want to come, you can't keep them from it.

Wolfe Kaufman

BYGONES

It used to be a good hotel, but that proves nothing—I used to be a good boy.

Mark Twain

CALCULATED RISK

Politicalese for "We have every hope and assurance that the plan will be successful, but if it doesn't work we knew all the time it wouldn't and said so."

James Thurber

CALIFORNIA POLITICAL EXTREMES

We have such a lush climate that both fruits and nuts flourish.

Jesse Unruh

33

CALMNESS

Charlotte, having seen his body,
Borne before her on a shutter,
Like a well-conducted person
Went on cutting bread and butter.

William Makepeace Thackeray

If you can keep your head while all about you are losing theirs,
you'll be the tallest drunk in the saloon.

Earl Wilson

CALUMNY

Vilify! Vilify! Some of it will always stick.

Beaumarchais

CAMPUS DEMONSTRATIONS

The reason that college students are doing so much demonstrating is that there is no one in class to teach them any more, and the students have nothing else to do.

Many professors are either writing a book, guest lecturing at another university, or taking a year off to write a report for the White House. Therefore, the professor has turned over his course to a graduate assistant who is working on his Ph.D., traveling on a Fulbright Scholarship, or picketing somewhere. So he has, in turn, turned the class over to one of the brighter students who is never there because he works on the college newspaper, or is a member of the Student Senate, or is a delegate to his national fraternity.

When the students arrive at class there is no one at the front of the room, so usually a Socialist student takes over the class and tells the students that it's about time they revolted against the System. The students pour out on the campus, heading for the administration building to protest to the chancellor of the university, who, unfortunately, is away trying to raise money for a new business administration building. The vice-chancellor, of course, is at the state capitol, testifying on new education bills, and the dean of men is at a convention in Phoenix. The dean of women is addressing a garden club in the next state, and the only one left in the administration building is the chief of campus police who isn't quite sure what the students are yelling about.

He arrests the ringleaders of the group—that's those who are standing in the front—and that plays right into the students' hands because now, with the arrests, they have something to demonstrate about.

In the meantime, the chancellor flies home to see if he can settle the matter. The students present him with a petition demanding the release of the arrested demonstrators. The chancellor is about to do this when the board of regents holds an emergency meeting and votes to back the chancellor who is "meting out punishment to the ringleaders." The faculty, which is made up of visiting professors from other schools, votes to support the students, and the chancellor finds himself in an impossible position. He therefore resigns, and accepts a grant from the Ford Foundation to make a study of higher education.

By this time, the demonstration starts petering out and the students begin wandering back to class, hoping there will be somebody there to teach them something. But even that Socialist student who started the demonstration is not there. He's been booked on a lecture tour to talk about free speech at other universities. So everyone decides to go to Washington and picket the White House over its policy on Vietnam.

Anon professor

CANCER

Cigarets are killers that travel in packs.

Mary S. Ott

CANDOR

I think it good plain English, without fraud,
To call a spade a spade, a bawd a bawd.
John Taylor ("A Kicksey Winsey")

CANNIBAL

A cannibal is a man who loves his neighbor with sauce.
Jean Rigaux

An assassin who has an excuse.
Pierre Valdagne

CAPITAL

Capital is dead labor, that, vampire-like, only lives by sucking living labor.
Karl Marx, 1867

Call it what you will, incentives are what get people to work harder.
Nikita S. Khrushchev, 1960

CAPITALISM/SOCIALISM

The inherent vice of capitalism is the unequal sharing of blessings; the inherent vice of socialism is the equal sharing of miseries.
Winston Churchill

35

THE CAPITOL

Washington, that grand old benevolent National Asylum for the Helpless.

Mark Twain

CARE-LESS

Let the world slide, let the world go:
A fig for care, and a fig for woe!
If I can't pay, why, I can owe,
And death makes equal the high and low.

John Heywood

CARES

Many of our cares are but a morbid way of looking at our privileges.

Sir Walter Scott

THOMAS CARLYLE

Carlyle finally compressed his Gospel of Silence into thirty handsome octavos.

John Morley

CARRIAGE

Sometimes a proud bearing is only the result of a stiff neck.

Eberhard Seybold

CARVING

Carving should not be made a matter of brute force. Never wrestle with any dish whatsoever; in other words, keep your head and if you find yourself becoming excited, stop and count to a hundred.

Sir James Barrie

CASTANETS

Are woods that dance.

Matteo

CATS

A harmless necessary cat....

Shakespeare

I cannot honestly report that I have ever seen a feline matron of this class (alley) washing her face when in an interesting condition.

Dickens

CAUTION

If thou canst not see the bottom, wade not.

Proverb

Keep no more cats than will catch mice.

Proverb

Put not your foot in it.

Proverb

CELEBRITY

How dreary to be somebody!
How public, like a frog
To tell your name the livelong day
To an admiring bog!

Emily Dickinson

Fame is a colored patch on a ragged garment.

Aleksander Pushkin

There is . . . a new sort of fame in our day that has never quite been known before. It is a fame seemingly invented out of whole cloth, based on nothing and needing only a press agent to keep it alive. This new species of fame does not wait for a man to win a race or a worldly prize before riveting its neon light on his head.

People in our day become famous who are no more than advertisements, and they advertise not genius but existence.

They are famous for stopping in hotels, for holding hands in public, for speaking to each other, for having babies, for getting invited to parties. This is true not only of movie stars but of statesmen and mountain climbers. . . .

A depersonalized citizenry avid for identity has invented this new type of fame. The lonely city dwellers, whose human faces are lost in the shuffle of world problems and mechanized existence, elect representatives to live for them.

Ben Hecht

CELLS

The way to remember a body cell from a prison cell is that they are in people instead of people in them.

Anon, Jr.

CENSORSHIP

Damn all expurgated books; the dirtiest book of all is the expurgated book.

Walt Whitman

Censorship ends in logical completeness when nobody is allowed to read any books except the books nobody can read.

Shaw

And art made tongue-tied by authority.

Shakespeare

It seems to me we were all better off when the Postal Department used to deliver the mail and left it to a Higher Authority to deliver us from evil.

Herbert L. Block

CENTURIES

The eighteenth century was a swindler century.

Thomas Carlyle

CEREMONY

Don't take a gilded sword to cut a radish.

Japanese proverb

CHANGING TIMES

The old-fashioned wife darned her husband's socks. The modern one socks her darn husband.

Anon

CHANGE

If times are changing so fast, how come we're still sitting around watching the same movies we saw twenty years ago?

Frank Freeman

CHARACTER

Is itching but not scratching.

Don Quinn

CHARITY

Charity creates a multitude of sins.

Wilde

God cheereth a loving giver.

LLL

CHARM

Charm of manner is a sex attribute which has become a habit.

Elbert Hubbard

All charming people are spoiled; it is the secret of their charm.

Wilde

If you have charm, you don't need to have anything else; and if you don't have it, it doesn't matter what else you have.

Sir James Barrie

—Except money.

LLL

CHASTITY

Of all sexual aberrations, perhaps the most peculiar is chastity.

Remy de Gourmont

CHEATING

If a man is worth doing at all, he is worth doing well.

LLL

CHEERFULNESS

'Tis easy enough to be pleasant,
When life flows by with a whistle,
But the man worth while
Is the man with a smile,
When he sits down on a thistle.

LLL

CHEMISTRY

In making water, it takes everything from H to O.

Anon, Jr.

Another name for magnesium silicate is talc. We call it talc because who would want to put magnesium silicate on a little baby?

Anon, Jr.

CHEQUES

We regret we are unable to accept cheques due to frequent disappointments.

Tiddy Dol's Eating House, London

CHICKEN

A rooster who lays eggs.

Anon, Jr.

CHILDREN

If children grew up according to early indications, we should have nothing but geniuses.

Goethe

We are all geniuses up to the age of ten.

Aldous Huxley

There are only two things a child will share willingly—communicable diseases and his mother's age.

Dr. Benjamin Spock

They ignore you if you're right, but they will blame you if you're wrong.
They despise you if you're weak, but they will hate you if you're strong.
Their logic is remorseless, but they don't know what you mean.
They're the enemies of order, but dependent on routine.
They will jeer at you, embarrass you, impoverish and flout you,
And for all you know they may grow up and write a book about you.

Barbara Young

Children and watches must not be constantly wound up—you must let them run.

Jean Paul

Little children should be serene and not scared.

R. I. Kimmons

Out of the mouths of babes come things you wouldn't want your neighbors to hear.

Mrs. H. Meade

Children love to learn, but hate to be taught.

Anon

Bear in mind that children of all ages have one thing in common—they close their ears to advice and open their eyes to example.

Anon parent

Babies do not want to hear about babies; they like to be told of giants and castles.

Samuel Johnson

All children wear the sign: "I want to be important NOW." Many of our juvenile delinquency problems arise because nobody reads the sign.

Dan Pursuit

Some of our modern children are so precocious, the birds and bees should study them.

Chester L. Marks

The owl thinks all her young ones beauties.

Spanish proverb

Many parents fear they will lose their children's love by crossing them. But only by helping children curb their impulses, and by guiding them to better use of their energies, can parents gain that love. Parents hear so much criticism of parents that they are afraid of frustrating a child's growing independence of thought, afraid to start a wearing argument, afraid of open rebellion. But parents and children are happiest and most secure when parents are in firm control.

Sidonie Matsner Gruenberg with Llewellyn Miller

The behavior of some children suggests that their parents embarked on the sea of matrimony without a paddle.

Anon

The parents of another era who taught the child to swim by tossing him in the water is succeeded by the kind who gives him a car to teach him to drive.

Senator Soaper

A child is being properly educated only when he is learning to become independent of his parents.

Adm. H. G. Rickover

I think, at a child's birth, if a mother could ask a fairy godmother to endow it with the most useful gift, that gift would be curiosity.

Eleanor Roosevelt

Parents spend the first part of a child's life getting him to walk and talk, and the rest of his childhood getting him to sit down and shut up.

Anon

If you want children to improve, let them overhear the nice things you say about them to others.

Dr. Haim Ginott

We like little children because they tear out as soon as they get what they want.

Kin Hubbard

Today's kid is in a hot house, hot school, hot school bus. His parents are afraid he'll have a concussion if he's hit with a snowflake.

Bonnie Prudden

The best time for parents to put the children to bed is when they still have the strength.

Homer Phillips

A man finds out what is meant by a spitting image when he tries to feed cereal to his infant.

Imogene Fey

Oh, for an hour of Herod!

Anthony Hope, upon emerging from a performance of Peter Pan

There are no children we love more passionately than those born of our own minds, those of whom we are both father and mother.

Sum-up of Montaigne by Guel de Balzac

CHILDREN/PARENTS

One of the most unmistakable effects of a child's presence in the household is that the worthy parents turn into complete idiots. Without the child, they might have been mere imbeciles.

George Courteline

CHOICE

I had rather have a fool to make me merry than experience to make me sad.

Shakespeare

When you have to make a choice and don't make it, that is in itself a choice.

William James

You don't want me as a dream?—Then you'll have me as a nightmare!

Tristan Corbière

One must choose in life between boredom and suffering.

Mme. de Staël

Every mind has its choice between truth and repose.

LLL

Better the arrow pierce your breast than your back.

Japanese proverb

Better still—duck.

LLL

CHOOSING A MATE

Only choose in marriage a woman whom you would choose as a friend if she were a man.

Joseph Joubert

CHRISTIANS/PAGANS

Christians are no better than pagans, but they blame themselves more.
They do almost as much evil, but they do it with a bad conscience.
All that is gained is a little more squeamishness.

Henri Frédéric Amiel

CHRISTMAS

I'll be spending a typical American Christmas. My tree is from Canada, the ornaments from Hong Kong. The lights come from Japan—and the idea from Bethlehem!

Robert Orben

CHRISTMAS SHOPPING

No. 1 item on the U.S. Government Printing Office "Holiday Gift List" during one Christmas season was "Poisonous Snakes of the World."

LLL

42

CHURCH

Empty front pews in the average church indicate that the congregation is afraid of what it may hear, and desires to be as close as possible to a convenient exit.

Douglas Meador

A sparrow fluttering about the church is an antagonist which the most profound theologian in Europe is wholly unable to overcome.

Sydney Smith

The observances of the church concerning feasts and fasts are tolerably well kept since the rich keep the feasts and the poor the fasts.

Sydney Smith

There stood the yellowed spire
Against the dark sky,
The moon over it.
Dotting the i.

Alfred de Musset

A spire whose "silent finger points to heaven."

William Wordsworth

While I cannot be regarded as a pillar, I must be regarded as a buttress of the church, because I support it from the outside.

Lord Melbourne

Who builds a church to God, and not to fame,
Will never mark the marble with his name.

Alexander Pope

The pursuit of happiness belongs to us,
but we must climb around or over the church to get it.

Heywood Broun

CHURCH BELLS

There is no family in America without a clock, and consequently there is no fair pretext for the usual Sunday medley of dreadful sound that issues from our steeples.

Mark Twain

CHURCH COLLECTION

With one hand he put
A penny in the urn of poverty,
And with the other took a shilling out.

Robert Pollok

CHURCHYARD

Nowhere probably is there more true feeling, and nowhere worse taste, than in a churchyard.

Benjamin Jowett

CIRCUMSTANCES

Circumstances alter faces.

Carolyn Wells

CIRCUS

Clowns are pegs to hang circuses on.

P. T. Barnum

CITIES

Too many people try to build buildings for all eternity. We should design structures—perhaps whole cities—to be written off more quickly. Since housing needs change from generation to generation, we ought to plan a disposable city rather than attempt to make our cities monuments.

J. Marshall Miller

A great city, a great loneliness.

Unknown Latin author

One New York cabbie, or two California realtors, or three Philadelphia lawyers are a match for the devil.

LLL

CITY/COUNTRY

A twofold national problem is how to preserve the wilderness in the country and get rid of the jungle in the cities.

Bill Vaughan

CITY HALL

Due to the large quantity of business transacted by the city council, we most respectfully request that anyone wishing to insult the council please limit himself to 15 minutes or to 15 insults, whichever is shorter.

Sign in office of Mayor Travis LaRue, Austin, Texas

CITY LIFE

Cities degrade us by magnifying trifles;
Life is dragged down to a fracas of pitiful cares and disasters.

Ralph Waldo Emerson

Life in the modern city has become a symbol of the fact that man can become adapted to starless skies, treeless avenues, shapeless buildings, tasteless bread, joyless celebrations.

Rene Dubos

CIVIL WAR

A conflict which cost more than ten billion dollars. For less than half, the freedom of all the four million slaves could have been purchased.

Charles and Mary Beard

CIVILITY

Civility costs nothing, but few sell it at that price.

LLL

CIVILIZATION

In deploring the state of the world, perhaps we are expecting too much of the human race too soon. On dark days, it is worth remembering that the word "civilization" itself was coined by a Frenchman only two hundred years ago.

Sydney H. Harris

Heaps of agonizing human maggots, struggling with one another for scraps of food.

John Ruskin

I know I am among civilized men because they are fighting so savagely.

Voltaire

Is a kind of rock-climbing experience; take three steps up and drop down two.

Lord Clark of Saltwood

Civilization is a movement and not a condition, a voyage and not a harbor.

Arnold Toynbee

CLARITY

Everybody calls "clear" those ideas which have the same degree of confusion as his own.

Marcel Proust

CLASSIFIED AD

Pink Diamond, about ¼ K. $150. Microscope, $30.

Sacramento Bee

CLASSIC/ROMANTIC

To understand oneself is the classic form of consolation; to elude oneself is the romantic.

George Santayana

CLASS REUNION

A class reunion is the same old faces with more new teeth.

Anon

CLEANLINESS

Cleanliness is next to the gas-station.

LLL

A white glove often conceals a dirty hand.

Italian saying

45

CLERGYMEN

Some ministers would make good martyrs; they are so dry they would burn well.

Charles Spurgeon

CLEVERNESS

The Athenians do not mind a man being clever, as long as he keeps it to himself.

Plato

CLIMBING

The higher the ape goes, the more he shows his tail.

Proverb

CLOTHES

The woman who can spot at fifty paces the slightest inconsistency in a husband's explanation of why he was late getting home, who can recall with computer accuracy what he said to that blonde at a party four years ago—that same woman seems to become oblivious to the hypocritical about-face of designers who blithely abandon, even denounce, the very fashions they cheered but a short time before.

Norman Lobsenz

It is an interesting question how far men would retain their relative rank if they were divested of their clothes.

Thoreau

The tulip and the butterfly
Appear in gayer coats than I:
Let me be dressed fine as I will,
Flies, worms, and flowers exceed me still.

Isaac Watts

Nowadays you can't tell whether a girl is wearing a high miniskirt or a low lobster bib.

Anon

One good thing about having one suit of clothes—you've always got your pencil.

Kin Hubbard

COCKTAILS

For a Cannibal Martini, take ⅓ vermouth, ⅔ gin, and into this drop a small girl named Olive.

Fred Allen

COFFEE

Black as the devil,
Hot as hell,

Pure as an angel,
Sweet as love.

Talleyrand

COLD CURES

Whiskey is the most popular of all the remedies that won't cure a cold.

Jerry Vale

COLLEGE

Two college presidents were comparing experiences. "When I retire," declared one, "I would like to be superintendent of an orphan asylum. Then I wouldn't get letters from parents."

"That's not a bad ambition," replied the other, "but when I retire I want to be a warden of a penitentiary—the alumni never willingly come back to visit."

Anon

Words addressed by Indiana University to the parents of freshmen-to-be: "This is not a remedial institution to rectify parental failure. We can't instill character where you haven't; we can't insure self-discipline in one year if you have indulged your child for eighteen; we can't inject a desire for learning if you, by preference and example, have allowed your child to develop intellectual immunity."

I can remember when the academic life was a meadow of mediation in an island of tranquility. Now the president and faculty get combat pay.

Hubert Humphrey

A place where we pass from adolescence to adultery.

Professor R. Barry

I find that the three major administrative problems on a campus are sex for the students, athletics for the alumni, and parking for the faculty.

Clark Kerr

COLORS

Onionskin pink n: a light brown that is stronger and slightly redder and darker than alesan, stronger and slightly yellower and darker than blush, lighter, stronger, and slightly redder than French beige; and redder, stronger, and slightly lighter than cork.

Webster's Third New International Dictionary

COLUMBUS

Made hope reasonable.

Francis Bacon

COMFORT

A good cigar is as great a comfort to a man as a good cry is to a woman.

Bulwer-Lytton

Bring not a bagpipe to a man in trouble.

English proverb

COMMAS AND PERIODS

Commas are used when you have to take a breath, and periods are used when you want to stop and think.

Anon, Jr.

COMMENTATORS

Oh! rather give me commentators plain,
Who with no deep researches vex the brain;
Who from the dark and doubtful love to run
And hold their glimmering tapers to the sun.

George Crabbe (1754–1832)

COMMERCE

Who buys had need of two eyes,
But one's enough to sell the stuff.

Proverb

Highways and streets have not all the thieves; shops have ten for one.

English proverb

Double-dealing is when you buy something wholesale and sell it retail.

Anon, Jr.

Checks are bouncing higher than ever.

Raymond Schuessler

COMMON SENSE

It is a thousand times better to have common sense without education than to have education without common sense.

Robert G. Ingersoll

The crown of all faculties is common sense. It is not enough to do the right thing, it must be done at the right time, and place. Talent knows what to do; tact knows when and how to do it.

William Matthews

COMMUNICATIONS

Newspaper reading is an activity that leads to gradual loss of memory, since most people read the newspapers with the subconscious wish of trying to forget as fast as possible all they read.

S. G. Warburg

COMMUNICATION TREND

People who travel in foreign countries encounter many difficulties with strange languages. One traveler discovered that by learning how to say "thank you" in the languages of the countries in which he traveled he was able to avoid considerable trouble. These two words were a passport to the hearts of all foreigners. In one season he learned to say "thank you" in seventeen languages.

Anon

COMPETENCE

Do it well, that thou may'st not do it twice.

English proverb

COMPANY

Hearts that are delicate and kind and tongues that are neither —these make the finest company in the world.

L. P. Smith

I love good creditable acquaintance;
I love to be the worst of the company.

Swift

I live in the crowd of jollity, not so much to enjoy company as to shun myself.

Samuel Johnson

Consolation, for the condemned, is to be one of many.

Italian proverb

Better be quarreling than lonesome.

Irish proverb

A crowd is not company, and faces are but a gallery of pictures, and talk but a tinkling cymbal, where there is no love.

Bacon

Better to be alone than in no company.

LLL

COMPARISON

'Tis comparison that makes men happy or miserable.

Swiss proverb

Hope is as cheap as despair.

Jewish proverb

Better late than never
Better never late.

LLL

As cauliflower to cabbage, so is repartee to back talk.

Anon

COMPARISON/DEGREES

Man, woman, and devil, are the three degrees of comparison.

Proverb

COMPENSATION

Make a virtue of necessity.

Proverb

COMPETENCE

He's not the best carpenter who makes the most chips.

Proverb

COMPLACENCY

Is pleasure accompanied by the idea of oneself as cause.

Baruch Spinoza

COMPLEX

He that has a great nose thinks everybody is speaking of it.

English proverb

COMPLIMENTS

When I walk with you I feel as if I had a flower in my buttonhole.

Thackeray

Both of us are close to Heaven, Madame;
You are beautiful, and I am old.

Victor Hugo

I can live for two months on a good compliment.

Mark Twain

Some folks pay a compliment like they went down in their pocket for it.

Kin Hubbard

COMPOSURE

We were saying, yesterday—

Luis de Leon, on resuming a lecture at Salamanca University after five years' imprisonment

COMPUTER

To err is human; to really foul things up requires a computer.

Bill Vaughan

Use of the computer in planning marriages is nothing new.
Many a young man has been hooked by a calculating mother.

Clyde Moore

One good reason why computers can do more work than people
is that they never have to stop to answer the telephone.

Ollie M. James

CON MAN

He shakes your hand to pump money out of your pocket.

Anon

CONCEALMENT

We use ideas merely to justify our evil, and speech merely to
conceal our ideas.

Voltaire

CONCEIT

Every man has a right to be conceited until he is successful.

Benjamin Disraeli

He is so full of himself that he is quite empty.

Anon

When a proud man hears another praised, he thinks himself
injured.

English proverb

CONCENTRATION CAMP

A concentration camp is a cage where animals keep men.

Don Quinn

CONDIMENTS

Horseradish is the brutal excitative of a simple people—the
English.

Lorna Bunyard

CONDUCT

Think much, speak little, and write less.

Proverb

CONFESSION

Good for the soul—but bad for the heel.

Agnes Guilfoyle

We confess little faults in order to suggest that we have no big
ones.

La Rochefoucauld

I am a fool, I love anything that is good.

Anon

CONFIDENCE

I have the most perfect confidence in your indiscretion.

Sydney Smith

CONFORM!

Oh, let us love our occupations,
Bless the squire and his relations,
Live upon our daily rations,
And always know our proper stations.

Charles Dickens

CONFORMITY

Everybody is criticizing conformity these days, but there is one good thing about it. You can practice it without making a spectacle of yourself.

Anon

Tolerably early in life I discovered that one of the unpardonable sins, in the eyes of most people, is for a man to go about unlabeled. The world regards such a person as the police do an unmuzzled dog.

T. H. Huxley

To those capable only of ordinary actions, everything that is very much out of the ordinary seems possible only after it is accomplished.

Cardinal de Retz

Every being cries out to be read differently.

Simone Weil

How glorious it is—and also how painful—to be an exception.

Alfred de Musset

People differ. Some object to the fan dancer, and others to the fan.

Elizabeth W. Spalding

You had better be a round peg in a square hole than a square peg in a square hole. The latter is in for life, while the first is only an indeterminate sentence.

Elbert Hubbard

Commandment Number One of any truly civilized society is this: Let people be different.

David Grayson

The beaten path is most crowded.

LLL

CONGRESS

Some politicians, if their constituents were cannibals, would promise them missionaries for dinner.

H. L. Mencken

It could probably be shown by facts and figures that there is no distinctly native American criminal class except Congress.

Mark Twain

CONSEQUENCES

When you have bought one fine thing you must buy ten more, that your appearance may be all of a piece.

English proverb

CONSCIENCE

Is the hag that rides my dreams.

John Dryden

A quiet conscience sleeps in thunder.

English proverb

A guilty conscience is the mother of invention.

Carolyn Wells

A grand eloquence, little conscience.

English proverb

My conscience hath a thousand several tongues,
And every tongue brings in a several tale,
And every tale condemns me for a villain.

Shakespeare

CONSERVATIVE

He entertains a new thought as if it were his mother-in-law.

LLL

Generally young men are regarded as radicals. This is a popular misconception. The most conservative persons I ever met are college undergraduates.

Woodrow Wilson, 1914

CONSERVATION

The Nation behaves well if it treats the natural resources as assets which it must turn over to the next generation increased, and not impaired, in value.

Theodore Roosevelt, 1910

CONSOLATION

Every silver lining
Has its dark cloud.

Sophie Levinson

A wooden bed is better than a golden coffin.

CONSOLATION PRIZE

Nothing so bad as not to be good for something.

Proverb

CONSTANCY

To say that you can love one person all your life is just like saying that one candle will continue burning as long as you live.

Leo Tolstoy

Stubbornly I sought icicles in fire, Softness in diamonds, constancy in Women, Pity in Hades, and sunshine at night.

Seigneur du Bartas

CONSTITUTION

What's the Constitution among friends?

Timothy Campbell (New York congressman)

A bad constitution is infinitely better than the best despot.

LLL

CONSULTANT

An expert called in when nobody wants to take the blame for what is going wrong.

Quoted by Sidney J. Harris

CONTEMPLATION

Contemplation in any sense is a casualty of the American way of life. We simply do not have time for it. We read poetry as we would a detective story. We listen to opera, chamber music and symphonies on our FM's while we do the morning dishes or prepare income tax statements. We visit art museums as we would tour the Grand Canyon. We watch movies and television with only a rare critical thought. . . . Our nation has so much leisure time that it has a "leisure problem" and yet it lacks the essential leisure of contemplation.

Rev. Andrew M. Greeley

CONTENTION

A clash of doctrines is not a disaster—it is an opportunity.

Alfred North Whitehead

The loud voice often wins the quarrel.

Japanese proverb

CONTRADICTION

One often contradicts an opinion when what is really uncongenial is the tone in which it was conveyed.

Nietzsche

CONTROVERSY

When a thing ceases to be a subject of controversy, it ceases to be a subject of interest.

William Hazlitt

CONVERSATION

The wit of Conversation consists more in finding it in others than in showing a great deal yourself: he who goes from your conversation pleased with himself and his own wit, is perfectly pleased with you.

La Bruyère

. . . the conversation was dull, as is always the case when we are speaking only favorably of our fellow men.

Pierre Ambroise François Choderlos de Laclos

Conversation is a form of communication in which some men never stop to think and many women never think to stop.

Anon

We'll talk without listening to each other, that is the best way to get along.

Alfred de Musset

A good memory and a tongue tied in the middle is a combination which gives immortality to conversation.

Mark Twain

If the art of conversation stood a little higher we would have a lower birthrate.

Stanislaw J. Lec

Strike while the irony is hot.

Don Quinn

It has been estimated that from the first "good morning" to the last "good night" the average man engages in approximately thirty conversations a day.

Roy S. Dunton

Conversation is the slowest form of human communication.

Don Herold

CONVENTIONS

Going to an out-of-town convention with your wife is like going fishing with a game warden.

Anon

CONVICTS' SONG

True patriots all; for be it understood
We left our country for our country's good.

George Barrington, Australia, 1796

COOKING

The broiling of beefsteaks has of late become a gentleman's sport with the result that our steaks are getting better and better. For reasons we shan't go into, a certain amount of show-off seems inevitable whenever a man is given a free hand in culinary matters, so there is now as much fuss surrounding the broiling of a steak as there has been about the salad bowl since our gentlemen took over in that field.

Sheila Hibben, 1941

The wife who drives from the back seat isn't any worse than the husband who cooks from the dining room.

Anon wife

Don't fire till you see the whites of their eggs.

LLL

COOLNESS

If I didn't panic when I found out that I was a human being, I'm never going to.

James Thurber

COOPERATION

No matter how great a warrior he is, a chief cannot do battle without his Indians.

Anon

CORNS

Better cut the shoe than pinch the foot.

English saying

CORNWALL

The devil will not come into Cornwall, for fear of being put into a pie.

Cornish proverb

CORPORATIONS

Corporations, which should be the carefully restrained creatures of the law and the servants of the people, are fast becoming the people's masters.

Grover Cleveland

The Communist party is the biggest corporation of all.

John Dos Passos

CORRECTION

Rebuke with soft words and hard arguments.

Proverb

CORRESPONDENCE

Nine-tenths of the letters in which people speak unreservedly of their inmost feelings are written after ten at night.

Thomas Hardy

CORRUPTION

Bad officials are ones elected by good citizens who do not vote.

George Jean Nathan

COSMETICS

A girl whose cheeks are covered with paint,
Has an advantage with me over one who ain't.

Ogden Nash

COST

The lion's skin is never cheap.

Proverb

COST OF LIVING

When I first started working I used to dream of the day when I might be earning the salary I'm starving on now.

Anon

The only thing that continues to give us more for our money is a weighing machine.

George Clark

COSTS

The way production costs are soaring, the fellow who used to "get it wholesale" now can buy it cheaper abroad.

Anon

COUNSEL

The advice of their elders to young men is very apt to be as unreal as a list of the hundred best books.

O. W. Holmes, Jr.

We might be more eager to accept good advice if it didn't continually interfere with our plans.

LLL

COUNTERFEIT

Men make counterfeit money; in many more cases money makes counterfeit men.

Sidney J. Harris

You may as well say, that's a valiant flea that dare eat his breakfast on the lip of a lion.

Shakespeare

I have never thought much of the courage of a lion-tamer; inside the cage he is, at least, safe from other men.

Shaw

Unfortunately courage is all too often composed of equal parts of bourbon and water.

Douglas Meador

THE COUNTRY

Compared to the city, the country looks like the world without its clothes on.

Douglas Jerrold

COURTESY

Is a form of polite behavior practiced by civilized people when they have time.

Anon

Politeness is a pleasant way for a man to get nowhere with a girl.

Anon

COURTSHIP

As the boy wave said to the girl wave: "Don't you think we're fit to be tide?"

LLL

Not the lover but his language wins the lady.

Japanese proverb

She is pretty to walk with,
And witty to talk with,
And pleasant, too, to think on.

Sir John Suckling

The taste of the first kiss disappointed me like a fruit tasted for the first time. It is not in novelty, it is in habit that we find the greatest pleasures.

Raymond Radiguet

A kiss that speaks volumes is seldom a first edition.

Clare J. Whiting

My lady, time is passing, time is passing. Well—not time, of course, but we are getting on.

Pierre de Ronsard

Happy the wooing that's not long in doing.

English proverb

He who would the daughter win
Should look at the mother before he begin.

LLL

COWARDICE

Fear of corrupting the mind of the younger generation is the loftiest form of cowardice.

Holbrook Jackson

CRAFT

It must be a wily mouse that can breed in a cat's ear.

Proverb

CRANK

Anybody of any originality, whatsoever, from Christopher Columbus to the man who rolls his own cigarettes.

Victorian gentleman

CREATION

God made everything out of nothing.
But the nothingness shows through.

Paul Valery

In the question of which came first, the chicken or the egg, I'm sure the chicken came before the egg, because I can see God creating a chicken, but I can't see Him laying an egg.

Anon, Jr.

CREDIT

Who wants to be wealthy
And miss the enthrallment
Enjoyed when you pay up
That final installment?

S. Omar Barker

The faith that exists
Between men and man
Is responsible for
The installment plan.

M. E. Mullen

Living upon trust is the way to pay double.

Proverb

CREDO

The world is as ugly as sin—and almost as delightful.

Frederick Locker-Lampson

CREDULITY

The most positive men are the most credulous.

Alexander Pope

CRICKET

I do not play cricket because it requires me to assume such indecent postures.

Oscar Wilde

CRIME

Steal money, you're a thief.
Steal a country, you're a king.

Japanese proverb

The robb'd that smiles, steals something from the thief.

Shakespeare

A threadbare coat is armour proof against highwaymen.

English saying

Give a thief enough rope and he'll steal it.

LLL

If you can't do the sentence, don't do the job.

"Charlie Coker"

The only way to make sure that crime doesn't pay is to have the government take it over and run it.

Ernest Bevin

The trouble these days is there's no arrest for the wicked.

Raymond J. Cvikota

CRIME-VIRTUE

A crime persevered in a thousand centuries ceases to be a crime, and becomes a virtue.

Mark Twain

CRISES

There is always another crisis around the corner.

Harry Truman

CRITICISM

Don't be afraid of criticism. Anyone who can fill out a laundry slip thinks of himself as a writer. Those who can't fill out a laundry slip think of themselves as critics.

George Seaton

I regard reviews as a kind of infant's disease to which new-born books are subject.

Georg C. Lichtenberg

How much better the world would be if we'd let opportunity do all the knocking.

Anon

To speak ill of others is a dishonest way of praising ourselves.

Will Durant

Criticism is the disapproval of people, not for having faults, but for having faults different from our own.

Anon

To avoid criticism, do nothing, say nothing, be nothing.

Elbert Hubbard

Of all the cants which are canted in this canting world, though the cant of hypocrisy may be the worst, the cant of criticism is the most tormenting.

Laurence Sterne

Criticism is what you get when you have everything else.

Anon

But you get more when you have nothing.

LLL

CRITICS

All critics should be assassinated.

Man Ray

It is probably not necessary for a critic to be insane to survive all those opening nights but I assure you that it helps.

Alexander Woollcott

He who is without sin among you, let him stone the first cast.

Anon

I never read a book before reviewing it; it prejudices one so.

Sydney Smith

As soon seek roses in December—ice in June
Hope constancy in wind, or corn in chaff,
Believe a woman, or an epitaph,
Or any other thing that's false, before
You trust in critics.

Lord Byron

A man is a critic when he cannot be an artist, just as a man becomes a stool pigeon when he cannot be a soldier.

Gustave Flaubert

The lot of critics is to be remembered by what they failed to understand.

George Moore

Critics are like brushers of other men's clothes.

British saying

CROWN

For within the hollow crown
That rounds the mortal temples of a king
Keeps Death his court.

Shakespeare

CRUELTY

There is no feast without cruelty.

Nietzsche

There is no laughter without cruelty.

LLL

CRUSTACEANS

More than any other of God's creatures, the crab has formulated the perfect philosophy of life. Whenever he is confronted with a great moral crisis in life, he first makes up his mind what is right and then goes sidewise as fast as he can.

Oliver Herford

CRYING

I wept when I was born, and every day shews why.

English saying

CUBA

It was true that the Cuban people were in miserable conditions under the Batista dictatorship, but Castro's dictatorship has made it worse.

Juanita Castro, his younger sister

CUNNING

He is far gone in cunning who makes other people believe he is but indifferently cunning.

Jean de La Bruyère

Nothing doth more hurt in a state than that cunning men pass for wise.

Bacon

CURIOSITY

Half the world does not know how the other half lives, but is trying to find out.

Ed Howe

The things most people want to know about are usually none of their business.

Shaw

Childhood and genius have the same master-organ in common —inquisitiveness.

Bulwer-Lytton

A bright eye indicates curiosity; a black eye, too much.

Anon

CURRENT AFFAIRS

With all those expert columnists
I've carefully perused,
I wish I were as well-informed
As I am well-confused!

Thomas Usk

CURSE

I wish my deadly foe no worse
Than want of friends and empty purse.

Nickolas Briton

CURSING

Take not God's name in vain; select a time when it will have effect.

Ambrose Bierce

He cursed him at board, he cursed him in bed;
From the sole of his foot to the crown of his head;
He cursed him in sleeping; that every night
He should dream of the devil, and wake in a fright;
He cursed him in eating; he cursed him in drinking;
He cursed him in coughing, in sneezing, in winking;
He cursed him in sitting; in standing; in lying;
He cursed him in walking, in riding, in flying;
He cursed him in living, he cursed him in dying!

Richard Harris Barham ("The Jackdaw of Rheims")

If ever I utter an oath again may my soul be blasted to eternal damnation.

Shaw

63

DADDY

What they call a banker who has been careless with his deposits.

Anon

DAMAGE

Great damage is usually caused by those who are too scrupulous to do small harm.

Cardinal de Retz

DANDRUFF

Don't blame your hair for what your scalp is doing to your head.

Ad

DANGER

We run carelessly to the precipice, after we have put something before us to prevent us from seeing it.

Blaise Pascal

DARKNESS

When it is dark enough, you can see the stars.

Charles A. Beard

THE DAY

Be reverent towards each day. Love it, respect it, do not sully it, do not hinder it from coming to flower. Love it even when it is gray and sad.

Romain Rolland

I consider the day a total loss if I don't catch hell about something.

LLL

To sensible men, every day is a day of reckoning.

John W. Gardner

DAY VS. NIGHT

The day has eyes, the night has ears.

Jewish proverb

DAYDREAMS

How many of our daydreams would darken into nightmares, were there any danger of their coming true.

L. P. Smith

DAYS

This was one of the rye-bread days, all dull and damp without.
Margaret Fuller

Those were the good old days—I was so unhappy then.
Claude Carloman de Rulhière

DAYS OF THE WEEK

Monday's child is wild of hair,
Tuesday's child nearly bare,
Wednesday's child awful weird,
Thursday's child long of beard,
Friday's child full of hell,
Saturday's child how it do smell!
And a child that's born on the Sabbath day
Is slight and light and fey and gay.

LLL

DEATH

And nothing can we call our own but death,
And that small model of the barren earth
Which serves as paste and cover to our bones.
For God's sake, let us sit upon the ground,
And tell sad stories of the death of kings.
Shakespeare

If the rich could hire other people to die for them, the poor could make a wonderful living.
Yiddish proverb

The long habit of living indisposeth us for dying.
Thomas Browne

The dead tiger leaves his pelt; man his reputation.
Japanese proverb

Dead men hear no tales; posthumous fame is an Irish bull.
Israel Zangwill

The tyrant dies and his rule is over; the martyr dies and his rule begins.

Sören Kierkegaard

The deep sleep in that bed
From which no morro's mischief knocks them up.
Dante Gabriel Rossetti

The good die first,
And they whose hearts are dry as summer dust
Burn to the socket.
William Wordsworth

I have lived without thinking,
Following without blinking
The natural ways of my flesh.
To me it's an absurdity
That death would stoop to think of me
Who never stopped to think of death.

Mathurin Régnier

Better to die of good wine and good company than of slow disease and doctor's doses.

Thackeray

DEATH/ENEMIES

I'm lonesome; they are all dying; I have hardly a warm personal enemy left.

Whistler

DEBT

The most momentous question before this country today, it has been said, is "How much is the down payment?" Interestingly enough, at the celebration of the Chinese New Year, one of the most honored observations is that of paying off all old debts. And we send missionaries to China!

Anon

If it isn't the sheriff, it's the finance company. I've got more attachments on me than a vacuum cleaner.

John Barrymore

Say nothing of my debts unless you mean to pay them.

Spanish proverb

What you don't owe won't hurt you.

Anon

DECAY

It is an immutable rule that when dynasties arise in the desert they are crude, poor, rancorous, and enterprising. After they acquire power, they become urbane, civilized, charitable, and ineffectual, and are toppled by some new broken sheik. Nor can the established ruler do anything about it—the historical process of decay began when he dethroned his predecessor.

Ibn Khaldun

DECEPTION

You are never so easily fooled as when you are trying to fool someone else.

La Rochefoucauld

Deceiving of a deceiver is no knavery.

English saying

Oh, what a tangled web we weave,
When bras we put on to deceive!

LLL

DECOR

The hall in the Menora Temple where the meeting was held is one of those decorative wonders peculiar to Brooklyn and Queens, a blend of Miami Beach and Mafioso . . . just what God would have done if he'd had the right decorator.

Joe Flaherty

DECORATIONS

The Legion of Honor is an award for grocers and bureaucrats.

Gustave Courbet

DEDUCTIONS

The kind of fallout that really disturbs most citizens is what gets dropped out of their pay checks.

Anon

DEFICIT

A deficit is what you have when you haven't as much as when you had nothing.

Anon

DELIBERATION

Go not for every grief to the physician, for every quarrel to the lawyer, nor for every thirst to the pot.

English proverb

DEMOCRACY

A democracy is a place where we have complete control over how we pay our taxes—cash, check, or money order.

Anon

Is a mode of government that gives every man a right to be his own oppressor.

James Russell Lowell

DEMOCRATS

The Democratic party at its worst is better for the country than the Republican party at its best.

Lyndon Johnson

DEMOCRACY-ARISTOCRACY

Democracy means government by the uneducated, while aristocracy means government by the badly educated.

G. K. Chesterton

DESIRE

Better go away longing than loathing.

English saying

Maids want nothing but husbands, and when they have them, they want everything.

Proverb

There are three wants which can never be satisfied: that of the rich, who wants something more; that of the sick, who wants something different; and that of the traveler, who says, "Anywhere but here."

Emerson

DESPERATION

Need teaches things unlawful.

Seneca

He that is carried down the torrent catcheth at every thing.

English proverb

DESTINY

Too many people confuse bad management with destiny.

Anon

There is a divinity which shapes our ends rough, hew them as we will.

LLL

DETERMINATION

Determination, tenacity, resolution, and strength can be the victims of a weak bladder.

LLL

DETRACTION

Detraction is a weed that grows only on dunghills.

English proverb

THE DEVIL

Wickedness with beauty is the devil's hook baited.

Proverb

An Italianized Englishman is a devil incarnate.

English proverb

If there were only some shorter and more direct route to the devil, it would save an awful lot of sorrow and anxiety in this world.

Kin Hubbard

DICKENS

While Christmas shopping, I asked a pretty college freshman in our local bookstore during the holiday rush for a copy of Dickens' *Christmas Carol*. Smiling sweetly she said, "Oh, he didn't write songs—he wrote books."

Annabel Cowan

DICTATORS

Ride to and fro upon tigers which they dare not dismount and the tigers are getting hungry.

Winston Churchill, 1936

DIET

The girl who went on a milk diet now weighs 59 quarts and 1 pint.

Lane Olinghouse

There's no better diet than eating only as much as you can afford.

Franklin P. Jones

DIFFERENCE

I have lived long enough to see that difference begets hatred.

Stendhal

There is but an inch of difference between the cushioned chamber and the padded cell.

G. K. Chesterton

There is not the thickness of a sixpence between good and evil.

Proverb

DIFFICULTIES

As a final incentive before giving up a difficult task, try to imagine it successfully accomplished by someone you violently dislike.

K. Zenios

Nothing difficult is ever easy.

Anon TV commentator

DIGESTION

The fate of a nation has often depended upon the good or bad digestion of a prime minister.

Voltaire

DIGITS

The fingers must be educated, the thumb is born knowing.

Chazal

DILEMMA

One of my daughters is mad at me because I won't let her wear a bra yet, and the other is mad because I won't let her throw hers away.

Anon mother, reported by Robert Sylvester

DINING

Wine is the intellectual part of a meal while meat is the material.

Alexandre Dumas père

DINING OUT

It is a great pleasure to eat, and have nothing to pay.

Proverb

DIPLOMAT

A man who can pull the wool over his wife's eyes with the right yarn.

Anon

DIPLOMATS

Are simply buyers and sellers of world herring.

Maksim Litvinov

DIPLOMACY

When a diplomat says yes, he means perhaps; when he says perhaps, he means no; and when he says no, he is no diplomat.

Anon diplomat

American diplomacy is easy on the brain but hell on the feet.

Charles Dawes

DISAPPOINTMENT

Nothing is as good as it seems beforehand.

George Eliot

DISCIPLINE

By systematic discipline all men may be made heroes.

Emerson

DISCONTENT

What makes us discontented with our condition is the absurdly exaggerated idea we have of the happiness of others.

Proverb

Discontents arise from our desires oftener than from our wants.

English proverb

DISCRETION

When you shut one eye, you do not hear everything.

Swiss proverb

Wear a horn and blow it not.

Spanish proverb

When you have got an elephant by the hind leg, and he is trying to run away, it is best to let him run.

Abraham Lincoln

DISCRIMINATION

Life would be tolerable were it not for its amusements.

Sir George Cornewall Lewis

DISILLUSION

Where love fails, we espy all faults.

Proverb

DISLIKE

I could never learn to like her—except on a raft at sea, with no other provisions in sight.

Mark Twain

DISPUTES

Arguments are vocal disagreements which are to be avoided, since they are always vulgar, and often convincing.

Wilde

DISSENSION

Never argue at the dinner table, for the one who is not hungry always gets the best of the argument.

Richard Whately

DISTRACTIONS

Music helps not the toothache.

Proverb

DISTURBANCES

No one likes to be disturbed at meals or love.

Lord Byron

DIVERSIONS

A golf course is an outdoor insane asylum peopled by ad men suffering from the delusion that eventually they will conquer the game. The more violent cases think they already have.

Peter Lind Hayes

DIVORCE

That's when a husband no longer has to bring the money home to his wife—he can mail it.

Morty Craft

DIZZINESS

He that is giddy thinks the world turns round.

English proverb

DO-GOODERS

In the eyes of a ruler, a man who is in a position to do good is just as dangerous and almost as criminal as one who intends to do harm.

Cardinal de Retz

DO-NOTHING

It is doubtless a formidable advantage never to have done anything, but it can be carried too far.

Antoine Rivaroli

DOCTORS

English physicians kill you, the French let you die.

Lord Melbourne

It is hard to say whether the doctors of law or divinity have made the greatest advances in the lucrative business of mystery.

Edmund Burke

DOGS

Newfoundland dogs are good to save children from drowning, but you must have a pond of water handy and a child, or else there will be no profit in boarding a Newfoundland.

Josh Billings

To his dog, every man is Napoleon; hence the constant popularity of dogs.

Aldous Huxley

Don't make the mistake of treating your dogs like humans, or they'll treat you like dogs.

Martha Scott

DOING

Whatsoever thy hand findeth to do, do it with thy might; for there is no work, nor device, nor knowledge, nor wisdom, in the grave.

Ecclesiastes

DOLLARS AND SENSE

He that gets money before he gets wit, will be but a short while master of it.

English proverb

DOLLAR-DIFFERENCE

Money does make all the difference. If you have two jobs and you're rich, you have diversified interests. If you have two jobs and you're poor, you're moonlighting.

Anon

DOMESTIC ECONOMY

Eliza Jones of Birmingham, England, was saved from bankruptcy by bank officials who put her financial affairs in order. She gave this excuse for going into debt: "I was trying to keep up with the Smiths next door."

DON QUIXOTE

Cervantes smiled Spain's chivalry away.

Lord Byron

DONOHUE'S LAW

What's worth doing is worth doing for money.

Joseph Donohue

DOORMEN

A doorman is a genius who opens your taxi door with one hand, helps you in with the other and still has a hand left waiting for the tip.

Earl Wilson

DOUBT

When in doubt, tell the truth.

Mark Twain

DRAMA

The thirty-seventh dramatic situation:
To become aware that one's mother is a virgin.

Alfred Jarry

DREAMS

Dreaming permits each and every one of us to be quietly and safely sane every night of our lives.

LLL

We use up too much artistic effort in our dreams; in consequence our waking life is often poor.

Nietzsche

I am so unhappy at the present time that in my dreams I am indescribably happy.

Sören Kierkegaard

In dreams I do not recollect that state of feeling so common when awake, of thinking on one subject and looking at another.

Samuel Taylor Coleridge

The inquiry into a dream is another dream.

Halifax

My life's dream has been a perpetual nightmare.

Voltaire

He dreamed he was eating Shredded Wheat and woke up to find the mattress half gone.

Fred Allen

DREAM OVER
Awakened, he descends the far side of the dream.

Victor Hugo

DRESS
Good clothes open all doors.

British proverb

It is not the gay coat makes the gentleman.

French proverb

He that is proud of his fine clothes gets his reputation from his tailor.

English proverb

Nine tailors make a man.

English proverb

DRINKING
Wine is a simple but elegant means of getting tight.

Anon Englishman

Don't make your nose blush for the sins of your mouth.

Anon AAA

Wine is the drink of the gods. Milk is the drink of babies, tea the drink of women. And water the drink of beasts.

John S. Blackie

A glass of water is worth a ton of wine.

Italian proverb

He drank like a fish, if drinking nothing but water could be so described.

Alfred Housman

The rapturous, wild, and ineffable pleasure
Of drinking at somebody else's expense.

H. S. Leigh ("Stanzas to an Intoxicated Fly")

By and by you sober down, and then you perceive that you have been drunk on the smell of somebody else's cork.

Mark Twain

When the wine is in, the wit is out.

Proverb

Save at the spigot and waste at the bunghole, and you'll have a barrel of fun.

LLL

Skid rows represent only 15 per cent of the alcoholics. The other 85 per cent are behind Venetian blinds, protected by their families, and never reaching the jail blotters.

Emmet Daly, Assistant Attorney General, California

I drank to forget, not to be obsessed by your face. . . . Alas! When I was drunk, I saw you double.

Marcel Achard

Better belly burst than good liquor be lost.

Jonathan Swift

He who drinks boilermakers tonight will hear the noise of the construction work in the morning.

John Kisela

He who goes forth with a fifth on the Fourth may not come forth on the Fifth.

Anon

I've formed a new organization called Alcoholics Unanimous. If you don't feel like a drink, you ring another member and he comes over to persuade you.

Richard Harris

Never drink on an empty wallet.

LLL

DRIVING

If soldiers were asked to do in battle what the average motorist does on weekends for fun, the officer in charge would be court-martialed for brutality.

Malcolm Muggeridge

It seems to make an auto driver mad if he misses you.

Kin Hubbard

The driving is like the driving of Jehu the son of Nimski; for he driveth furiously.

2 Kings

DUELING

I thoroughly disapprove of duels. I consider them unwise and I know they are dangerous. Also, sinful. If a man should challenge me now I would go to that man and take him kindly and forgivingly by the hand and lead him to a quiet retired spot and kill him.

Mark Twain

DUTY

Once a rigid idea of duty has got inside a narrow mind, it can never again get out.

Joubert

When a stupid man is doing something he is ashamed of, he always declares that it is his duty.

Shaw

DYNASTY

To drown in the East River.

Mod Mod Dictionary

EARLY DEFINITION

A Communist is one who has yearnings
For equal division of unequal earnings.

Ebenezer Elliott, 1781–1849

EARLY RISING

The early bird wishes he'd let someone else get up first.

Mrs. A. Simmons

EATING

Grub first, then ethics.

Bertolt Brecht

Better a good dinner than a fine coat.

French saying

Better some of the pudding than none of the pie.

English proverb

Better a mouse in the pot than no flesh at all.

British proverb

Better lose a supper than have a hundred physicians.

Spanish proverb

That all-softening, overpowering knell,
The tocsin of the soul—the dinner bell.

Lord Byron

If you can judge a country by what it eats, a country where
there is no free lunch is no longer a free country.

Arthur "Bugs" Baer

I look upon it, that he who does not mind his belly will hardly
mind anything else.

Samuel Johnson

A good stomach is the best sauce.

English proverb

If it were not for the belly, the back might wear gold.

German proverb

A dainty stomach beggars the purse.

Proverb

A full purse makes the mouth run over.

Anon

The gourmand puts his purse into his belly; and the miser his
belly into his purse.

Anon

Every cook praises his own broth.

English saying

Too many cooks make a hash of the broth.

Mrs. W. Haigh

Plain cooking cannot be entrusted to plain cooks.

Countess Morphy

Nothing helps scenery like ham and eggs.

Mark Twain

I always eat peas with honey
I've done it all my life.
Of course it makes them taste funny,
But they don't fall off the knife.

Anon

You first parents of the human race . . . who ruined yourself
for an apple, what might you not have done for a truffled
turkey?

Brillat-Savarin

The acceptance of foods depends on their fit in the existing cultural pattern. For instance, if you want to achieve acceptance in a society which regards fried grasshoppers as the ultimate in food elegance, then you must provide a product which looks and tastes and has the texture of fried grasshoppers.

James A. Sumner, president, General Mills

Everyone acts the way he eats.

LLL

There's somebody at every dinner party who eats all the celery.

Kin Hubbard

It is amusing to see boys eat—when you have not got to pay for it.

Jerome K. Jerome

Bread of a day, ale of a month and wine of a year.

English saying

He who indulges, bulges.

Eleanor S. J. Rydberg

EAVESDROPPING

Listen at the keyhole, and you'll hear news of yourself.

Proverb

ECONOMICS

Economics is like being lost in the woods. How can you tell where you are going when you don't even know where you are?

Anon

A recession is a depression that got bogged down in prosperity.

Walt Streightiff

What this country needs is a good five-dollar nickel.

LLL

ECONOMISTS

If all economists were laid end to end, they would not reach a conclusion.

Shaw

ECONOMY

The secret of economy is to live as cheaply the first few days after payday as you lived the last few days before.

Anon

ECSTASY

An ecstasy is a thing that will not go into words; it feels like music, and one cannot tell about music so that another person can get the feeling of it.

Mark Twain

EDEN

God created man, and, finding him not sufficiently alone, gave him a female companion to make him feel his solitude more keenly.

Paul Valery

EDUCATION

To teach is also to learn.

Japanese proverb

Never let your schooling interfere with your education.

LLL

It is harder to conceal ignorance than to acquire knowledge.

Arnold H. Glasow

Nothing in education is so astonishing as the amount of ignorance it accumulates in the form of inert facts.

The Education of Henry Adams

As a result of all his education, of all he sees and hears around him, the child absorbs such an amount of lies and stupidities, mingled with essential truths, that the first duty of the adolescent who wants to be a healthy man is to disgorge everything.

Romain Rolland

The principal goal of education is to create men who are capable of doing *new* things, not simply of repeating what other generations have done.

Jean Piaget

The object of teaching a child is to enable him to get along without a teacher.

Elbert Hubbard

The greatest school that ever existed, it has been said, consisted of Socrates standing on a street corner with one or two interlocutors.

Richard M. Weaver

In the pursuit of quality in education people have tried faith, prayer, and old phonograph records. None has worked. A few school districts are now trying money and they are achieving remarkable success.

Dr. Paul Mort

If the cost of a college education continues to snowball for many more years, a person can make a profit by remaining ignorant.

Anon

Our colleges would have no expansion problem if the relation between getting a higher income and getting a higher education was eliminated.

LLL

Education has become such a fetish . . . that many parents are pushing their children far beyond their capacity. . . . At the rate we are going, we are headed for a society of all generals and no privates.

Vance Packard

"Whom are you?" said he, for he had been to night school.

George Ade

One of the teacher's constant tasks is to take a roomful of live wires and see that they are grounded.

Anon teacher

Education is the process of casting false pearls before real swine.

Professor Irwin Edman

Has reached such a high point that many people believe ROTC stands for Riots On The Campus.

Wick Fowler

Let every sheep keep his own skin.

Henry Thoreau, upon declining his diploma from Harvard

Sexual enlightenment is justified insofar as girls cannot learn too soon how children do not come into the world.

Karl Kraus

Fools are not born—they are educated.

Elbert Hubbard

Who does not teach his child a trade brings him up to steal.

Anon burglar

A man who has never gone to school may steal from a freight car; but if he has a university education, he may steal the whole railroad.

Theodore Roosevelt

Criminals springing from our schools and colleges are more brazen, more vicious, and more desperate than ever before in the history of any civilized community.

Warden Lewis Lawes of Sing Sing Prison

One learns by lying.

The ship that makes her voyage without the loss of a spar or a rope, teaches little; but there is a whole world of information in the log of a vessel with a great hole in her, all her masts carried away, the captain invariably drunk, and the crew mutinous.

Charles Lever

EFFICIENCY

There is nothing so useless as doing efficiently that which should not be done at all.

Peter F. Drucker

Efficiency experts—
At least those I've known—
Can cope with my troubles
But not with their own.

Anon

Why is it that there is never enough time to do a job right, but always enough time to do it over?

Anon

EGOTISM

Glass blowers will never produce anything as fragile as the human ego.

Arnold H. Glasow

Talk to a man about himself and he will listen for hours.

Benjamin Disraeli

The poet, of all sorts of artificers, is the fondest of his works.

Proverb

Of all the lovely sounds on earth—
The song of birds, rain's anodyne—
The sweetest is a human voice!
Bewitching, undulating—mine!

Leslie Millichamp

ELEPHANTS

Do not capture mice.

Latin proverb

ELEVATION

Perched on the loftiest throne in the world, we are still sitting on our own behind.

Montaigne

81

ELEVENTH COMMANDMENT
Thou Shalt Not Park From Here to the Corner.

Sign outside South Haven, Michigan, church entrance

ELOCUTION
Papa, potatoes, poultry, prunes, and prism, are all very good words for the lips : especially prunes and prism.

Charles Dickens

EMOLUMENTS
Tips are wages we pay other people's help.

Anon

EMOTIONS
The advantage of the emotions is that they lead us astray.

Wilde

EMPATHY
Empathy is akin to sympathy, but whereas sympathy says, "I feel as you do," empathy says, "I know how you feel." In other words, empathy enables us to use our heads more than our hearts, and allows us to appreciate another person's feelings without becoming emotionally involved with him.

R. W. Armstrong

EMPLOYMENT TESTS
Many top businessmen would be out of a job if they had to take personality and capability tests given applicants for employment or promotion in their own companies.

Samuel Feinberg

EMPLOYER-EMPLOYEE
If he works for you, you work for him.

Japanese proverb

ENEMIES
To have a good enemy, choose a friend: he knows where to strike.

Diane de Poitiers

Unwilling friend, let not your spite abate;
Help me with scorn, and strengthen me with hate.

John Davidson

ENERGY

Extreme busyness, whether at school or college, kirk or market, is a symptom of deficient vitality.

Robert Louis Stevenson

ENGLAND

A not uncommon experience for a young Englishman is to sit on a sofa with his girl friend in the half darkness while she tells him she has found a shop that sells the most revealing black mini-skirt with slits up the side, really fab, worn with a white see-through skinny sweater that has a hole in the middle and a plunging neckline, and some super fishnet stockings, and a frothy lace petticoat with an op-art silk lining. Inexpressibly intrigued, he attempts to kiss her. And gets his face smacked.

David Frost and Antony Jay

THE ENGLISH

Are a hardy race that considers plain boiled turnips to be food.

William Wallace Irwin

The English are people who employ insolence to cover emptiness.

Whistler

The English have an extraordinary ability for flying into a great calm.

Alexander Woollcott

The English have a miraculous power of turning wine into water.

Oscar Wilde

The English instinctively admire any man who has no talent and is modest about it.

James Agate

If an earthquake were to engulf England tomorrow, the English would manage to meet and dine somewhere among the rubbish, just to celebrate the event.

Douglas Jerrold

Englishmen never will be slaves; they are free to do whatever the Government and public opinion allow them to do.

Shaw

The English country gentleman galloping after a fox—the unspeakable in full pursuit of the uneatable.

Oscar Wilde

ENGLISH/IRISH

If one could only teach the English how to talk and the Irish how to listen, society would be quite civilized.

Oscar Wilde

THE ENGLISH LANGUAGE

England and America are two countries separated by the same language.

Shaw

ENGLISH SUMMER

The way to endure summer in England is to have it framed and glazed in a comfortable room.

Horace Walpole

ENGLISH WINTER

Ending in July, to recommence in August.

Lord Byron

ENGLISHMEN

An Englishman thinks he is moral when he is only uncomfortable.

Shaw

ENJOYMENT

Enjoy yourself a little, while the fool seeks for more.

Spanish proverb

ENTERPRISE

What America really needs is more young people who will carry to their jobs the same enthusiasm for getting ahead that they display in traffic.

Anon

ENTERTAINMENT

The most difficult character in comedy is the fool, and he who plays the part must be no simpleton.

Cervantes

If you want to make people weep, you must weep yourself. If you want to make people laugh, your face must remain serious.

Casanova

Worth seeing? Yes; but not worth going to see.

Samuel Johnson

Nothing draws a family closer together than a twelve-inch TV set in a twenty-five-foot living room.

Quoted by Earl Wilson

It's a wise child that knows no television.

LLL

ENTHUSIASM

I prefer the errors of enthusiasm to the indifference of wisdom.

Anatole France

ENVY

Everything may be borne except another's good fortune.

LLL

The greatest mischief you can do the envious is to do well.

Proverb

There is nothing more universally commended than a fine day; the reason is, people can commend it without envy.

William Shenstone

EPIGRAM

A grain of truth in the twinkling of an eye.

Anon

EPITAPHS

Let's talk of graves, of worms, and epitaphs.

Shakespeare

Nobles and heralds, by your leave,
Here lies what once was Matthew Prior;
The son of Adam and of Eve:
Can Bourbon or Nassau claim higher?

Matthew Prior

This is the epitaph I want on my tomb: "Here lies one of the most intelligent animals who ever appeared on the face of the earth."

Benito Mussolini, 1941

Here lies John McDonald
Born a man.
Died a grocer.

On tombstone in Scotland

This is the grave of Mike O'Day
Who died maintaining his right of way.
His right was clear, his will was strong,
But he's just as dead as if he'd been wrong.

Anon

Stranger, regard this spot with gravity—
Dentist Green's filling his last cavity.

I'm Smith of Stoke, and sixty-odd,
I've lived without a dame
From youth-time on; and would to God
My dad had done the same.

Thomas Hardy

Here lies Will Smith—and what's something rarish,
He was born, bred, and hanged, all in the same parish.

Anon

Here lies the body of Mary Ann Lowder,
She burst while drinking a Seidlitz powder.
Called from the world to her heavenly rest,
She should have waited till it effervesced.

Anon

Here lie I and my four daughters,
Killed by drinking Cheltenham waters.
Had we but stuck to Epsom salts,
We wouldn't have been in these here vaults.

Anon

Little Pam has gone to rest,
Safe at last on Abraham's breast,
Which may be nuts for Little Pam,
But is certainly rough on Abraham.

Anon

Here lies a poor woman who was always tired,
She lived in a house where help wasn't hired:
Her last words on earth were: "Dear friends, I am going
To where there's no cooking, or washing, or sewing,
For everything there is exact to my wishes,
For where they don't eat there's no washing of dishes.
I'll be where loud anthems will always be ringing,
But having no voice I'll be quit of the singing.
Don't mourn for me now, don't mourn for me never,
I am going to do nothing for ever and ever."

Anon

Beneath this stone, a lump of clay,
 lies Arabella Young,
Who on the twenty-fourth of May,
 began to hold her tongue.

On tombstone in English graveyard

Here lies my wife, a sad slattern and shrew;
If I said I regretted her, I should lie, too.

On tombstone in Yorkshire cemetery

Here lies my wife: here let her lie!
Now she's at rest, and so am I.

Intended for John Dryden's (1631–1700) wife

Here lies my wife, oh, how fine.
For her own repose, as well as mine!

Jacques Du Lovens, 1583–1650

Here lies my wife,
And lies and lies and lies and lies.
I wish, instead,
That she were dead.

Anon husband

EPITHETS

When a mother calls her own child "bastard!"—you may believe her.

Anon

EQUALITY

Golden lads and girls all must,
As chimney-sweepers, come to dust.

Shakespeare

EROS

Spelled backwards gives you an idea of how it affects beginners.

Anon

ERROR

To disavow an error is to invent retroactively.

Goethe

A little inaccuracy sometimes saves tons of explanation.

Saki

To err is human, but isn't it divine?

D. Crewe

ESCAPADE

'Tis a naughty night to swim in.

Shakespeare

ESCAPE

A witty French bishop was once asked why he kept up a country home which he seldom visited. "Do you not know," he replied, "that I must have some place where, tho I never go to it, I can always imagine that I might be happier than where I am?"

Anon

ESPIONAGE

Spy and the world spies with you; get caught and you're on your own.

G. Brown

THE ESTABLISHMENT

The trouble with most people is, they bow to what is called authority; they have a certain reverence for the old because it is old. They think a man is better for being dead, especially if he has been dead a long time. They think the fathers of their nation were the greatest and best of all mankind. All these things they implicitly believe because it is popular and patriotic, and because they were told so when they were very small, and remember distinctly hearing mother read it out of a book.

Robert Ingersoll

ETERNITY

What man is capable of the insane self-conceit of believing that an eternity of himself would be tolerable even to himself?

Shaw

EUROPE

A place where they name a street after you one day and chase you down it the next.

Arthur "Bugs" Baer

EVENTS

The dull period in the life of an event is when it ceases to be news and has not begun to be history.

Thomas Hardy

EVERYBODY

We are all in the gutter, but some of us are looking at the stars.

Wilde

EVIDENCE

Words are but wind, but seeing is believing.

Proverb

EVIL

The belief in a supernatural source of evil is not necessary; men alone are quite capable of every wickedness.

Joseph Conrad

Ever since the world began, it has been mostly wickedness that has made the headlines. How many people even know that Adam and Eve had a third son, who never got into trouble?

Sydney J. Harris

Of two evils choose the prettier.

Carolyn Wells

Of two evils, when we tell ourselves we are choosing the lesser, we usually mean we are choosing the more comfortable.

Sydney J. Harris

Evil is *live* spelled backwards.

Anon

EVIL/VIRTUE

Men's evil manners live in brass: their virtues
We write in water.

Shakespeare

EXAGGERATION

There are some people so addicted to exaggeration that they can't tell the truth without lying.

Josh Billings

EXAMINING THE MAFIA

We're trying to determine what the facts are regardless of the answers. I think the persistent taking of the Fifth Amendment is an indication of something.

N.Y. State Senator John Hughes (R-Syracuse)

EXAMPLE

Few things are harder to put up with than the annoyance of a good example.

Mark Twain

EXCELLENCE

The society which scorns excellence in plumbing, because plumbing is a humble activity, and tolerates shoddiness in philosophy, because it is an exalted activity, will have neither good plumbing nor good philosophy. Neither its pipes nor its theories will hold water.

John W. Gardner

EXCESS

To gild refined gold, to paint the lily,
To throw a perfume on the violet,
To smooth the ice, or add another hue
Unto the rainbow, or with taper-light
To seek the beauteous eye of heaven to garnish,
Is wasteful and ridiculous excess.

Shakespeare

EXCUSES

Who pardons the bad, injures the good.

English proverb

Bad excuses are worse than none.

English proverb

EXERCISE

The only exercise I get is when I take the studs out of one shirt and put them in another.

Ring Lardner

EXPECTATIONS

A cathedral, a wave of a storm, a dancer's leap, never turn out to be as high as we had hoped.

Proust

EXPERIENCE

He who stumbles twice over one stone, deserves to break his shins.

Proverb

We should be careful to get out of an experience only the wisdom that is in it—and stay there, lest we be like the cat that sits down on a hot stove-lid. She will never sit down on a hot stove-lid again—and that is well; but also she will never sit down on a cold one any more.

Mark Twain

Experience increases our wisdom but doesn't reduce our follies.

Josh Billings

The child sees everything which has to be experienced and learned as a doorway. So does the adult. But what to the child is an entrance is to the adult only a passage.

Nietzsche

"Live and Learn" is a fine old bit of advice, but the trouble with it today is that we have time for one or the other but not for both.

Hugh Allen

The only thing experience teaches us is that experience teaches us nothing.

André Maurois

EXPERTS

Even when the experts all agree, they may well be mistaken.

Bertrand Russell

EYES

He had but one eye, and the popular prejudice runs in favor of two.

Charles Dickens

The iris is the pleasant part of the eye, like in iris eyes are smiling.

Anon, Jr.

THE FACE

Chins are exclusively a human feature, not to be found among the beasts. If they had chins, most animals would look like each other. Man was given a chin to prevent the personality of his mouth and eyes from overwhelming the rest of his face, to prevent each individual from becoming a species unto himself.

Chazal

If the eyes are often the organ through which the intelligence shines, the nose is generally the organ which most readily publishes stupidity.

Proust

A house when gone to wrack and ruin
May be repaired and made a new one.
Alas! for ruins of the face
No such rebuilding e'er takes place.

Jean de la Fontaine

He had the sort of a face that, once seen, is never remembered.

Wilde

FACT

There is no sadder sight in the world than to see a beautiful theory killed by a brutal fact.

Thomas H. Huxley

Facts apart from their relationships are like labels on empty bottles.

Sven Halla

My mind is already made up! Don't confuse me with the facts.

Wall sign

FALLING

No one ever stumbled lying snug in bed.

Japanese proverb

Except for virgins.

LLL

FAILURE

Not failure, but low aim is crime.

Lowell

FAIR PLAY

All is unfair in love and war.

LLL

FAKER

He was born with a silver spoon in his mouth—but it had someone else's initials.

Anon

FALSEHOOD

If a child tells a lie, tell him that he has told a lie, but don't call him a liar. If you define him as a liar, you break down his confidence in his own character.

Jean Paul Richter

He who sticks to a lie for self-protection is as if he clung to a lightning rod in a thunderstorm.

Anon

FALSIES

Are the bust that money can buy.

Bob Levinson

FAME

Is nothing but the sum of all misunderstandings collected around a name.

Rainer Maria Rilke

Desire of glory is the last garment that even wise men put off.

English proverb

From a report of the Jane Austen Society: an account of the pitiable plight of an English tradesman who rented a house in Winchester where the distinguished author of *Pride and Prejudice* had once dwelt.

This shopkeeper, it seems, approached the trustees of Winchester College, from whom he rented the building, with the request that they put up some sort of informative plaque on the premises. "American tourists keep coming into my shop to ask if it is the Jane Austen house," he explained. "They take up my time and never buy anything. It's a great nuisance."

So a neat plaque was provided, with the succinct inscription:

Home of
Jane Austen
1775–1817

In a fortnight the shopkeeper was back. "Take down the plaque!" he pleaded.

"What's the matter," he was asked, "didn't it help?"

"Twice as many people are coming in," lamented the tradesman, "only now they are Englishmen. They keep coming in to ask, 'Who was Jane Austen?' "

Anon

Human nature is so well disposed toward those in interesting situations, that a young person who either marries or dies, is sure to be kindly spoken of.

Jane Austen

Every man has a lurking wish to appear considerable in his native place.

Samuel Johnson

Many a man's name appears in the paper only three times: when he's too young to read, when he's too dazed to read, and when he's too dead to read.

Anon

FAMILIARITY

Is a magician that is cruel to beauty, but kind to ugliness.

Ouida

Familiarity breeds contempt—and children.

Mark Twain

FAMILY

He that hath wife and children hath given hostages to fortune, for they are impediments to great enterprises, either of virtue or mischief.

Francis Bacon, a bachelor

Many children, and little bread, is a painful pleasure.

Proverb

It is a poor family that hath neither a whore nor a thief in it.

Proverb

FAMILY TREE

He that boasteth of his ancestors, confesseth he hath no virtue of his own.

English proverb

He that hath one of his family hanged, may not say to his neighbor, Hang up this fish.

Proverb

FAMOUS LAST WORDS

National Socialism does not harbor the slightest aggressive intent towards any European nation.

Adolf Hitler

Though you would often in the Fifteenth Century have heard the snobbish Roman say, in a would-be off-hand tone, "I'm dining with the Borgias tonight," no Roman was ever able to say "I dined last night with the Borgias."

Max Beerbohm

FANATIC

A fanatic is a fan who has gotten out of hand.

LLL

FARCE

Farce creates people who are so intellectually simple as to hide in packing cases or pretend to be their own aunts.

G. K. Chesterton

FAREWELL

It is amazing how nice people are to you when they know you are going away.

Michael Arlen

FARMING

One good thing about living on a farm is that you can fight with your wife without being heard.

Kin Hubbard

FASCISM

Is capitalism in decay.

Nikolai Lenin

FASCISM/COMMUNISM

I never could believe that Providence had sent a few men into the world ready booted and spurred to ride, and millions ready saddled and bridled to be ridden.

Richard Rumbold

FASHION

Never in the history of fashion has so little material been raised so high to reveal so much that needs to be covered so badly.

Jim Klobuchar

The only women who dress to please their husbands are wearing last year's clothes.

Anon

FAT WIFE

A bulge in a girdled cage.

Anon

FATE

No one knows what will happen to him before sunset.

Turkish proverb

FATHER-SON

Diogenes struck the father when the son swore.

Robert Burton

It's a wise son that owes his own father.

Anon

FATIGUE

William James, the great psychologist, once pointed out that many people get tired at a certain time every day because they have made it a habit to get tired at that particular time, not because they are really tired.

Gola Roberts

FAULT-FINDING

Everyone's faults are not written on their foreheads.

English proverb

If the best man's faults were written on his forehead, it would make him go out and buy a hat.

Gaelic proverb

FAVORS

I never forget a favor
Altho I must admit it
Does seem to have more flavor
When I'm the one who did it!

S. Omar Barker

FEAR

Fear can be headier than whiskey, once a man has acquired a taste for it.

Donald Downes

He that hath been bitten by a serpent is afraid of a rope.

English proverb

We fear something before we hate it; a child who fears noises becomes a man who hates noises.

Cyril Connolly

When we are afraid, we say that we are cautious. When others are afraid, we say that they are cowardly.

Marcel Archard

Suspicion always haunts the guilty mind;
The thief doth fear each bush an officer.

Shakespeare

FEELING

A man ought to feel what he's saying. I never heard a man yell "ouch" without enthusiasm.

Frank Clark

FEELINGS

I wish there were windows to my soul, so that you could see some of my feelings.

Artemus Ward

FEET

A pedestrian is a man in danger of his life; a walker is a man in possession of his soul.

David McCord

FELINE ANIMALS

Cats are the crabgrass on the lawn of civilization.

Snoopy

FELLOWSHIP

What men call good fellowship is commonly but the virtue of pigs in a litter which lie close together to keep each other warm.

Thoreau

FEMALE

A woman is only a collocation of animal cells formed into the female humanity-producing beast.

James Dickey

FERMENT

Where passion is high, there reason is low.

Proverb

FEVER

Once Antigonus was told his son, Demetrius, was ill, and went to see him. At the door he met some young beauty. Going in, he sat down by the bed and took his pulse. "The fever," said Demetrius, "has just left me." "Oh, yes," replied the father, "I met it going out at the door."

Plutarch

FICTION

Truth is stranger than fiction; fiction is obliged to stick to possibilities, truth isn't.

Mark Twain

Life in the city is an abrasive experience and fiction consists of abrasion.

Jonathan Baumbach

When I sit down at the typewriter, I am out to change the world.

John Oliver Killens

FIGHTING

It takes two to make a quarrel, one if it's a woman.

LLL

FINAGLE'S LAW

Once a job has been fouled up, anything done to improve it only makes it worse.

Anon

FIRE FIGHTING

To cast oil into the fire is not the way to quench it.

Irish Proverb

FINANCE

Most banks will gladly grant a loan;
In fact, they often speed it;
The only thing that they require
Is proof that you don't need it.

F. G. Kernan

FISH/MAN

3rd Fish: Master, I marvel how the fishes live in the sea.
1st Fish: Why, as men do a-land; the great ones eat up the little ones.

Shakespeare

FISHING

Fish are not to be caught with a bird-call.

English saying

We may say of angling as Dr. Boteler said of strawberries, "Doubtless God could have made a better berry, but doubtless God never did."

Izaak Walton

Is a laborious way of taking it easy.

Franklin P. Jones

FLATTERERS

Flatterers look like friends, as wolves like dogs.

George Chapman

Flatterers are cats that lick before and scratch behind.

American proverb

FLATTERY

He who fondles you more than usual has either deceived you or wants to do so.

French proverb

'Tis an old maxim in the schools,
That flattery's the food of fools;
Yet now and then your men of wit
Will condescend to take a bit.

Jonathan Swift

A little flattery will support a man through great fatigue.

James Monroe

What really flatters a man is that you think him worth flattering.

Shaw

Flattery is warming yourself by an artificial fireplace.

LLL

FLEXIBILITY

Better to bend than break.

English proverb

FLIGHT

The only victory over love.

French proverb

FLIRTS

The smiles of a pretty woman are the tears of the purse.

Venetian proverb

FLOUR POWER

Honest millers have golden thumbs.

Belgian proverb

FLYING

We have already begun to fly; several persons, here and there, have found the secret of fitting wings to themselves, of setting them in motion, so that they are held up in the air and are carried across streams . . . the art of flying is only just being born; it will be perfected, and some day we will go as far as the moon.

Bernard Le Bovier de Fontenelle, 1657–1757

FLYING OBJECTS

Birds are costing the U.S. Air Force about $10 million a year in aircraft damage.

Society of Automotive Engineers

FOLLY

A foolish man may be known by six things: anger without cause, speech without profit, change without progress, inquiry without object, putting trust in a stranger, and mistaking foes for friends.

Arabian proverb

The ultimate result of shielding men from the effects of folly is to fill the world with fools.

Herbert Spencer

FOOD

Asparagus inspires gentle thoughts.

Charles Lamb

Even were a cook to cook a fly, he would keep the breast for himself.

Polish proverb

Where would we be without salt?

James A. Beard

FOOLS

A fellow who is always declaring he's no fool usually has his suspicions.

Wilson Mizner

See the happy moron
   He doesn't give a damn;
I wish I was a moron,
   My God! Perhaps I am!

Anon of course

If all fools wore white caps, we should look like a flock of geese.

Proverb

Nature never makes any blunders; when she makes a fool, she means it.

Josh Billings

Any fool can make a rule, and every fool will mind it.

Thoreau

He is not a wise man who cannot play the fool on occasion.

English proverb

Every man is a damn fool for at least five minutes every day; wisdom consists in not exceeding the limit.

Elbert Hubbard

Every man plays the fool once in his life, but to marry is playing the fool all one's life long.

William Congreve

A man may be a fool and not know it—but not if he is married.

H. L. Mencken

Not all men are fools—some are bachelors.

Anon

Answer not the fool in his error, for thine attempt to instruct him will rouse his hatred.

Arabic proverb

This man must be very ignorant, for he answers every question he is asked.

Voltaire

The *shlemiehl* lands on his back and bruises his nose.

Yiddish proverb

He was born silly and had a relapse.

Arthur "Bugs" Baer

He that makes himself an ass must not take it ill if men ride him.

English proverb

A learned fool is one who has read everything and simply remembered it.

Josh Billings

A blockhead is never bored; he always has himself to think about.

Remy de Gourmont

A fool never admires himself so much as when he has committed some folly.

Chinese proverb

Money never made a fool of anybody; it only shows them up.

Kin Hubbard

A fool is half a prophet.

Yiddish proverb

What is a fool? Perhaps simply an undemanding mind, which is satisfied with little. Could it be that a fool is really wise?

Paul Valery

FOOLHARDINESS

An action or venture that fools and youths mistake for courage.

Harry Ruby

If you leap into a well, Providence is not bound to fetch you out.

Proverb

FOOLISHNESS

Folly taxes us four times as much as Congress.

Anon, 1900

Congress has caught up!

Anon, 1970

FOREVER

In a love affair, is at least over the weekend.

Anon

FORGETTING

Forgetting of a wrong is a mild revenge.

English saying

FORKED TONGUE

She speaks poniards, and every word stabs.

Shakespeare

FORMAL ADDRESS

When a teacher calls a boy by his entire name, it means trouble.

Mark Twain

FORTUNE

Dame Fortune is a fickle gipsy,
And always blind, and often tipsy;
Sometimes, for years and years together,
She'll bless you with the sunniest weather,
Bestowing honour, pudding, pence,
You can't imagine why or whence;—
Then in a moment—Presto, Pass!—
You find yourself right on your ass.

LLL, adapted from W. M. Praed

FORTUNES

He who swells in prosperity will shrink in adversity.

Proverb

FORTUNE-TELLERS

Show me a rich fortune-teller.

LLL

FRANCE

A nation of small, slow, stingy people, with at least one virtue, foresight.

Anon editor of the Matin

In France, we threaten the man who rings the alarm bell and leave him in peace who starts the fire.

Sébastien Chamfort

FREEDOM

Some fancy they may achieve freedom by doing as they please, by living undisciplined, uncontrolled lives. And they are surprised when they end up enslaved by some habit, some stronger mind, some malicious evil which resides within themselves or in society. As one writer put it, "They think they are emancipated, when they are only unbuttoned."

O. Carroll Arnold

Men rattle their chains to show that they are free.

Anon

The truly free man is the one who will turn down an invitation to dinner without giving an excuse.

Jules Renard

FREEDOM AND WOMEN

Eventually women will learn that there's no such thing as freedom. Their husbands are just as fastened to the deck as they are.

Katherine Ann Porter

FREEDOM OF PRINT

Let people talk, let them blame you, condemn you, imprison you, even hang you, but publish what you think. It is not a right, but a duty, a strict obligation laid upon anyone who thinks, to express what he thinks in public for the common good. . . . To speak is a good thing, to write it better, to print an excellent thing.

Paul Louis Courier

FREEDOM OF SPEECH

Provided I do not write about the government, religion, politics, morals, people in power, official institutions, the Opera, the other theatres, or about anybody attached to anything, I am free to print anything, subject to the inspection of two or three censors.

Figaro

THE FRENCH

A blaspheming Frenchman is a spectacle more pleasing to the Lord than a praying Englishman.

Heinrich Heine

No Frenchman of any standing is to be found in the gutter.

Robin Sokal

FRENCH ACADEMY

The French Academy is the secret longing of all men of letters. It is a mistress against whom they compose songs and epigrams, until they have obtained her favors. Once they have had her, they are no longer interested.

Voltaire

THE FRENCH AND THE SPANISH

The French are wiser than they seem, and the Spaniards seem wiser than they are.

Francis Bacon

FRESH AIR

Fresh air and innocence are good, if you don't take too much of them—but I always remember that most of the achievements and pleasures of life are in bad air.

O. W. Holmes, Jr.

FRIENDS

One friend in a lifetime is much; two are many; three are hardly possible.

Henry Adams

The best mirror is an old friend.

Proverb

But the best friend is not an old mirror.

LLL

Give me the avowed, the erect, the manly foe,
Bold I can meet—perhaps may turn his blow;
But of all plagues, good Heaven, thy wrath can send,
Save, save, oh! save me from the Candid Friend.

George Canning

There is no man so friendless but what he can find a friend
sincere enough to tell him disagreeable truths.

Bulwer-Lytton

There are some people who are very resourceful
At being remorseful
And who apparently feel that the best way to make friends
Is to do something terrible and then make amends.

Ogden Nash

A friend is someone whom we can always count on to count
on us.

François Perier

Friends are like fiddle-strings, they must not be screwed too
tight.

English proverb

When we are down and out, something always turns up—and
it's usually the noses of your friends.

Orson Welles

There are three faithful friends—an old wife, an old dog, and
ready money.

Franklin

It is in the thirties that we want friendship. In the forties, we
know they won't save us any more than love did.

F. Scott Fitzgerald

Go slowly to the entertainments of thy friends, but quickly to
their misfortunes.

Chilo

Friendships last when each friend thinks he has a slight
superiority over the other.

Anon

A friend is a speaking acquaintance who also listens.

Arnold H. Glasgow

FRIENDS/ENEMIES

Instead of loving your enemies, treat your friends a little
better.

Ed Howe

We were persuaded to become friends again; we embraced and
we have been mortal enemies ever since.

Lesage

FRIENDSHIP

We are so fond of one another because our ailments are the
same.

Jonathan Swift

If love is a taskmaster, friendship is the most discreet and
exquisite of chambermaids.

Jean Dutourd

Try your friend with a falsehood, and if he keeps it a secret,
tell him the truth.

Italian proverb

I can't be your friend and your flatterer too.

Proverb

Don't speak badly of my friends; I am capable of doing that
just as well as you.

Sacha Guitry

ROBERT FROST

Got a Pullet Surprise for his work.

Anon, Jr., reported by Art Linkletter

FRUITS

A cranberry is a cherry with an acid condition.

Fred Allen

FRUSTRATIONS

Photographers, along with dentists, are the two professions
never satisfied with what they do. Every dentist would like to
be a doctor and inside every photographer is a painter trying
to get out.

Pablo Picasso

FULFILLMENT

If we had everything we wanted, we wouldn't like what we
had.

William Feather

FULL HOUSE

A woman should have a prosaic husband and take a romantic
lover.

Stendhal

FUN

A few weeks ago he [Nixon] said he was having fun as President, for "fun is the opportunity to do things you couldn't do if you were not President."

Ted Lewis

Let us have wine and woman, mirth and laughter;
Sermons and soda-water the day after.

Lord Byron

FUN/FUNDS

Oh, what fun it is to have money!

Arthur Clough

FUNERALS

I have been to a funeral. I can't describe to you the howl which the widow set up at proper intervals.

Charles Lamb

FUNGUS

A mushroom is wood in its most delectable form.

LLL

FURS

No one in this world needs a mink coat but a mink.

Anon psychiatrist

FUTILITY

Most of us don't know what we want and spend our lives wondering why we don't get it.

Arnold H. Glasgow

It is hard to shave an egg.

Proverb

It's no good planting boiled potatoes.

Charles Spurgeon

It is lost labor to play a jig to an old cat.

Proverb

It is needless to pour water on a drown'd mouse.

Devonshire proverb

A stroke at every tree, without felling any.

Anon

THE FUTURE

My interest is in the future, because I am going to spend the rest of my life there.

Charles Kettering

Don't waste time looking back. Your eyes are in the front of your head.

Anon Englishman

Ten years from now you will be able to sit on a lawn that needs no mowing and reach up to pick a normal-sized peach from the low branches of a dwarf tree.

Dr. Jas. A. Lockhart, biologist at the California Institute of Technology,
1959

The trouble with the future is that it usually arrives before we are ready for it.

Arnold H. Glasgow

The future is no longer what it used to be.

Friedrich Hollander

GAMBLING

The roulette table pays nobody except him that keeps it. Nevertheless, a passion for gambling is common, though a passion for keeping roulette tables is unknown.

Shaw

If the Prince of Monaco has a roulette table, surely convicts may play cards.

Chekhov

He who gambles picks his own pocket.

Anon

The best throw of the dice is to throw them away.

Scottish proverb

GAMES

Life's too short for chess.

Henry James Byron

GARDEN OF EDEN

Eve: Do you love me?
Adam: Who else?

Anon eavesdropper

GARDENING

On the first day of springtime, my true love gives to me five packs of seed, four sacks of fertilizer, three cans of weed killer, two bottles of insect spray, and a pruning knife for the pear tree.

Dick West

Plant and the wife plants with you. Weed and you weed alone.

Denis Breeze

You can't teach an old dogweed new twigs.

Caesar Bottom

Old gardeners never die—they only spade away.

Mrs. Muriel Cox

GARDENS

Love of flowers and vegetables is not enough to make a man a good gardener. He must also hate weeds.

Eugene P. Bertin

The philosopher who said that work well done never needs doing over never weeded a garden.

Anon

GAY

The Gay Liberation Front's plan to take over the government of sparsely populated Alpine County in California by moving in thousands of gays to out-vote the locals is running into some big successes and some big hassles. More recruits are needed, if you're interested. . . .

Howard Smith

GENERALITIES—DETAIL

We think in generalities, but we live in detail.

Alfred North Whitehead

For parlor use, the vague generality is a lifesaver.

George Ade

GENERALS

As for being a General, well, at the age of four with paper hats and wooden swords we're all Generals. Only some of us never grow out of it.

Peter Ustinov

THE GENERATION GAP

Is the difference between a ukelele and an electric guitar.

Mitzi Gaynor

It's hard to know exactly when one generation ends, and the next one begins. But it's somewhere around nine o'clock at night.

Charles Ruffing

GENERATIONS

Every generation is a secret society and has incommunicable enthusiasms, tastes, and interests which are a mystery both to its predecessors and to posterity.

John Jay Chapman

GENEROSITY

Less of your courtesy and more of your purse.

Scottish proverb

GENETICS

The population explosion is simply love in boom.

Anon

GENIUS

The thinking of a genius does not proceed logically. It leaps with great ellipses. It pulls knowledge from God knows where.

Dorothy Thompson

Doing easily what others find difficult is talent; doing what is impossible for talent is genius.

Henri Amiel

Talk not of genius baffled. Genius is master of man.
Genius does what it must, and Talent does what it can.

Bulwer-Lytton (Last Words of a Sensitive Second-Rate Poet)

Everyone is a genius—at least once a year.

Lichtenberg

When a true genius appears in the world you may know him by this sign, that the dunces are all in confederacy against him.

Jonathan Swift

Good God! What a genius I had when I wrote that book.

Jonathan Swift

A man who is a genius and doesn't know it probably isn't.

Lec

The greatest minds are more dangerous than useful to the direction of affairs; unless they have more lead than quicksilver, they are of no value to the state.

Cardinal Richelieu

One of the strongest characteristics of genius is the power of lighting its own fire.

John Watson Foster

Inspiration and genius
Are not everything
While Mozart composed
The phone didn't ring.

May Richstone

The dearth of genius in America is owing to the continual teasing of mosquitoes.

Poe

GENTILITY

A true lady or gentleman remains at home with a grouch, same as if they had pneumonia.

Kin Hubbard

GENTLEMAN

This is the final test of a gentleman: his respect for those who can be of no possible service to him.

William L. Phelps

The manner of a vulgar man has freedom without ease; the manner of a gentleman has ease without freedom.

Lord Chesterfield

GEOGRAPHY

Egypt was started in the N.E. corner of Africa a long time ago and has occupied the same location to the present time, but sometimes under different management.

Anon, Jr.

Venice is a watering place kept up for the benefit of visitors.

Richard Wagner, c. 1860

Omaha is a little like Newark—without Newark's glamor.

Joan Rivers

GEOGRAPHY/POLLUTION

The river Rhine, it is well known
Doth wash your city of Cologne;
But tell me, nymphs! what power divine
Shall henceforth wash the river Rhine?

Coleridge

GEOMETRY

Teaches us to bisex angels.

Anon, Jr.

GEOPOLITICS

He that would England win, must with Ireland first begin.

English proverb

THE GEORGES

George the First was always reckoned
Vile, but viler George the Second;
And what mortal ever heard
Any good of George the Third?
When from earth the Fourth descended
God be praised, the Georges ended!

Walter Landor

GERMAN

Mastery of the art and spirit of the Germanic language enables
a man to travel all day in one sentence without changing cars.

Mark Twain

There are one hundred German expressions to express in-
toxication.

Schopenhauer (Handschriftlichem Nachlass)

A press campaign of four months will convince the German
people of the rightness of any idiocy you like to suggest.

Alfred von Kiderlen-Waechter

The Germans are responsible for everything that exists today,
for the sickliness and stupidity that oppose culture, the neuro-
sis, called nationalism, from which Europe suffers; they have
robbed Europe itself of its meaning and its intelligence. They
have led it into a blind alley.

Nietzsche

The Germans, a race eager for war.

Seneca the Younger

GIFTS

Little gifts maintain friendship; great ones maintain love.

Decoly

A blind man will not thank you for a looking glass.

English proverb

GILDING THE FILLY

Ugly women, finely dressed, are the uglier for it.

Italian proverb

GIRLS

Men often make passes
At girls who hold glasses.

LLL

Saying no the maiden shakes her head up and down.

Japanese proverb

Maidens and fish don't keep.

Japanese proverb

Adolescence is the age when a girl's voice changes from no to yes.

Anon

GIVING

He that bringeth a present, findeth the door open.

Scottish proverb

How many times have we heard, "Why, I've given him the shirt off my back and now look what he has done to me," or "I've given him the best years of my life and look what I get in return." If we bestow a gift or favor and expect a return for it, it is not a gift but a trade.

Anon giver

Some people who cast their bread upon the waters expect it to return as French toast.

Anon

It is more blessed to give the truth than to deceive.

LLL

GLOVES

Losing one glove is certainly painful but nothing compared to the pain of losing one, throwing away the other and finding the first one again.

Piet Hein

GO SLOW

Good and quickly seldom meet.

George Herbert, 1640

GOALS

On every side of us are men who hunt perpetually for their personal Northwest Passage, too often sacrificing health, strength, and life itself to the search; and who shall say that they are not happier in their vain but hopeful quest than wiser, duller folks who sit at home, venturing nothing and, with sour laughs, deriding the seekers for that fabled thorofare.

Kenneth Roberts

GOBBLEDYGOOK

Temperature Distribution in the Crystallization in Cylindrical Tubes, by Massachusetts Institute of Technology, Cambridge,

Mass., notes that numerical values of interface temperature rise as a function of the various parameters of a capillary crystallization experience are presented. These results should aid in the design and interpretation of future investigations of solidification kinetics by the capillary method.

U.S. Agency

GOD

God is a verb, not a noun.

Buckminister Fuller

I am always humbled by the infinite ingenuity of the lord, who can make a red barn cast a blue shadow.

E. B. White

God's works are good. This truth to prove
Around the world I need not move;
  I do it by the nearest pumpkin.

Jean de la Fontaine

Those who set out to serve both God and Mammon soon discover that there is no God.

Logan P. Smith

A God all mercy is a God unjust.

Edward Young

"The heavenly Father feedeth the fowls of the air"—and in winter He letteth them starve to death.

Jules Renard

An honest God is the noblest work of man.

Robert Ingersoll

How come if God is so all-powerful and omnipotent that he has such a short name.

Nina Weisman, Age Six

That God has managed to survive the inanities of the religions that do Him homage is truly a miraculous proof of His existence.

Ben Hecht

GOD AND WOMAN

The Bible says that the last thing God made was woman; He must have made her on a Saturday night—it shows fatigue.

Alexandre Dumas père

GOLD BAND

Oh! How many torments link in the small circle of a wedding ring.

Balzac

GOLDEN RULE

The golden rule is that there are no golden rules.

Shaw

GOLF

This is a terrible game. I'm glad I don't have to play again until tomorrow.

Anon duffer

GOLF CART

A method of transporting clubs that has one big advantage—it can't count.

Joachim Heinrich

GONERS

The absent are never without fault, nor the present without excuses.

Franklin

GOOD AND EVIL

The good should be grateful to the bad—for providing the world with a basis for comparison.

Sven Halla

The only good is knowledge and the only evil is ignorance.

Diogenes Laërtius

'Tis a good ill that comes alone.

Proverb

GOOD OLD DAYS

When policemen didn't hide at the side of a busy road but took their chances in traffic like anyone else.

Terry McCormick

GOODBYE

Farewell, a long farewell, to all my greatness;
This is the state of man: today he puts forth
The tender leaves of hope, tomorrow blossoms,
And bears his blushing honours thick upon him;
The third day, comes a frost, a killing frost..

Shakespeare

GOOD RESOLUTIONS

Are often checks drawn on an account with insufficient funds.

Jules Renard

GOOD TASTE

Good taste is the modesty of the mind; that is why it cannot be either imitated or acquired.

Émile de Girardin

GOODNESS

Be not simply good; be good for something.

Thoreau

Be good and you will be lonesome.

Mark Twain

GOOSE

The goose gabbles amid the melodious swans.

Virgil

GOSSIP

The difference between gossip and news depends on whether you hear it or tell it.

Anon

When a woman says, "I don't wish to mention any names," it ain't necessary.

Kin Hubbard

Wild horses couldn't drag a secret out of most women. Unfortunately, women seldom have lunch with wild horses.

Ivern Boyett

Gossip always travels faster over grapevines that are slightly sour.

Anon

There are two things that will be believed of any man whatsoever, and one of them is that he has taken to drink.

Booth Tarkington

None are so fond of secrets as those who do not mean to keep them.

Charles Calib Colton

"They say so" is half a lie.

Spanish proverb

There are many who dare not kill themselves for fear of what the neighbors will say.

Cyril Connolly

At every word a reputation dies.

Alexander Pope

GOURMET COOKING

There is no such thing as gourmet cooking. . . . Having started as a perfectly respectable part of the French language, it has been abused to serve as a label for the worst eccentricities and superficial elaborations of modern American cooking.

Michael Field

GOVERNMENT

The Nixon administration more and more resembles a badly run ship embarked on an endless series of disorganized shake-down cruises.

Richard Watts

Knowing exactly how much of the future can be introduced into the present is the secret of great government.

Victor Hugo

You are apprehensive of monarchy; I, of aristocracy. I would therefore have given more power to the President and less to the Senate.

John Adams

Tyranny is always better organized than freedom.

Charles Pierre Péguy

What right has government to take a hand in cultural things? Government's proper role is as a policeman. It has no business in housing. It would be better to subsidize transportation for poor people, so that they can live in outlying areas, than to put them in jail in the center of a city.

Frank Lloyd Wright

Bureaucracy is based on a willingness either to pass the buck or to spend it.

Mrs. Henry J. Serwat

Does it ever seem to you that your paycheck has turned into a receipt for your payroll deductions?

Anon

Modern political theory seems to hold that the way to keep the economy in the pink is to run the government in the red.

Nathan Nielsen

This is the age when, if you miss a day's work, the government loses almost as much as you do.

Anon

Everything now seems to be under federal control except the national debt and the budget.

Bob Goddard

Washington bureaucrats have finally figured out how to balance the budget. They're going to tilt the country.

Anon

The truth about government of the people, by the people, and for the people is that we are all being billed in triplicate. Which is not what Honest Abe had in mind.

Oren Arnold

Bureaucracy is a giant mechanism operated by pygmies.

Balzac

The republican form of government is the highest form of government; but because of this it requires the highest type of human nature—a type nowhere at present existing.

Herbert Spencer

A monarchy is a merchantman which sails well, but will sometimes strike on a rock, and go to the bottom; a republic is a raft which will never sink, but then your feet are always in the water.

Fisher Ames, in Congress 1795

A crisis a day keeps the Left Wing away.

Mrs. J. Smith

Govern a great nation as you would cook a small fish. Don't overdo it.

Lao-Tsze

He who hesitates would make a good Prime Minister.

T. Wells

In a democracy, the votes of the vicious and stupid count. But under any other system, they might be running the show.

Anon

There is an increased demand for codes of ethics in politics, although most office holders are sworn in with their hand resting on one.

Bill Vaughan

Any man who thinks he is going to be happy and prosperous by letting the Government take care of him should take a close look at the American Indian.

Anon

Democracy is the recurrent suspicion that more than half of the people are right more than half of the time.

E. B. White

Patrick Henry should come back to see what taxation *with* representation is like.

Anon

GRAFFITI

White walls are fools' writing paper.

Proverb

117

GRAMMAR

Pregnant is the past tense of virgin.

Anon

This is the sort of English up with which I will not put.

Sir Winston Churchill

GRAMMARIANS

. . . thou hast men about thee that usually talk of a noun and a verb and such abominable words as no Christian ear can endure to hear.

Shakespeare

GRASP

Take things always by their smooth handle.

Thomas Jefferson

GRASS

There is no riddle to surpass
The mystery of growing grass,
Which bravely thrusts its tender stalk
Thru tiny cracks along the walk,
And thrives in crannies of the wall,
And in the flower beds grows tall
And grows and grows, till summer's gone,
On everything except the lawn.

Curtis Heath

GRATITUDE

If you can't be thankful for what you receive, be thankful for what you escape.

Anon

I helped him when he was poor,
He never paid me back.
Yet though he owed me all he had,
He never objected to my presence.
Ah, what exquisite gratitude.

Nicholas Boileau-Despréaux

GREAT EXPECTORATIONS

Spit not against heaven, 'twill fall back in thy face.

Proverb

GREAT MEN

The two maxims of any great man at court are—always to keep his countenance and never to keep his word.

Jonathan Swift

If we didn't have ordinary men, how could we tell the great
ones?

Japanese proverb

Lives of great men all remind us
As we history's pages turn
That we often leave behind us
Letters which we ought to burn.

Harriet Fleischman

GREAT MINDS

When the human mind has achieved greatness and given evidence of extraordinary power in one domain, there is a tendency to credit it with similar power in all other domains.

John Tyndall

GREATNESS

No man ever yet became great by imitation.

Samuel Johnson

Great things are accomplished by those who do not feel the
impotence of man. This insensibility is a precious gift; but it
must be frankly admitted that, in this respect, our criminals
bear a certain resemblance to our heroes.

Paul Valery

GREED

The Chinese tell of a man of Peiping who dreamed of gold,
much gold, his heart's desire. He rose one day, and when the
sun was high he dressed in his finest garments and went to the
crowded market place. He stepped directly to the booth of a
gold dealer, snatched a bag full of gold coins, and walked
calmly away. The officials who arrested him were puzzled:
"Why did you rob the gold dealer in broad daylight?" they
asked. "And in the presence of so many people?"
  "I did not see any people," the man replied. "I saw only
gold."

Louis Binstock

GRIEF

It is foolish to tear one's hair in grief, as though sorrow would
be made less by baldness.

Cicero

GROWING UP

I remember, I remember
The fir-trees dark and high;

I used to think their slender tops
Were close against the sky;
It was a childish ignorance
But now 'tis little joy
To know I'm further off from heaven
Than when I was a boy.

Thomas Hood

Puberty—down in front.

LLL

GUESTS

Unbidden guests are often welcomest when they are gone.

Shakespeare

We never sit down to our pottage,
We never go calm to our rest,
But lo! at the door of our cottage,
The knock of the Guest.

Phyllis McGinley

GUGGENHEIM'S LAW NO. 1

Never make love to a woman before breakfast for two reasons. One, it is tiring. Two, you may meet someone else during the day that you like better.

Benjamin Guggenheim

GUGGENHEIM MUSEUM

Short of insisting that no pictures at all be shown, Frank Lloyd Wright could not have gone much further to create a structure sublime in its own right but ridiculous as a museum of art.

Lewis Mumford

GUILT

Every guilty person is his own hangman.

Seneca

So full of artless jealousy is guilt,
It spills itself in fearing to be spilt.

Shakespeare

GUN

Gun is short for "the Lady Gunhilda," an early cannon (1330) in the arsenal at Windsor.

Keith Read

GUNS vs. BUTTER

Guns will make us powerful; butter will only make us fat.

Herman Goering, 1936

HABIT

The fixity of a habit is generally in direct proportion to its absurdity.

Proust

Habit is habit, and not to be flung out of the window by any man, but coaxed downstairs a step at a time.

Mark Twain

HAIR

Young men object that they can't get a job if their hair is long. They ought to see how tough it is to get one when the hair is sparse and gray.

Bill Vaughan

A hair in the head is worth two in the brush.

Oliver Herford

He is false by nature that has a black head and a red beard.

English proverb

There was never a saint with red hair.

Russian proverb

Fair hair may have foul roots.

Russian proverb

Uneasy lies the head that wears the curlers.

Miss J. E. Battott

HALF TRUTH

Half truth. Whole lie.

Yiddish proverb

HAMLET

Hamlet's experiences simply could not have happened to a plumber.

Shaw

HANDICAPS

If I had the use of my legs, I should never have become a painter.

Henri Toulouse-Lautrec

HANDSOME

Handsome is what make-up does.

Miss E. Craig

HANDWRITING

My handwriting looks as if a swarm of ants, escaping from an ink bottle, had walked over a sheet of paper without wiping their legs.

Sydney Smith

HAPPINESS

Half riches, half poverty.

Eugene Ionesco

The moon.

Joseph Kessell

Living in peace with myself.

Georges Simenon

Is a vegetarian looking at the price of meat today.

Abel Green

Is getting a bill you've already paid, so you can sit down and write a nasty letter.

Peter Nero

To be happy, you must have taken the measure of your powers, tasted the fruits of your passion, and learned your place in the world.

Santayana

What makes men happy is loving to do what they have to do. This is a principle on which society is not founded.

Helvetius

If you observe a really happy man you will find him building a boat, writing a symphony, educating his son, growing double dahlias in his garden, or looking for dinosaur eggs in the Gobi desert. He will not be searching for happiness as if it were a collar button that has rolled under the radiator. He will have become aware that he is happy in the course of living twenty-four crowded hours of the day.

Dr. W. Beran Wolfe

Happy the man, and happy he alone,
He who can call today his own;
He who, secure within, can say:
"Tomorrow do thy worst, for I have lived today."

Horace

How happy some people would be
If they troubled themselves as little
About other people's business
As they do about their own.

Lichtenberg

They say that money doesn't bring happiness, but it's nice to be able to find out for yourself.

Anon banker

Is getting here in time.

Sign scrawled in Greenwich Village beer hall toilet

Grief can take care of itself; but to get the full value of a joy you must have somebody to divide it with.

Mark Twain

If happiness could be bought, few of us would have the price.

Anon

The happiest part of a man's life is what he passes lying awake in bed in the morning.

Samuel Johnson

Happiness ain't a thing in itself—it's only a contrast with something that ain't pleasant.

Mark Twain

For the happiest life, days should be rigorously planned, nights left open to chance.

Mignon McLaughlin

A lifetime of happiness! No man alive could bear it; it would be hell on earth.

Shaw

It is not enough to be happy; it is necessary, in addition, that others not be.

Jules Renard

O, how bitter a thing it is to look into happiness through another man's eyes!

Shakespeare

The most miserable people I have known have not been those who suffered from catastrophes—which they could blame on fate or accident—but those who had everything they wanted, except the power to enjoy it.

Sydney J. Harris

HAPPINESS/WISDOM

'Tis better to be happy than wise.

Latvian proverb

HARM

Great damage is usually caused by those who are too scrupulous to do small harm.

Cardinal de Retz

Better suffer a great evil than do a little one.

English saying

The offender never pardons.

George Herbert

HASTE

A hasty man never wants for woe.

English saying

Three things only are well done in haste: flying from the plague, escaping quarrels, and catching fleas.

Russian proverb

I have no time to be in a hurry.

John Wesley

He sows hurry and reaps indigestion.

Robert Louis Stevenson

More waist, less speed.

David Walters

HATRED

There is no greater hatred in the whole world than the hatred of ignorance for knowledge.

Galileo Galilei

In many cases, the political radical is one who first rejects the society of parents, then turns against all society and finds security in a group where all feel rejected. . . . Both Hitler and Karl Marx, the author of the Communist Manifesto, as well as Marx's collaborator, Friedrich Engels, grew up hating their fathers.

Dr. Andre E. Weil

HAZARD

What is necessary is never a risk.

Cardinal de Retz

Some had rather guess at much, than take the pains to learn a little.

Danish proverb

HEAD TO FOOT

Little wit in the head makes much work for the feet.

Proverb

HEALTH

A famous psychiatrist conducting a university course in psychopathology was asked by a student, "Doctor, you've told us about the abnormal person and his behavior; but what about the normal person? "If we ever find him," replied the psychiatrist, "We'll cure him."

Anon

There's lots of people in this world who spend so much time watching their health that they haven't the time to enjoy it.

Josh Billings

The only way to keep your health is to eat what you don't want, drink what you don't like, and do what you'd rather not.

Mark Twain

Invalids live the longest.

Japanese proverb

He is remarkably well, considering that he has been remarkably well for so many years.

Sydney Smith

HEALTH TIP

Wash your hands often, your feet seldom, and your head never.

John Ray, 1670

HEARING

We have two ears and only one tongue in order that we may hear more and speak less.

Diogenes

It isn't the things that go in one ear and out the other that hurt, as much as the things that go in one ear and get mixed up before they slip out of the mouth.

Anon

HEART

What is spoken of as "heart" is really a lot lower down.

LLL

HEART AND MOUTH

The heart of a fool is in his mouth, but the mouth of a wise man is in his heart.

Sirach

HEARTLESS HEELS

He that has no heart should have heels.

English proverb

HEAVEN/HELL

Many might go to Heaven with half the labor they go to Hell.

Jonson

HEAVENS BELOW!

If the sky fall, we shall catch larks.

Proverb

HEIGHT

When I was young, my producer, George Tyler, told me that were I four inches taller I could become one of the greatest actresses of my time. I decided to lick my size. A string of teachers pulled and stretched till I felt I was in a medieval torture chamber, I gained nary an inch—but my posture became military. I became the tallest five-foot woman in the world. And my refusal to be limited by my limitations enabled me to play Mary of Scotland, one of the tallest queens in history.

Helen Hayes

HELL

If there is no Hell, a good many preachers are obtaining money under false pretenses.

William A. Sunday

Is a place where the Germans are the police, the Swedish are the comedians, the Italians are the defense force, Frenchmen dig the roads, the Spanish run the railways, the Turks cook the food, the Irish are the waiters, the Greeks run the government, and the common language is Dutch.

British version

Not so bad as the road to it.

Yiddish proverb

The devil does a nice business for such a lousy location.

Dan Bennett

HELP

Considering the virtues that are required of a servant, does Your Excellency know many masters who would make acceptable valets?

Pierre Beaumarchais (The Marriage of Figaro)

HELPLESS

No one can feel as helpless as the owner of a sick goldfish.

Kin Hubbard

HEREDITY

The law of heredity is that all undesirable traits come from the other parent.

Anon

HEROES

Heroes are created by popular demand, sometimes out of the scantiest materials . . . such as the apple that William Tell

never shot, the ride that Paul Revere never finished, the flag
that Barbara Frietchie never waved.

G. W. Johnson

HERESY

Mock on, mock on, Voltaire, Rousseau;
Mock on, mock on; 'tis all in vain!
You throw the sand against the wind
And the wind blows it back again.

William Blake

HESITATION

The woman that deliberates is lost.

Joseph Addison

She who hesitates is won.

Anon

He who hesitates is bossed.

Sonia Chapman

HIBERNIAN HERNIA

A lethal rupture caused by lifting a barrel of Irish dew, one
drink at a time.

Desmond O'Hanrahan

HIGH PRESSURE

A study shows that stress does not cause high blood pressure.
It was conducted with rats, though, so it may not mean much
—rats are not in the people race.

Bill Vaughan

HIJACKING

You buy a ticket and board a plane for Miami, but you find
yourself landing in the airport in Havana. Your plane has
been hijacked. You pay your tuition and sign up for a course in
Shakespeare, but you find yourself listening to lectures and rap
sessions on the criminality of the American role in Southeast
Asia. Your education has been hijacked.

S. I. Hayakawa

HINDSIGHT

The time will come when Winter will ask us: "What were you
doing all the Summer?"

Bohemian proverb

HIPPIES

Hippies, fleeing from the rat race, living among the rats.

LLL

Are lost sheep, masquerading as shepherds.

Sam Levenson

HISTORY

Anybody can make history; only a great man can write it.

Oscar Wilde

If a man could say nothing against a character but what he could prove, history could not be written.

Samuel Johnson

The first qualification for a historian is to have no ability to invent.

Stendhal

Very few things happen at the right time, and the rest do not happen at all; the conscientious historian will correct these defects.

Herodotus

Cut off the human race from the knowledge and comprehension of its history, and its government will just turn into a monkey cage. We need the guidance of history. All our yesterdays, it is true, have only lighted fools the way to dusty death. But we need at least the dates of the yesterdays and the list of the fools.

Stephen Leacock

History teaches everything, even the future.

Alphonse de Lamartine

History is prophecy backward.

LLL

History proves that war is better at abolishing nations than nations are at abolishing wars.

Anon

The major fact about history is that in large part it appears criminal.

W. E. Arnold, Jr.

The first lesson of history is the good of evil.

Emerson

With history being made all the time, every day now seems to be the first anniversary of something awful.

Anon

In 1799 General Tamax received a proposal from Napoleon, who wished to enter the Russian service, but they were unable to agree, as Napoleon demanded the rank of major.

Tolstoi

History books which contain no lies are extremely tedious.

Anatole France

Happy the people whose annals are boring to read.

Montesquieu

So long as we read about revolutions in books, they all look very nice—like those landscapes which, as artistic engravings on white vellum, look so pure and friendly; dung heaps engraved on copper do not smell, and the eye can easily wade through an engraved morass.

Heinrich Heine

Human history becomes more and more a race between education and catastrophe.

H. G. Wells

If all the dreams which men had dreamed during a particular period were written down, they would give an accurate notion of the spirit which prevailed at the time.

Georg Hegel

Only the history of free peoples merits our attention; that of men under despotism is simply a collection of anecdotes.

Sébastien Chamfort

Perhaps in time the so-called Dark Ages will be thought of as including our own.

Lichtenberg

It costs us more to make history than the stuff is worth.

Pic Larmour

Most history is just gossip that has grown old gracefully.

Sydney J. Harris

The British never remember it; the Irish never forget it; the Russians never make it, and the Americans never learn from it.

Bishop Fulton J. Sheen

HIT AND MISS

The vulgar keep no account of your hits, but of your misses.

Proverb

HOLD THE THOUGHT

When I hear an ambulance siren, I have trained myself to think: "Someone is going to have a baby!"

Anon

HOLIDAYS

April fools have a day all their own, but the rest of us have to muddle along without any recognition.

Anon

If all the year were playing holidays
To sport would be as tedious as to work.

Shakespeare

HOLLYWOOD

Everywhere you look are advertisements for food or some mortuary. Even the benches at bus stops have ads offering a liberal credit plan for your funeral. In England they bury you or burn you or toss you away without making any fuss.

Dirk Bogarde

Is like a World's Fair that has been on a year too long.

Sonny Fox

HOLLYWOOD CENSORSHIP

Being a censor is like being a whore; everyone wants to know how you got into the business.

Jack Vizzard, ex-Hollywood censor

HOME

The average mortgage runs about twenty years, which gives the owner time, if he works on it every weekend, to get the place in shape to sell.

Gene Brown

HOME OWNERS

The fellow who owns his own home is always just coming out of a hardware store.

Kin Hubbard

HONESTY

It's strange that men should take up crime when there are so many legal ways to be dishonest.

Anon

Honesty is the rarest wealth anyone can possess, and yet all the honesty in the world ain't lawful tender for a loaf of bread.

Josh Billings

The world will be a better place when the Found ads in the newspapers begin to outnumber the Lost ads.

Lisa Kirk

Make yourself an honest man and then you may be sure there is one rascal less in the world.

Thomas Carlyle

There are times and countries when the only place for an honest man is in jail.

Thomas Mann

If you are honest because you think that is the best policy, your honesty has already been corrupted.

Sidney J. Harris

Honesty is the best policy?

HONESTY/DISHONESTY

It is impossible for a man to be cheated by anyone but himself.

Emerson

You can't cheat an honest man.

W. C. Fields

HONEYMOON

The honeymoon is over when he gets out of the car at the drive-in movie to wipe off the windshield.

Anon

HONOLULU

Psychiatrists are few in Honolulu and reputedly doing a lousy business. When life gets a little too oppressive in these parts, we just have another drink. If you don't look at trouble, it either goes away or else sticks around and becomes friendly like everybody else.

Robert Carson

HONOR

What is a gentleman but his word?

Proverb

Birds pay equal honours to all men.

English proverb

HOPE

He that places his faith in hope often lives on charity.

LLL

Hope is generally a wrong guide, though it is very good company by the way.

Halifax

My only hope lies in my despair.

Jean Racine

More are taken by hope than by cunning.

Vauvenargues

One door never shuts, but another opens.

Anon

HORN-TOOTING

Self-praise is no recommendation.

Proverb

131

HORSE SENSE

The true value of horse sense is shown by the fact that the horse was afraid of the auto during that period when the pedestrian laughed at it.

Anon

HORSEMANSHIP

The stupider the peasant, the better the horse understands him.

Chekhov

HORSEMANSHIP/MEDICINE

The best thing for the inside of a man is the outside of a horse.

Lord Henry Palmerston

HOSPITAL

A hospital should also have a recovery room adjoining the cashier's office.

Francis O' Walsh

HOSPITALITY

An unbidden guest must bring his stool with him.

English proverb

A good cup of coffee will get a town further with a stranger than a nifty boulevard.

Eugene P. Bertin

A host is like a general; it takes a mishap to reveal his genius.

Horace

A de luxe hotel is an institution designed to supply exclusiveness to the masses.

Oliver Herford

HOUSE OF COMMONS

There is hardly a person in the House of Commons worth painting, though many of them would be better for a little whitewashing.

Wilde

HOUSE RULES

If any pilgrim monk come from distant parts, with wish as a guest to dwell in the monastery, and will be content with the

132

customs which he finds in the place, and do not perchance by his lavishness disturb the monastery, but is simply content with what he finds, he shall be received for as long a time as he desires. If, indeed, he find fault with anything, or expose it, reasonably, and with the humility of charity, the Abbot shall discuss it prudently, lest perchance God had sent him for this very thing. But, if he have been found gossipy, and contumacious in the time of his sojourn as guest, it shall be said to him, honestly, that he must depart. If he does not go, let two stout monks, in the name of God, explain the matter to him.

Holy Rule of St. Benedict, posted in men's bar, National Press Club

HOUSING

The American Way: A "gracious living" sign on a new high-rent apartment means one thing—"no children allowed."

Dan Kidney

Before the craze for split-level homes a fellow kept it to himself if he lived over a garage.

Anon

HOUSING SHORTAGES

The foxes have holes, and the birds of the air have nests; but the Son of Man hath not where to lay his head.

Book of Matthew

HUMAN DEPLETION

Why not give every taxpayer who works for a living a depletion allowance? Every year that we work we get more and more depleted, so why can't we be given the same consideration as an oil well?

Rep. Thomas Rees (D-Calif.)

HUMAN NATURE

The end of the human race will be that it will eventually die of civilization.

Emerson

The Highly Fashionable and the Absolutely Vulgar are but two faces of the common coin of humanity.

H. G. Wells

HUMILITY

It is always the secure who are humble.

G. K. Chesterton

133

HUMOR

Modern man takes life far too seriously, and because he is too serious his world is full of troubles. The importance of humor should never be forgotten. For sense of humor changes the quality and character of our entire cultural life. . . . There is a purifying power in laughter—both for individuals and for nations. If they have a sense of humor, they have the key—to good sense, to simple thinking, to a peaceable temper, and to a cultured outlook on the world.

Lin Yutang

A sense of humor . . . is not so much the ability to appreciate humorous stories as it is the capacity to recognize the absurdity of the positions one gets into from time to time, together with skill in retreating from them with diginity.

Dana L. Farnsworth

HUNGER

The famished belly has no eyes.

Paul Leautaud

Twelve hours of hunger will reduce any saint, artist, or philosopher to the level of a highwayman.

Shaw in letter to Virginia Woolf

HUNGRY ARTISTS

Youngsters come to me. They asked, "How is an artist to live?" And I'd say what Duchaps always said: "Breathe. Keep doing it; sooner or later your work will sustain you."

Man Ray

HUNTING

It is as necessary, or rather more necessary, for most men to know how to capture mice, than how to take elephants.

Edward Topsell

Throwing your cap at a bird is not the way to catch it.

Proverb

If you run after two hares, you will catch neither.

Proverb

HURRY

Is a visible form of worry.

Arnold H. Glasow

HURT FEELINGS

The woman who is always having her feelings hurt is about as pleasant a companion as a pebble in a shoe.

Elbert Hubbard

HUSBAND

A man should be taller, older, heavier, uglier and hoarser than his wife.

E. W. Howe

All husbands are alike, but they have different faces so you can tell them apart.

Anon

He that hath a wife and children must not sit with his fingers in his mouth.

English proverb

The majority of husbands remind me of an orangutan trying to play the violin.

Balzac

The man had a grand job, but his wife complained because his average income was around midnight.

Anon

The married man must turn his staff into a stake.

Proverb

Nothing is more debasing for a real man than a plastic apron.

Viscountess Lewisham

A husband should tell his wife everything that he is sure she will find out, and before anyone else does.

Thomas Dewar

HUSBAND-WIFE

Observe the face of the wife to know the husband's character.

Proverb

A joint account is where you send your wife to the bank and kiss your money goodbye.

Anon

HYPOCHRONDRIA

He that is uneasy at every little pain is never without some ache.

English proverb

HYPOCRISY

Who paints me before blackens me behind.

Irish saying

May the man be damned and never grow fat,
Who wears two faces under one hat.

Proverb

Never trust a man who speaks well of everybody.

John Churton Collins

The friar preached against stealing when he had a pudding in his sleeve.

English proverb

ICE

A diamond is the only kind of ice that keeps a girl warm.

Elizabeth Taylor

IDEALISTS

When they come downstairs from their ivory towers, idealists are apt to walk straight into the gutter.

Logan P. Smith

The idealist is incorrigible: if he is thrown out of his heaven, he makes an ideal of his hell.

Nietzsche

He is so much of an idealist about his ideals that he can be a ruthless realist in his methods.

G. K. Chesterton

IDEAL WOMAN

One with lockjaw.

Ring Lardner

One who can mow the lawn, and put up the storm windows in December.

W. C. Fields

IDEAS

New ideas are for the most part like bad sixpences, and we spend our lives trying to pass them off on one another.

Samuel Butler (II)

Every time a man puts a new idea across he finds ten men who thought of it before he did—but they only thought of it.

Anon

One of the most hazardous of human occupations is the transferring of an idea from one mind to another. It's hazardous because you presuppose the existence of a second mind.

Christian Burckel

IDENTITY

I hate labels, and I wear no labels. When a man has to put something around his neck and say I AM, he isn't.

Pearl Bailey

IDLENESS

Is the finest thing in the world, provided one doesn't suffer from it.

Edgar Degas

The man with time to burn never gave the world any light.

Anon

IGNORANCE

He that knows least commonly presumes most.

English proverb

Everybody is ignorant, only on different subjects.

Will Rogers

Have the courage to be ignorant of a great number of things, in order to avoid the calamity of being ignorant of everything.

Sydney Smith

There is one thing to be said for ignorance—it sure causes a lot of interesting arguments.

Anon

A man's ignorance is as much his private property, and as precious in his own eyes, as his family Bible.

Oliver Wendell Holmes

ILL

All ill which doesn't affect me is only a dream.

Jules Renard

ILLNESS

Sickness tells us what we are.

Proverb

An hour of pain is as long as a day of pleasure.

English saying

Every invalid is a physician.

Irish proverb

I enjoy convalescence; it is the part that makes the illness worthwhile.

Shaw

ILLNESS-CURE

Keep up the spirits of your patient with the music of the viol and the psaltery, or by forging letters telling of the death of his enemies, or (if he be a cleric) by informing him that he has been made a bishop.

Henri de Mondeville

ILLUSION

The hardest thing to hide is something that is not there.

Eric Hoffer

IMAGINATION

Is what makes you think you're having a good time when you're only spending money.

Anon

A humble-bee in a cow-turd thinks himself a king.

English proverb

Anything one man can imagine, other men can make real.

Jules Verne

IMITATION

Is the sincerest form of competition.

LLL

Almost all absurdity of conduct arises from the imitation of those whom we cannot resemble.

Samuel Johnson

A man never knows what a fool he is until he hears himself imitated by one.

Sir Herbert Beerbohm Tree

IMMORAL

In primitive societies, immoral meant unusual, unexpected, and therefore shocking. And it would seem in so-called civilized societies, too.

James Laver

IMMORALITY

Is the morality of those who are having a better time.

H. L. Mencken

We are told by moralists with the plainest faces that immorality will spoil our looks.

Logan P. Smith

IMMORTALITY

To live in hearts we leave behind,
Is not to die.

Thomas Campbell

IMPLEMENTS

Pen and ink is wit's plough.

Proverb

IMPROMPTU EPITAPH ON OLIVER GOLDSMITH

Here lies Nolly Goldsmith, for shortness called Noll,
Who wrote like an angel, but talked like poor Poll.

David Garrick

IMPROVEMENT

Everyone thinks of changing the world, but no one thinks of
changing himself.

Leo Tolstoy

I used to think I was poor. Then they told me I wasn't poor,
I was needy. Then they told me it was self-defeating to think
of myself as needy, that I was culturally deprived. Then they
told me deprived was a bad image, that I was underprivileged.
Then they told me underprivileged was overused, that I was
disadvantaged. I still don't have a dime, but I do have a *great*
vocabulary.

Jules Feiffer

IMPROVING

I will not meddle with that I cannot mend.

Thomas Fuller

IMPULSE

Don't trust first impulses—they are always good.

Talleyrand

IMPULSIVENESS

One half the troubles of this life can be traced to saying "yes"
too quick, and not saying "no" soon enough.

Josh Billings

INFLUENCE

If you think you have influence, try ordering someone else's
dog around.

Anon

IN THE OPEN

Love, a cough, and the itch, cannot be hid.

Proverb

IN A RUT

To those capable only of ordinary actions, everything that is very much out of the ordinary seems possible only after it is accomplished.

Cardinal de Retz

IN THE WRONG

When a man is not liked, whatever he doth is amiss.

English proverb

INACTION

When day is done, you frequently find out that not much else has.

Anon Englishman

INCOME TAX

Another thing I'll never learn,
Altho it's plain to some, no doubt,
Is why they call it a "return"
When all I do is shell it out.

Ken Kraft

INCOMPATIBLE INCOME

There's nothing agrees worse
Than a proud mind and a beggar's purse.

Anon

INDEPENDENCE—RICHES

A man is rich in proportion to the number of things which he can afford to let alone.

Thoreau

INDIGESTION

The rebellions of the belly are the worst.

Bacon

Bolt in haste, belch at leisure.

LLL

INDIVIDUALITY

Read every day something no one else is reading. Think every day something no one else is thinking. It is bad for the mind to be always a part of a unanimity.

Christopher Morley

INDOLENCE

It is the common error of Socialists to overlook the natural indolence of mankind.

John Stuart Mill

Lazy people have no spare time.

Japanese proverb

INDUSTRY

It now takes a loaf and a half to be better than none.

Anon

INFATUATION

Love is an excruciating toothache of the brain.

Henry Murger

INFLATION

One of the benefits of inflation is that kids no longer get sick on a nickel's worth of candy.

Anon barber

A little inflation is like a little pregnancy—it keeps on growing.

Leon Henderson

The trouble with today's economy is that when a man is rich, it's all on paper. When he's broke, it's cash.

Sam Marconi

The trouble with inflation is that it now takes twice as much money to live beyond our means as it used to.

Anon

Some statistics are inaccurate, but any that deal with the cost of living are on the up and up.

Anon

In the old days, $10 worth of groceries would fill a pantry to bursting. Today, $10 worth of groceries won't even burst a shopping bag. Certainly shows how much stronger bags are now, doesn't it?

David Savage

All the talk going around about the high cost of living is just propaganda—put out by people who eat.

Anon

So far I haven't heard of anybody who wants to stop living on account of the cost.

Kin Hubbard

INFLATION SOLUTION

An American can still feed himself "adequately" for something in the neighborhood of $100 a year. His diet: 370 pounds of wheat flour; 57 cans of evaporated milk; 111 pounds of cabbage; 25 pounds of spinach, and 285 pounds of navy beans.

George Stigler, Columbia University economist

INHERITANCE

The worst misfortune that can happen to an ordinary man is to have an extraordinary father.

Austin O'Malley

INJUNCTION

Nobody has a right to speak more clearly than he thinks

Alfred North Whitehead

INJURY

If an injury has to be done to a man, it should be so severe that his vengeance need not be feared.

Machiavelli

INJUSTICE

Is the only blasphemy.

Robert Ingersoll

INNOCENCE

Itself sometimes hath need of a mask.

English proverb

INNS

The fairer the hostess, the fouler the reckoning.

British proverb

INQUISITIVE

To a man full of questions, make no answer at all.

Proverb

INSANITY

Insanity in individuals is something rare—but in groups, parties, nations and epochs it is the rule.

Nietzsche

INSCRIPTION

Messenger of Sympathy and Love, Servant of Parted Friends,

Consoler of the Lonely, Bond of the Scattered Family, Enlarger of the Common Life.

On U.S. Post Office, Washington, D. C.

INSECT WORLD

We hope that, when the insects take over the world, they will remember with gratitude how we took them along on all our picnics.

Bill Vaughan

The lightning-bug is brilliant, but he hasn't any mind;
He stumbles through existence with his head-light on behind.

Eugene F. Ware

A bee is never as busy as it seems; it's just that it can't buzz any slower.

Kin Hubbard

The fly sat upon the axle-tree of the chariot-wheel and said, "What a dust I raise."

Aesop, quoted by Bacon

INSOLENCE

When you have done a fault, be always pert and insolent, and behave yourself as if you were the injured person.

Jonathan Swift

INSPIRATION

A writer is rarely so well inspired as when he talks about himself.

Anatole France

INSULT

To praise princes for virtues they are lacking in is a way of insulting them with impunity.

La Rochefoucauld

Be so kind as to turn the matter over in what you are pleased to call your mind.

Richard Bethell, Lord Westbury

Just look at her—she's had eleven husbands, including three of her own.

Anon

I wish I'd known you when you were alive.

LLL

Thou hast a head, and so hath a pin.

Jonathan Swift

One insult pocketed soon produces another.

Thomas Jefferson

INSURANCE COMPANIES

Are like women. They conceive in pleasure and bring forth in pain.

Mme. Henri-Robert

INTEGRITY

Is praised and starves.

Juvenal

INTELLECTUAL

A highbrow is a person who enjoys a thing until it becomes popular.

Anon

INTELLIGENCE

The voice of the intelligence is soft and weak, said Freud: It is drowned out by the roar of fear. It is ignored by the voice of desire. It is contradicted by the voice of shame. It is hissed away by hate and extinguished by anger. Most of all, it is silenced by ignorance.

Karl Menninger

Intelligence has been defined by the psychologists as the capacity to learn. That is nonsense. Intelligence is the capacity to wonder.

Hy Sherman

INTEMPERANCE

Bacchus has drowned more men than Neptune.

Garibaldi

INTERPRETATIONS

There is more ado to interpret interpretations, than to interpret things; and more books upon books than upon any other subject.

Michel de Montaigne (1533–1592)

INVENTIONS

If it hadn't been for Edison, we'd be watching television by candlelight.

Anon

IRELAND

In some parts of Ireland, the sleep which knows no waking is always followed by a wake which knows no sleeping.

Mary Little

144

THE IRISH

For the great Gaels of Ireland
Are the men that God made mad,
For all their wars are merry,
And all their songs are sad.

G. K. Chesterton

An Irishman can be worried by the consciousness that there is nothing to worry about.

Austin O'Malley

The Irish are a fair people; they never speak well of one another.

Samuel Johnson

Put an Irishman on the spit, and you can always get another Irishman to turn him.

Shaw

The Irish do not want anyone to wish them well; they want everyone to wish their enemies ill.

Harold Nicolson

ISRAEL

When Israel, of the Lord beloved,
Out from the land of bondage came,
Her fathers' God before her moved,
An awful guide in smoke and flame.

Sir Walter Scott

ITALY

Is a country of fifty-five million actors, the worst of whom are on the stage.

Orson Welles

The Creator made Italy from designs by Michelangelo.

Mark Twain

Venice would be a fine city—if it were only drained.

Ulysses S. Grant

I-TALK

Neither speak well nor ill of yourself. If well, men will not believe you; if ill, they will believe a great deal more than you say.

Proverb

JACOBIN

A steady patriot of the world alone,
The friend of every country but his own.

George Canning

JAPANESE PROVERB

Even the finest shoe makes a terrible hat.

JEALOUSY

A jealous man's horns hang in his eyes.

English proverb

JEHOVAH

Is the most fascinating character in all fiction.

Oliver Herford

JESTING

The wise make jests, and fools repeat them.

Proverb

JET AGE PLANNING

Means building an air terminal so that you must walk a mile in order that your luggage will be at the exit before you are.

LLL

JET TRAVEL

The highest form of civilization.

LLL

JEWELS

Diamonds are found on the backs of diamond-back rattle-snakes. That is why they cost so much.

Anon, Jr.

THE JEWS

Are a frightened people. Nineteen centuries of Christian love have broken down their nerves.

Israel Zangwill, c. 1900

JOURNALISM

A journalist is a grumbler, a censurer, a giver of advice, a regent of sovereigns, a tutor of nations. Four hostile news-papers are more to be feared than a thousand bayonets.

Napoleon Bonaparte

Writing about the Nixon Administration is about as exciting as covering the Prudential Life Assurance Co.

Art Buchwald

A journalist is stimulated by a deadline; he writes worse when he has time.

Karl Kraus

146

Journalists say a thing that they know isn't true, in the hope
that if they keep on saying it long enough it will be true.

Arnold Bennett

Most journalists are restless voyeurs who see the warts on the
world, the imperfections on people and places ... gloom is their
game, the spectacle their passion, normality their nemesis.

Gay Talese

JOURNALISM/LITERATURE

The difference between journalism and literature is that journalism is unreadable and literature is not read.

Wilde

JOURNEY

The fool wanders; the wise man travels.

Proverb

The end of a thousand mile journey is the last step.

Scarritt Adams

JUDGE

Advice of salty old judge to young lawyer: "To be a good
judge, you must have inestimable good judgment, a sense of
fair play and a darn good bladder."

Mrs. Loyal C. Payne

JUDGMENT

The good judgment of some people will never wear out. They
don't use it often enough.

Anon

Thou art weighed in the balance, and oft found wanton.

LLL

JUNK MAIL

Instead of an unlisted phone, I need an unlisted address.

Carmichael

JUSTICE

Laws catch flies, but let hornets go free.

Proverb

And hungry judges soon the sentence sign.
And wretches hang that jurymen may dine.

Alexander Pope

JUVENILE DELINQUENCY

Another way to reduce juvenile delinquency sharply would be
to quit coddling hard-boiled eggs.

Anon

KEYS

The frustrating thing is that the key to success doesn't always fit your ignition.

Roger C. Meyer

KIDS

When children stand quiet, they have done some harm.

English proverb

KINDNESS

If you're naturally kind you attract a lot of people you don't like.

William Feather

KINGS

The whole institution of royalty is dying out because kings have no union.

LLL

KISS

Lord! I wonder what fool it was that first invented kissing.

Jonathan Swift

If you can kiss the mistress, never kiss the maid.

Proverb

KNOWLEDGE

... knowledge is power ... knowledge is safety, and ... knowledge is happiness.

Thomas Jefferson

One part of knowledge consists in being ignorant of such things as are not worthy to be known.

Proverb

"A little knowledge is a dangerous thing." That is why so many persons don't fool with it.

Dan Kidney

If a little knowledge is dangerous, where is the man who has so much as to be out of danger?

Thomas Huxley

You can know ten things by learning one.

Japanese proverb

He who knows others is learned;
He who knows himself is wise.

Lao-Tsze

After learning the tricks of the trade, many of us think we know the trade.

William Feather

The trouble with most folks isn't so much their ignorance, as knowing so many things that ain't so.

Josh Billings

KNOWLEDGE/IGNORANCE

What you don't know won't help you much either.

Dan Bennett

LABOR

Labor is the capital of our workingmen.

Grover Cleveland

Not to oversee workmen, is to leave them your purse open.

Italian proverb

LAND RUSH

Some surveyors looked around, and you know what they discovered on my property? Parking space!

Oscar Homolka

LANGUAGE

The words in his mouth were smoother than butter, but margarine was in his heart.

LLL

I speak Spanish to God, Italian to women, French to men, and German to my horse.

Charles V

English is a funny language. A fat chance and a slim chance are the same thing.

Jack Herbert

If English was good enough for Jesus, it is good enough for you.

Arkansas town school superintendent, refusing request that foreign languages be taught in high school

LARCENY

Don't plug your ears when you go to steal a bell.

Japanese Proverb

LAST WORDS

Alas, I am dying beyond my means.

Wilde

I go to seek a great perhaps.

Ring down the curtain, the farce is over.

Also, François Rabelais

I feel nothing but a great difficulty in dying.

LAS VEGAS

Las Vegas is a strip of lights bounded by slot machines. The only town I know where Western Union has messages already printed for sending home for money.

LAUGHTER

Of all God's gifts to men, laughter is one of the most subtle and is one of the most precious. It has neither nationality nor religion. As an equalizer, it has no equal. Even science which can do so many things can't teach us to laugh.

Laughing is the cheapest luxury man enjoys. It stirs up the blood, expands the chest, electrifies the nerves, clears away the cobwebs from the brain, and gives the whole system a cleansing rehabilitation.

We must use laughter discreetly, because there is much power in laughter. The Eskimos do not punish a thief; they laugh at him. There is, consequently, very little stealing among Eskimos.

A sense of humor keen enough to show a man his own absurdities, as well as those of other people, will keep him from the commission of all sins, or nearly all, save those that are worth committing.

I love such mirth as does not make friends ashamed to look upon one another next morning.

Good jests bite like lambs, not like dogs.

Laugh and the world laughs with you—cry and you sell 3 million records.

Laughter is surplus energy, released by fear appeased.

The humorist runs with the hare; the satirist hunts with the hounds.

Father Ronald A. Knox

He who laughs, lasts.

Anon

LAWS

Laws should be like clothes. They should be made to fit the people they are meant to serve.

Clarence Darrow

There is no man so good, who, were he to submit all his thoughts and actions to the laws would not deserve hanging ten times in his life.

Montaigne

Reading the fine print may give you an education—not reading it will give you experience.

V. M. Kelley

A fox should not be on the jury at a goose's trial.

English proverb

One eye-witness is better than ten hearsays.

Legal proverb

Witnesses are expensive, not everyone can afford them.

Jean Racine

False folk should have many witnesses.

Scottish proverb

Written laws are like spiders' webs, and will, like them, only entangle and hold the poor and weak, while the rich and powerful will easily break through them.

Anacharsis

The law doth punish man or woman
That steals the goose from off the common,
But lets the greater felon loose,
That steals the common from the goose.

Anon, 1764

I was never ruined but twice: once when I lost a lawsuit, and once when I won one.

Voltaire

May you have a lawsuit in which you know you are in the right.

Gypsy curse

Gentlemen, it is lawful to rape your wife.

Herbert Bayard Swope

It's hard to explain to kids why a nation that spends billions for nuclear bombs is still trying to outlaw firecrackers.

Anon

LAWYER

When there's a rift in the lute, the business of the lawyer is to widen the rift and gather the loot.

Arthur Hays

A lawyer is a learned gentleman who rescues your estate from your enemies and keeps it himself.

Lord Brougham

A divorce lawyer is the man who referees the fight and winds up with the purse.

Anon

If there were no bad people, there would be no good lawyers.

Dickens

The robes of lawyers are lined with the obstinacy of clients.

English proverb

It is the trade of lawyers to question everything, yield nothing, and to talk by the hour.

Thomas Jefferson

When you have no basis for an argument, abuse the plaintiff.

Cicero

Only painters and lawyers can change white to black.

Japanese Proverb

He saw a lawyer killing a viper
On a dunghill hard by his own stable;
And the Devil smiled, for it put him in mind
Of Cain and his brother Abel.

Coleridge

Lawyers are the only persons in whom ignorance of the law is not punished.

Jeremy Bentham

LAWYERS AND SOLICITORS

The difference between a lawyer and a solicitor is simply that of a crocodile and an alligator.

English proverb

LAZINESS

Laziness implies a lot of intelligence. It is the normal healthy attitude of a man with nothing to do.

Sir Heneage Oglivie, age seventy-two

LEADER

A good leader can't get too far ahead of his followers.

F. D. Roosevelt

Who comes earliest leads the way.

Japanese Proverb

Great actions are not always true sons of great and mighty resolutions.

Samuel Butler (I)

The world will only, in the end, follow those who have despised as well as served it.

Samuel Butler (II)

Followers subordinate themselves, not because the leader is utterly different, but because he is the same, only more so.

Paul Pigors

There is no trick to being a captain as long as the sea is quiet.

Benjamin II

The leader is a stimulus, but he is also a response.

Eduard C. Lindeman

Something is happening to our country. We aren't producing leaders like we used to. A new chief executive officer today, exhausted by the climb to the peak, falls down on the mountaintop and goes to sleep.

Robert Townsend

LEARNING

It is always in season for old men to learn.

Aeschylus

Some people will never learn anything because they understand everything too soon.

Anon

When I thought I had been learning how to live, I had only been learning how to die.

Leonardo da Vinci

LEARNING VS. KNOWLEDGE

There is much more learning than knowledge in the world.

Belgian proverb

LEGITIMACY

Mothers may have illegitimate children, but fathers simply have natural sons.

Elbert Hubbard

LETTER

I have received no more than one or two letters in my life that were worth the postage.

Thoreau

LETTER TO CONGRESS

The Supreme Court should be confined to interrupting the law, rather than making it.

Anon

LETTER WRITING

They prosper who burn in the morning
The letters they wrote over night.

Ronald Arthur Hopwood

LIBERTY

Is life so dear, or peace so sweet, as to be purchased at the price of chains and slavery? Forbid it, Almighty God! I know not what course others may take; but, as for me, give me liberty, or give me death!

Patrick Henry

LIBRARY

No place affords a more striking conviction of the vanity of human hopes, than a public library.

Samuel Johnson

The library has been variously and sentimentally called the storehouse of all knowledge and the treasure house of the mind. Its real virtue, however, is that as a repository it preserves error as well as truth and nonsense as well as sense.

Harry Golden

LIE/TRUTH

A good lie finds more believers than a bad truth.

German proverb

LIE LOW

Where there is whispering, there is lying.

Proverb

(A. J.) LIEBLING'S LAW

If you just try long enough and hard enough, you can always manage to boot yourself in the posterior.

LIES

The ordinary decent Parisian male lies ten times a day, the ordinary decent female twenty times a day, the man of fashion a hundred times a day. It has never been possible to calculate how many times a day the lady of fashion lies.

Hippolyte Taine

LIFE

The universe is like a safe to which there is a combination—
but the combination is locked up in the safe.

Peter DeVries

Every day is a little life, and our whole life is but a day
repeated.

Anon

We are no more than candles burning in the wind.

Japanese proverb

Life is simply a bad quarter of an hour made up of exquisite
moments.

Mauvais

Life is far too important a thing ever to talk seriously about.

Wilde

Life is a dream—but don't wake me.

Yiddish proverb

Life is a child that has to be rocked in its cradle until it finally
falls asleep.

Voltaire

Life is not long, and too much of it must not pass in idle de-
liberation how it shall be spent.

Samuel Johnson

To dream is happiness; to wake is life.

Victor Hugo

Life is a greedy pursuit of trifles.

Sherwood Anderson

Life is one long process of getting tired.

Samuel Butler (II)

The art of life is the avoiding of pain.

Thomas Jefferson

The years don't last as long as you think they are going to.

Walter Lippmann at age eighty

Life is too short to be small.

Benjamin Disraeli

A man of sixty has spent twenty years in bed and over three
years in eating.

Arnold Bennett

It is better to wear out one's shoes than one's sheets.

Genoese proverb

The play is the tragedy, "Man,"
And its Hero, the Conqueror Worm.

Edgar Allan Poe

For men must work, and women must weep,
And the sooner it's over, the sooner to sleep.

Charles Kingsley

Time flies, death urges, knells call, heaven invites, Hell threatens.

Edward Young

It is a funny thing about life: if you refuse to accept anything but the best you very often get it.

Somerset Maugham

Give us the luxuries of life and we will dispense with the necessaries.

John Lothrop Motley

If one considered life as a simple loan, one would perhaps be less exacting.

Eugene Delacroix

Life is the greatest bargain; we get it for nothing.

Yiddish proverb

He that will live in this world must be endowed with the three rare qualities of dissimulation, equivocation, and mental reservation.

Aphra Behn

Half our mistakes in life arise from feeling where we ought to think, and thinking where we ought to feel.

John Collins

It is better to burn the candle at both ends, and in the middle, too, than to put it away in the closet and let the mice eat it.

Henry van Dyke

Life can only be understood backwards, but it must be lived forwards.

Sören Kierkegaard

It happens in life, as in grammar, that the exceptions outnumber the rules.

Remy de Gourmont

There are people who so arrange their lives that they feed themselves only on side dishes.

Ortega y Gasset

The first forty years of life give us the text; the next thirty supply the commentary.

Schopenhauer

My theory is to enjoy life, but the practice is against it.

Charles Lamb

LIFE TODAY

Finding a way to live the simple life today is man's most complicated task.

Henry A. Courtney

Never look behind you. Something may be gaining on you.

Sachel Paige

Today we use 300 horsepower to move a 150-pound man one block to purchase a one-ounce package of cigarettes—complete with filter tips so he won't know he's smoking.

John B. Macdonald

A lot of today's frustration is caused by a surplus of simple answers, coupled with a tremendous shortage of simple problems.

Paul Sweeney

LIFE/DEATH

Who has but a short time to live
No longer needs to dissemble.

Philippe Quinault

Pay as you go, unless you are going for good.

Anon

Everything peters out in a song.

Figaro

Only the young die good.

Oliver Herford

LIGHT

There is not enough darkness in all the world to put out the light of even one small candle.

Robert Alden

LIGHTNING

Lightning never strikes twice in the same place, because after the first time the place is gone.

Anon

LIMERICKS

After being a judge in a limerick contest, director Mike Nichols said: "It was easy. We just threw out the dirty ones and gave the prize to the one that was left."

There was a young man of Montrose,
Who had pockets in none of his clothes,
   When asked by his lass
   Where he carried his brass,
He said, "Darling, I pay through the nose."

Arnold Bennett

I sat next to the duchess at tea;
It was just as I feared it would be:
   Her rumblings abdominal
   Were truly phenomenal,
And everyone thought it was me.

attributed to Woodrow Wilson

In New Orleans dwelled a young Creole
Who, when asked if her hair was all reole,
   Replied with a shrug
   "Just give it a tug
And decide by the way that I squeol."

Alben Barkley

According to experts, the oyster
In its shell—or crustacean cloister—
   May frequently be
   Either he or a she
Or both, if it should be its choice ter.

Berton Braley

There once was an old man of Lyme
Who married three wives at a time;
   When asked, "Why a third?"
   He replied, "One's absurd,
And bigamy, sir, is a crime."

W. C. Monthouse

There was a coed of Cayenne
Who ate onions, blue cheese and Sen-Sen
   Till a bad fright one day
   Took her breath quite away
And we hope she won't find it again.

Anon

There's a wonderful family called Stein
There's Gert and there's Epp and there's Ein
   Gert's poems are bunk,
   Epp's statues are junk,
And no one can understand Ein.

Anon

There once was a sculptor named Phidias
Whose manners in art were invidious:
   He carved Aphrodite
   Without any nightie,
Which startled the ultrafastidious.

Anon

There was a young man of Japan
Whose limericks never would scan;
   When they said it was so,
   He replied: "Yes, I know,

158

But I always try to get as many words into the last line as
ever I possibly can."

Anon

LIMERICK AND SEQUEL

There was an old man of Nantucket
Who kept all his cash in a bucket;
 But his daughter, named Nan
 Ran away with a man
And as for the bucket, Nantucket.

Pa followed the pair to Pawtucket
(The man and the girl with the bucket)
 And he said to the man,
 "You're welcome to Nan,"
But as for the bucket, Pawtucket.

Anon

LION

A great jaw set on four powerful springs of short, massive legs.

Hippolyte Taine

LISTENING

Two men were walking along a crowded sidewalk in a down-
town business area. Suddenly one exclaimed: "Listen to the
lovely sound of that cricket." But the other could not hear.
He asked his companion how he could detect the sound of a
cricket amid the din of people and traffic. The first man, who
was a zoologist, had trained himself to listen to the voices of
nature. But he didn't explain. He simply took a coin out of
his pocket and dropped it to the sidewalk, whereupon a dozen
people began to look about them. "We hear," he said, "what
we listen for."

Kermit L. Long

Listening is a magnetic and strange thing, a creative force.
The friends who listen to us are the ones we move toward, and
we want to sit in their radius. When we are listened to, it
creates us, makes us unfold and expand. I discovered this a few
years ago. Before that, when I went to a party I would think
anxiously: "Now try hard, be lively." But now I tell myself
to listen with affection to anyone who talks to me. This person
is showing me his soul. It is a little dry and meager and full
of grinding talk just now, but soon he will begin to think. He
will show his true self; will be wonderfully alive.

Dr. Karl Menninger

159

The funny thing about human beings is that we tend to respect the intelligence of, and eventually to like, those who listen attentively to our ideas even if they continue to disagree with us.

S. I. Hayakawa

He that speaks, sows; he that hears, reaps.

Proverb

Hear twice before you speak once.

Scottish proverb

Listen, or thy tongue will keep thee deaf.

American Indian proverb

LITERATURE

The reason why so few good books are written is that so few people who can write know anything.

Walter Bagehot

How vain it is to sit down to write when you have not stood up to live.

Thoreau

Some of the new books are so down to earth they should be plowed under.

Anna Herbert

Sperone-Speroni explains very well why a writer's form of expression may seem quite clear to him yet obscure to the reader; the reader is advancing from language to thought, the writer from thought to language.

Sébastien Roch Nicolas Chamfort

When once the itch of literature comes over a man, nothing can cure it but the scratching of a pen.

Samuel Lover

To hold a pen is to be at war.

Voltaire

Devotees of grammatical studies have not been distinguished for any very remarkable felicities of expression.

Louisa May Alcott

Our American professors like their literature clear, cold, pure, and very dead.

Sinclair Lewis

To write simply is as difficult as to be good.

Somerset Maugham

If you can describe clearly without a diagram the proper way of making this or that knot, then you are a master of the English tongue.

Hilaire Belloc

When we encounter a natural style we are always surprised and delighted, for we thought to see an author and found a man.

Blaise Pascal

When I wrote the *Charterhouse,* to get the right tone and to sound natural I read two or three pages of the Civil Code every morning.

Stendhal

Big book, big evil.

Callimachus

American Novel: A story in which two people want each other from the beginning but don't get each other until the end of the book.

French Novel: A story in which the two people get together right at the beginning, but from then until the end of the book they don't want each other any more.

Russian Novel: A story in which the two people don't want each other or get each other—and for 800 pages brood about it.

Erich Maria Remarque

There is a great discovery still to be made in literature, that of paying literary men by the quantity they do not write.

Thomas Carlyle

People do not deserve to have good writing, they are so pleased with bad.

Emerson

I wonder why murder is considered less immoral than fornication in literature.

George Moore

If *Hamlet* had been written these days it would probably have been called *The Strange Affair at Elsinore.*

Sir James Barrie

LITERARY TRENDS

Perhaps I have hit on a reason for my waning love of novels of which I was not aware before—that they have substituted gynecology for romance.

Ben Hecht

LITERARY ACCLAIM

This author has got it made;
No vestige of doubt now lurks.
For consider this accolade:
His books are known as Works.

Georgie Starbuck Galbraith

LIVE AND LOVE

To live is like to love—all reason is against it, and all healthy instinct is for it.

Samuel Butler (II)

LIVING

Never let your head hang down. Never give up and sit down and grieve. Find another way. And don't pray when it rains if you don't pray when the sun shines.

Sachel Paige

Were we to take as much pains to be what we ought, as we do to disguise what we are, we might appear like ourselves without being at the trouble of any disguise at all.

La Rochefoucauld

We crucify ourselves between two thieves: regret for yesterday and fear of tomorrow.

Fulton Oursler

How easy it is for a man to die rich, if he will but be contented to live miserable.

Henry Fielding

The trouble with most people is that they're working so hard for a living they don't have time to live.

Helen Leffer

I am here to live aloud.

Emile Zola

Living? We'll leave that to the servants.

Philippe Auguste Villiers de L'Isle-Adam

LIVING TODAY

Not only is there no God, but try getting a plumber on weekends.

Anon

LOAN/LENT

Owe money to be paid at Easter, and Lent will seem short.

Italian proverb

LOGIC

Get your facts first, and then you can distort them as much as you please.

Mark Twain

"For example" is not proof.

Yiddish proverb

LONDON

London is the city where they purvey the most inaccurate news and produce the worst possible arguments, based on information which is entirely false.

Voltaire

What's not destroyed by time's devouring hand?
Where's Troy, and where's the Maypole in the Strand?
Peas, cabbages, and turnips once grew, where
Now stands New Bond Street, and a newer square;
Such piles of buildings now rise up and down,
London itself seems going out of town.

James Bramston

When a man is tired of London he is tired of Life; for there is in London all that life can afford.

Samuel Johnson

There are only five women in London worth talking to, and two of these can't be admitted into decent society.

Oscar Wilde

Trafalgar Square is a place found by thousands of pigeons, washed by fountains that soak the population when the wind catches them, and deep in peanut shells.

V. S. Pritchett

A tourist fell in Fleet Street and injured his arm. While not too serious, the visitor asked the next passerby for the address of the nearest physician. "Turn up Hind Court into Gough Square. There's a doctor on the left-hand side. You'll see the name on a plate outside."

The tourist followed directions and found the house readily enough. And there was the plaque, as stated. It read:

Home of
Dr. Samuel Johnson
1709–1784

LONDON BRIDGE

Four thousand people cross London Bridge daily, mostly fools.

Carlyle

LONDON CLUBS

Those mausoleums of inactive masculinity are places for men who prefer armchairs to women.

V. S. Pritchett

LONDON, MISLEADING INFO FOR TOURISTS

If you take a taxi, the driver will be only too willing to give your shoes a polish while waiting at the traffic lights.

R. J. Phillips

Visitors in London hotels are expected by the management to hang the bed-linen out of the windows to air.

Alex Castle

Prostitutes are now seen only occasionally. On certain days, however, they come out in force, easily recognised by the little favours they sell from trays.

P. W. R. Foot

On first entering an Underground train, it is customary to shake hands with every passenger.

R. J. Phillips

Try the famous echo in the British Museum Reading Room.

Gerald Hoffnung

LONELINESS

Loneliness wouldn't be so hard to fight, if I didn't have to do it all by myself.

Meek, via Howie Schneider

Why should I feel lonely? Is not our planet in the Milky Way?

Thoreau

What fools call loneliness, wise men know as solitude.

Ching Chow

LONG AGO

When the village square was a place—not a person.

Ralph Newman

LONGEVITY

There is no shortcut to longevity; to achieve it is the work of a lifetime.

James Crichton-Browne

Mirth and motion prolong life.

Balkan proverb

Eat everything, drink everything and don't worry about anything. It's always nice to have a shot just before breakfast.

Mrs. Galsomina Del Vecchio, age 108

People always wonder how I have achieved such a ripe age [100] and I can only say I never felt the urge to partake of the grape, the grain, or the weed, but I do eat everything.

Mrs. Mary Borah

LOOKING

Let us not look back in anger, nor forward in fear, but around in awareness.

James Thurber

Handsome frequently is as ugly does.

LOOSE TALK

His talk was like a spring, which runs
With rapid change from rocks to roses:
It slipped from politics to puns,
It passed from Mahomet to Moses.

Winthrop Praed

He who says what he likes, hears what he does not like.

Proverb

LOSS

He who loses money, loses much; he who loses a friend, loses more; but he who loses his spirits, loses all.

English proverb

He that loseth a wife and a farthing hath a great loss of a farthing.

English proverb

LOUD MOUTH

He that has the worst cause makes the most noise.

English proverb

LOVE

Love has but one word and it never repeats itself.

Lacordaire

Love is more easily illustrated than defined.

Anon

Speak low if you speak love.

Shakespeare

No sooner met, but they looked; no sooner looked, but they loved; no sooner loved, but they sighed; no sooner sighed, but they asked one another the reason.

Ditto

They hugged each other very tightly, exchanging kisses rendered surpassingly salty by their tears. This is thought by some to add relish, as with peanuts, by bringing out the sweetness.

John Collier

When she saw him, she felt a stab in her heart that persons who have never been dazed by love take for a metaphor.

Abel Hermant

The Americans, like the English, probably make love worse than any other race.

Walt Whitman

Love is all—love and life in the sun,
Love is the main thing, the mistress does not matter:
What matters the bottle so long as we get drunk?

Alfred de Musset

Love is like war; easy to begin but very hard to stop.

H. L. Mencken

Love is woman's eternal spring and man's eternal fall.

Helen Rowland

Love is the egotism of two.

French saying

Never the time and the place
    And the loved one all together!

Robert Browning

In love, there is always one who kisses and one who offers the cheek.

French proverb

Why is it better to love than to be loved? It is surer!

Sacha Guitry

Our love is like the misty rain that falls softly—but floods the river.

African proverb

Love does not consist in gazing at each other but in looking together in the same direction.

Saint Exupery

O, how this spring of love resembleth
The uncertain glory of an April day!

Shakespeare

Love, like butter, goes well with bread.

Yiddish proverb

Love is like mushrooms. One doesn't know if they belong to the good or bad sort until it is too late.

Tristan Bernard

Love never dies of starvation but often of indigestion.

Ninon de Lenclos

One doesn't die from love. Sometimes one dies from another's love when he buys a revolver.

Marcel Pagnol

Blue eyes say, "Love me or I die"; black eyes say, "Love me or I kill thee."

Spanish proverb

True love is like a ghost; everybody talks about it but few have seen it.

La Rochefoucauld

No one has ever loved anyone the way everyone wants to be loved.

Mignon McLaughlin

Be loving without zeal. She will come to you by herself. Know then when to take her by force the day she intended to give herself to you.

Pierre Louys

To obtain a woman who loves you, you must treat her as if she didn't.

Pierre de Beaumarchais

In Love's wars, he who flieth is conqueror.

Proverb

In matters of love, there is nothing more persuasive than a courageous stupidity.

Balzac

The pleasure of making love increases the indifference felt towards the partner.

Claire Lardinois

I made no advances to her, but she accepted them.

Louis Scutenaire

A wise woman never yields by appointment.

Stendhal

Don't think that every sad-eyed woman has loved and lost— she may have got him.

Anon

The woman one loves always smells good.

Remy de Gourmont

He that will win his dame must know
As love does when he bends his bow;
With one hand thrust the gal from you
With the other pull her to.

After Samuel Butler, (I)

Let the man who does not wish to be idle fall in love.

Ovid

Heaven grant us patience with a man in love!

Kipling

A man should never tear his hair
When jilted by his lady fair.
She isn't apt to be enthralled
The least bit more if he is bald.

Richard Wheeler

As soon as you cannot keep anything from a woman, you love her.

Paul Géraldy

A gentleman in love may behave like a madman but not like a dunce.

La Rochefoucauld

The magic of first love is our ignorance that it can never end.

Benjamin Disraeli

Escape me?
Never—
Beloved!
While I am I, and you are you.

Robert Browning

There can be no great love without great pain.

Anon

A man has no business to marry a woman who can't make him miserable. It means she can't make him happy.

Anon

When there are rings under the eyes, the place is taken.

Willy

When my love swears that she is made of truth, I do believe her though I know she lies.

Shakespeare

Better to be a young man's darling than an old man's slave.

LLL

Love your neighbor
All your life;
A much sweeter labor
Is to love his wife.

LLL

How I missed her, how I missed her,
How I missed my Clementine!
But I kissed her little sister,
And forgot my Clementine.

Percy Montrose

When we want to read of the deeds that are done for love, whither do we turn? To the murder column.

Shaw

Love is a bind.

LLL

I could not love thee, Dear, so much
Lov'd I not honor less.

LLL

A fence between makes love more keen.

Anon

Oh, what a ravishing thing is the beginning of an Amour!

Aphra Behn

To love and win is the best thing; to love and lose, the next best.

Thackeray

What is irritating about love is that it is a crime that requires an accomplice.

Baudelaire

One should always be in love; that is the reason one should never marry.

Wilde

I have loved
Three whole days together;
And am like to love three more,
If it prove fair weather.

Sir John Suckling

Faults are thick where love is thin.

English saying

At the gate where suspicion enters, love goes out.

English proverb

The only big difference in the game of love over the last few thousand years is that they've changed trumps from clubs to diamonds.

Anon

The ideal love affair is one conducted by post.

Shaw

The end of passion is the beginning of repentance.

Spanish proverb

The best proof that experience is useless is that the end of one love does not disgust us from beginning another.

Paul Bourget

Love in haste, detest at leisure.

Lord Byron

LOVE NOW

At no time in history has so large a proportion of humanity rated love so highly.

Morton M. Hunt

LOVE-CONSTANCY

Then talk not Inconstancy,
    False Hearts and broken Vows;
If I, by Miracle, can be
This live-long minute true to thee,
    'Tis all that Heav'n allows.

Earl of Rochester

She gave herself, he took her: the third party was time, who made cuckolds of them both.

Chazal

LOVE/EATING

The loves of some people are but the result of good suppers.

Anon

LOVE/HATE

Love, friendship, respect do not unite people as much as a common hatred for something.

Chekhov

LOVE/HATE/INDIFFERENCE

The true opposite of love is not hate but indifference. Hate, bad as it is, at least treats the neighbor as a *thou*, whereas indifference turns the neighbor into an *it*, a thing. This is why we may say that there is actually one thing worse than evil itself, and that is indifference to evil. In human relations the nadir of morality, the lowest point as far as Christian ethics is concerned, is manifest in the phrase, "I couldn't care less."

Joseph Fletcher

LOVE LETTER

It is well to write love letters. There are certain things which it is not easy to ask your mistress face to face, like for money, for instance.

Henri de Régnier

The only love letters which have any use are letters of goodbye.

Etienne Rey

In love, to write is dangerous, without mentioning that it is also useless.

Alexandre Dumas fils

LOVE-LORN

Heighdy! heighdy!
Misery me, lackadaydee!
He slipped no sup, and he craved no crumb,
As he sighed for the love of a ladye!

Sir William Gilbert

LOVE MATCHES

Love matches are made by people who are content, for a month of honey, to condemn themselves to a life of vinegar.

Countess of Blessington

LOVE, MORE ABOUT

Love is a sweet tyranny, because the lover endureth his torments willingly.

Proverb

LOVE TALK

Don't say: "And you know, you are the first" because he would pretend to believe it but that would be sheer courtesy. But say: "Before I knew you, I didn't know what it was" because that men always believe.

Georges-Armand Masson

LOVE AND FOOLS

Only a man who has loved a woman of genius can appreciate what happiness there is in loving a fool.

Talleyrand

LOVER

All the world loves a lover—unless he's in a telephone booth.

Dave Tomick

LOVER AND MISTRESS

To have a new mistress is a pleasure only surpassed by that of ridding yourself of an old one.

William Wicherley

LOVING

You say to me-wards your affection's strong;
Pray love me little, so you love me long.

Robert Herrick

LOW AND HIGH

   Verily
I swear, 'tis better to be lowly born,
And range with humble livers in content,
Than to be perk'd up in a glist'ring grief,
And wear a golden sorrow.

Shakespeare

LOYALTY

Loyalty implies loyalty in misfortune; and when a soldier has accepted any nation's uniform he has already accepted its defeat.

G. K. Chesterton

LOYALTY/ANIMALS

To be sure, the dog is loyal. But why, on that account, should we take him as an example? He is loyal to men, not to other dogs.

Karl Kraus

LUCK

Throw a lucky man into the sea, and he will come up with a fish in his mouth.

Arab proverb

You need a strong stomach to digest good luck.

Russian proverb

The only sure thing about luck is that it will change.

Wilson Mizner

The nature of my luck's been such—
I'm pitiful to see.
I've been up against the wall so much
The handwriting's on me.

Leonard K. Schiff

If I dealt in candles, the sun would never set.

Yiddish proverb

Luck is like having a rice dumpling fly into your mouth.

Japanese proverb

Greater luck hath no man than this, that he lay down his wife at the right moment.

Samuel Butler (II)

MARTIN LUTHER

Luther was guilty of two great crimes—he struck the Pope in his crown, and the monks in their belly.

Desiderius Erasmus

LUXURY

Every luxury must be paid for, and everything is a luxury, starting with being in the world.

Cesare Pavese

Every extra thing you own is extra trouble.

Japanese proverb

LYING

Any fool can tell the truth, but it requires a man of some sense to know how to lie well.

Samuel Butler (II)

With a man, a lie is a last resort; with a woman, it's First Aid.

Gelette Burgess

Liars begin by imposing upon others, but end by deceiving themselves.

Proverb

The visionary lies to himself, the liar only to others.

Nietzsche

No man has a good enough memory to make a successful liar.

Lincoln

I do not mind lying, but I hate inaccuracy.

Samuel Butler (II)

A little inaccuracy sometimes saves tons of explanation.

Saki

M vs. N

There is a big difference between m and n. Take the word "acme." With three loops you are at the top, but with two loops, you only have pimples.

Anon, Jr.

MADNESS

Avarice, ambition, lust, etc., are species of madness.

Benedict Spinoza

MADNESS OF CROWDS

There is no fence against a panic.

Italian proverb

MAGIC

Magic is something we do to ourselves.

Aleister Crowley

MAIDEN'S PRAYER

Love me lots,
Love me little,
Only leave me not
Fatter in the middle.

LLL

MAJORITY

The most dangerous foe to truth and freedom in our midst is the compact majority. Yes, the damned, compact, liberal majority.

Henrik Ibsen

Desperate courage makes one a majority.

Andrew Jackson

MALICE

In the adversity of our best friends we often find something which does not displease us.

de la Rochefoucauld

MAN

Is, of all the animals, the supreme opportunist.

Desmond Morris

Man is the only one that knows nothing, that can learn nothing without being taught. He can neither speak nor walk nor eat, and in short he can do nothing at the prompting of nature only, but weep.

Pliny the Elder

Man's greatest weakness is love of life.

Molière

Man was created a little lower than the angels, and has been getting a little lower ever since.

Josh Billings

The organ of the accumulated smut and sneakery of 10,000 generations of weaseling souls.

Philip Wylie

Man is the second strongest sex in the world.

Phillip Barry

Man survives where swine perish, and laughs where gods go mad.

Dostoevski

Only man has dignity; only man, therefore, can be funny.

Father Knox

Man is still the most inexpensive, nonlinear, all-purpose computing system that is capable of being mass-produced by unskilled labor.

Anon

In each human heart are a tiger, a pig, an ass, and a nightingale; diversity of character is to do their unequal activity.

Ambrose Bierce

Too often man handles life as he does bad weather. He whiles away the time as he waits for it to stop.

Alfred Polgar

Nature gave men two ends—one to sit on and one to think with. Ever since then man's success or failure has been dependent on the one he used most.

George R. Kirkpatrick

Every man hath a fool in his sleeve.

Old English saying

Whenever man begins to doubt himself, he does something so stupid that he is reassured.

Lec

We have retained so many behavioral traits inherited from our Stone Age ancestors that the best relic we have of early man is modern man.

Dr. David Hamburg

It takes one woman twenty years to make a man of her son, and another woman twenty minutes to make a fool of him.

Helen Rowland

We drink when we're not thirsty, and we make love at any old time—these are the only differences between us and the other animals.

Beaumarchais

The ability to make love frivolously is the chief characteristic which distinguishes human beings from the beasts.

Heywood Broun

The most colossal joke is grave, censorious, senatorial, soul-possessing Man, 'rect on his two spindles.

Dylan Thomas

Plato having defined man to be a two-legged animal without feathers, Diogenes plucked a cock, and, bringing him into the school, said, "Here is Plato's man." From which there was added to the definition, "with broad, flat nails."

Diogenes Laërtius

Like a man made after supper of a cheese-paring: when he was naked, he was, for all the world, like a forked radish, with a head fantastically carved upon it with a knife.

Shakespeare

Man is a somewhat altered fish, a slightly remodeled ape.

George R. Stewart

An ape with possibilities.

Roy Chapman Andrews

Man is an intensely vocal, acutely exploratory, over-crowded ape.

Desmond Morris

Man is the only animal that refuses to be weaned.

U.S. Dairy Assn.

Man is nature's sole mistake.

Alexander Pope

The three stages of man: When you are young, when you are middle-aged, and finally when people tell you how well you look.

Harry Golden

A human being is an ingenious assemblage of portable plumbing.

Christopher Morley

MAN/WOMAN

The mutual relations of the two sexes seems to us to be at least as important as the mutual relations of any two governments in the world.

Lord Macaulay

Women have more imagination than men. They need it to tell us how wonderful we are.

Arnold H. Glasgow

When both husband and wife wear pants it is not difficult to tell them apart. He is the one who is listening.

Anon

Women, when they have made a sheep of a man, always tell him that he is a lion with a will of iron.

Balzac

No man can understand why a woman should prefer a good reputation to a good time.

Helen Rowland

A man is a person who will pay two dollars for a one-dollar item he wants. A woman will pay one dollar for a two-dollar item she doesn't want.

William Binger

The wife carries the husband on her face; the husband carries the wife on his shirt.

Roumanian saying

Women and small men are hard to handle.

Japanese proverb

For men at worst differ as Heaven and Earth,
But women, worst and best, as Heaven and Hell.

Tennyson

Men, some to business, some to pleasure take;
But every woman is at heart a rake.

Alexander Pope

A reformed rake makes the best husband.

English proverb

MAN'S LIFE

At given points in a man's life, he must take it by the scruff of the neck and shake it.

Moss Hart

MANAGEMENT

To manage men, one ought to have a sharp mind in a velvet sheath.

George Eliot

MANKIND

Man is an accidental by-product of an unintelligible cosmic process.

H. L. Mencken

I hate mankind, for I think myself one of the best of them, and I know how bad I am.

Samuel Johnson

No portion of mankind ever was as good as it thought itself or as bad as it was thought by its enemies.

Sir Sarvepalli Radhakrishnan

MANNERS

An English gentleman is a man who may shake his dog's paw, but not his servant's hand.

Colin Wilson

Bad manners simply indicate that you care a good deal more for the food than the society at the table.

Gelett Burgess

Neither burn incense nor break wind.

Japanese proverb

MARCH

If you kill one flea in March you will kill a hundred.

Proverb

March comes in with adder-heads and goes out with peacocks' tails.

Proverb

MARK TWAIN

Mark Twain's "1601" was a covert way of scribbling dirty words on Tom Sawyer's fence.

Justin Kaplan

MARRIAGE

Marriage is sometimes like a boxing card. The preliminaries are frequently better than the main event.

Anon

Marriage is the only known business in which a man takes his boss along on his vacation.

Anon

To marry once is a duty, twice a folly, thrice is madness.

Dutch proverb

Marry such women as seem good to you, two, three or four, but if you fear you will not be equitable, then only one.

The Koran

"Come, Come," said Tom's father, "at your time of life,
There's no longer excuse for thus playing the rake—
It is time you should think, boy, of taking a wife"—
"Why, so it is, father—whose wife shall I take?"

Thomas Moore

By all means marry; if you get a good wife, you'll become happy; if you get a bad one, you'll become a philosopher.

Socrates

When you're a married man, Samivel, you'll understand a good many things as you don't understand now; but vether it's worth goin' through so much, to learn so little, as the charity-boy said ven he got to the end of the alphabet, is a matter o' taste.

Charles Dickens

Doant thou marry for munny, but goa wheer munny is!

Tennyson

Home life as we understand it is no more natural to us than a cage is natural to a cockatoo.

Shaw

His designs were strictly honorable; that is, to rob a lady of her fortune by way of marriage.

Henry Fielding

The music at a wedding procession always reminds me of the music of soldiers going into battle.

Heine

Strange to say what delight we married people have to see these poor fools decoyed into our condition.

Samuel Pepys

If you're afraid of loneliness do not marry.

Chekhov

There are some good marriages, but practically no delightful ones.

La Rochefoucauld

Marriage has many pains, but celibacy has no pleasures.

Samuel Johnson

The trouble with marriage is that, while every woman is at heart a mother, every man is at heart a bachelor.

E. V. Lucas

What a pity it is that nobody knows how to manage a wife but a bachelor.

George Colman [the elder]

It doesn't much signify whom one marries, for one is sure to find out next morning that it was someone else.

Samuel Rogers

A man finds himself seven years older the day after his marriage.

Bacon

If you would have a happy family life, remember two things: in matters of principle, stand like a rock; in matters of taste, swim with the current.

Thomas Jefferson

Go down the ladder when thou marriest a wife; go up when thou choosest a friend.

English proverb

A deaf husband and a blind wife are always a happy couple.

Danish proverb

It is better to marry a quiet fool than a witty scold.

Anon

Every one can tame a shrew but he that hath her.

English proverb

Almost any man can support the girl he marries, but the problem is—what's *he* going to live on?

Joseph Salak

So heavy is the chain of wedlock that it needs two to carry it, and sometimes three.

Dumas

Before marriage, a man will lie awake all night thinking about something you said; after marriage, he'll fall asleep before you finish saying it.

Helen Rowland

The secret of marriage is they murder you and then you apologize for it.

Oscar Levant

It's a myth that brides blush. Actually, their faces are flushed with victory.

Roger Allen

Marriage is neither heaven nor hell; it is simply purgatory.

Lincoln

MARRIAGE AND PRIESTHOOD

A married priest would run the risk of having interests in common with his fellow citizens, a state of things not at all in keeping with the profound and sacred views of the Holy Catholic Church.

Voltaire

MASTER

No man can serve two masters. This is the law which prohibits bigamy.

Anon

MATRIMONY

'Tis safest in matrimony to begin with a little aversion.

Richard Sheridan

Formerly a man wondered if he could afford to marry; now he wonders if he can get along without a working wife.

Carl Ellstam

MATURITY

A person remains immature, whatever his age, as long as he thinks of himself as an exception to the human race.

Harry A. Overstreet

Few people know how to be old.

La Rochefoucauld

The trick is to grow up without growing old.

Frank Lloyd Wright

By the time a man finds greener pastures, he also finds he can't climb the fence.

Irv Scheel

MAXIMS

What are the proper proportions of a maxim? A minimum of sound to a maximum of sense.

Mark Twain

People who live in chateaux
Shouldn't throw tomateaux.

Morton

A loafer always has the correct time.

Kin Hubbard

A good listener is not only popular everywhere, but after a while he knows something.

Wilson Mizner

Don't talk about yourself; it will be done when you leave.

Addison Mizner

Lack of pep is often mistaken for patience.

Kin Hubbard

The world ain't getting no worse; we've only got better facilities.

Kin Hubbard

MEDICINE

I was well, would be better, took physic, and died.

English proverb

Diet cures more than the lancet.

British saying

The people you see waiting in the lobbies of doctors' offices are, in a vast majority of cases, suffering through poisoning caused by an excess of food. Coupled with this go the bad results of imperfect breathing, improper use of stimulants, lack of exercise, irregular sleep, or holding the thought of fear, jealousy, and hate. All of these things, or any one of them, will, in very many persons, cause fever, chills, congestion, cold feet, and faulty elimination.

Elbert Hubbard, c. 1900

To the physician, each man, each woman, is an amplification of one organ.

Emerson

Physicians of the Utmost Fame
Were called at once; but when they came
They answered, as they took their Fees,
"There is no Cure for this Disease."

Hilaire Belloc

Nature, time, and patience are the three great physicians.

Bulgarian proverb

A doctor is a man licensed to make grave mistakes.

LLL

I am dying with the help of too many physicians.

Alexander the Great

Doctors will have more lives to answer for in the next world than even we generals.

Napoleon Bonaparte

One doctor makes work for another.

Anon

There are worse occupations in the world than feeling a woman's pulse.

Laurence Sterne

A doctor used to say: "Only heirs really pay well."

Chamfort

He's a devout believer in the department of witchcraft called medical science.

Shaw

Doctors make the worst patients.

British saying

The best doctor is the one you run for and can't find.

Diderot

Saying "Gesundheit!" doesn't really help the common cold— but it's about as good as anything the doctors have come up with.

Earl Wilson

We've made great medical progress in the last generation. What used to be merely an itch is now an allergy.

Anon

Asthma is a disease that has practically the same symptoms as passion, except that with asthma it lasts longer.

Anon

Tree surgeons are taught to wear safety belts so they won't fall out of patients.

Anon

There is no fun like getting out of the hospital. A lot of living is to be caught up with, and there is a sense of delirious freedom. To take a pill or not take a pill is our own business and no officious person is around to write down Gestapo-like reports on whether we went to the bathroom or not. Everything is our own business now. Getting out of the hospital is tops in human experience and happiness.

Harry Golden

But who is there to shake you awake at 2 A.M. to give you your sleeping pill?

LLL

Mary had a little lamb. The doctor fainted.

Anon

THE MEEK

It's going to be fun to watch and see how long the meek can keep the earth after they inherit it.

Don Quinn

When the time comes for the meek to inherit the earth, the inheritance taxes will be so high, they won't want it.

Anon

182

MEMORIAL DAY

At the end of this month, we will once again be engaged in a great holiday weekend, testing whether this motorist, or any motorist, can long endure.

Anon

MEMORIES

We should never remember the benefits we have conferred, nor forget the favors received.

Proverb

Pleasant memories must be arranged for in advance.

Anon

When to the session of sweet silent thought,
I summon up remembrance of things past.

William Shakespeare

I've a grand memory for forgetting.

Robert Louis Stevenson

The existence of forgetting has never been proved: we only know that some things do not come to our mind when we want them to.

Nietzsche

A great memory does not make a mind any more than a dictionary is a piece of literature.

John Henry Newman

All complain of want of memory, but none of want of judgment.

English saying

Women and elephants never forget.

Dorothy Parker

It's a poor sort of memory that only works backward.

Lewis Carroll

MEN

I like men to behave like men. I like them strong and childish.

Françoise Sagan

One puzzling thing about men—they allow their sex instinct to drive them to where their intelligence never would take them.

Joan Fontaine

Whenever I meet a man who would make a good husband, he is.

Anon spinster

The minute a man is convinced that he is interesting, he isn't.

Stephen Leacock

There are two kinds of men who never amount to much: those who cannot do what they are told, and those who can do nothing else.

Cyrus H. K. Curtis

Men are no more than mischievous baboons.

Dr. William Harvey

Men hunt, women fish.

Victor Hugo

MEN/ANIMALS

Animals have these advantages over man: They have no theologians to instruct them, their funerals cost them nothing, and no one starts lawsuits over their wills.

Voltaire

MEN/WOMEN

Time and circumstance, which enlarge the views of most men, narrow the views of women almost invariably.

Thomas Hardy

MERCHANDISE

Pleasing ware is half sold.

Proverb

METALLURGY

Is the study of how to keep people from being allergic to metals.

Anon, Jr.

METAPHYSICS

Is an attempt to prove the incredible by an appeal to the unintelligible.

H. L. Mencken

When one man speaks to someone who does not understand him, and when the first ceases to understand, we have metaphysics.

Voltaire

METEOROLOGY

A weather vane tells the direction of the wind. When the wind blows in various directions, use a varicose vane.

Anon, Jr.

MIDDLE AGE

Is when you have met so many people that every new person you meet reminds you of someone else, and usually is.

Ogden Nash

You've reached middle age when all you exercise is caution.

Anon

If you go all out and wind up all in, that's middle age.

Anon

THE MIDDLE EAST

Is a region where oil is thicker than blood.

James Holland

MILEAGE

If it costs one cent to ride a thousand miles, a trip around the world would cost 25 cents; to the moon, $2.38; to the sun, only $930; but a trip to the nearest star would cost two hundred and sixty million dollars.

Anon travel agent

THE MILITARY

Overgrown military establishments . . . under any form of government, are inauspicious to liberty and . . . particularly hostile to Republican Liberty.

George Washington

THE MILKY WAY

Was discovered by Louis Pasteur.

Anon, Jr.

MILLION

When the million applaud, you ask yourself what harm you have done; when they censure you, what good.

Charles Caleb Colton

THE MIND

There are boxes in the mind with labels on them: "To study on a favorable occasion"; "Never to be thought about"; "Useless to go into further"; "Contents unexamined"; "Pointless business"; "Urgent"; "Dangerous"; "Delicate"; "Impossible"; "Abandoned"; "Reserved"; "For others"; "My forte"; etc.

Paul Valery

Our minds are lazier than our bodies.

La Rochefoucauld

The mind is an iceberg—it floats with only one-seventh of its bulk above water.

Freud

The conscious mind may be compared to a fountain playing in the sun and falling back into the great subterranean pool of the subconscious from which it rises.

Freud

A narrow mind has a broad tongue.

Arabic proverb

We have all forgotten more than we remember.

Proverb

What is on your mind, if you'll forgive the overstatement.

Fred Allen

MIND AND BODY

We have rudiments of reverence for the human body, but we consider as nothing the rape of the human mind.

Eric Hoffer

MINISTER

A clergyman is an interpreter of religion who does not believe that the Bible means what it says; he is always convinced that it says what he means.

Shaw

MIRACLES

It would have approached nearer to the idea of miracle if Jonah had swallowed the whale.

Thomas Paine

The most wonderful thing about miracles is that they sometimes happen.

Chesterton

MIRROR

That man, who flees from truth, should have invented the mirror is the greatest of historical miracles.

Friedrich Hebbel

For there was never yet fair woman but she made mouths in a glass.

Shakespeare

The place where everyone sees his best friend.

Yiddish proverb

Your looking glass will tell you what none of your friends will.

Proverb

MISADVENTURE

Who perisheth in needless danger, is the devil's martyr.

English proverb

MISERS

A miser is a guy with unready cash.

Stanley Levinson

MISERY

Is getting a copy of Johnny Carson's new book, *Misery is a Blind Date*, and discovering that out of forty-six jokes only four are funny.

Muriel Stevens

Misery acquaints a man with strange bedfellows.

Shakespeare

If misery loves company, misery has company enough.

Thoreau

If you have attended the free lectures of the College of Misery, for a short time even, and have paid attention to what you have seen with your own eyes and heard with your own ears, you will reap firm faith and learn more than you can express in words.

Vincent Van Gogh

The secret of being miserable is to have leisure to bother about whether you are happy or not.

Shaw

MISFORTUNE

One of the greatest weaknesses of those who suffer misfortune through their own fault is that they almost always try to find excuses before looking for remedies; as a result they often find remedies too late.

Cardinal de Retz

We all have enough strength to bear the misfortune of others.

La Rochefoucauld

MISHAPS

Like knives, mishaps either serve us or cut us, as we grasp them by the blade or the handle.

Lowell

MISPRINTS

A misprint (attributed to an anonymous typesetter on *The London Times*, but probably apocryphyl) is said to have occurred in a contemporary report of the opening of Waterloo Bridge by Queen Victoria. The Queen, the newspaper had intended to say, was the first person to *pass* over the bridge. (My italics—and I hope the printers get it right this time.)

Fritz Spiegl

MISTAKES

The error of the past is the success of the future. A mistake is evidence that someone tried to do something.

Anon

We usually call our blunders mistakes, and our friends style our mistakes blunders.

Henry Wheatley

The greatest mistake made by people in love is to believe that either one of the two will always make the other happy.

Anon

There is nothing wrong with making mistakes; just don't respond with encores.

Anon

MIXED EMOTIONS

The best definition is watching your mother-in-law drive over a cliff in your new Cadillac.

Long John Nebel

MIXED METAPHORS

None so blind as those who won't listen.

LLL

People who live in stone houses should never throw glasses.

LLL

MIXED MOTTOS

Better a hen today than an egg tomorrow.

LLL

MODERATION

Even moderation ought not to be practiced to excess.

Anon

MODERN AGE

A baby born nowadays faces the possibility of hearing music and voices every moment of his life. With radio or television in the house, radio in cars, portable radios that go anywhere, piped music in restaurants and factories, one can pass years without ever experiencing silence.

Wheeler McMillen

Pioneer legislation of the week: A bill passed by the lower house of the Iowa legislature provides a year in jail, $1,000 fine or both for drunken water skiing.

Sports Illustrated

The impossibility of yesterday has become the luxury of today and the necessity of tomorrow.

Anon

MODERN PAINTINGS

Are like women. You'll never enjoy them if you try to understand them.

Harold Coffin

MODERN WITCHES BREW

Into concrete mixer throw
Brick from shoddy bungalow,
Thrice three chunks of orange peel
Gathered from the beach at Deal,
Foot of hare untimely slain
On the outer traffic lane,
Cast-off paper from a toffee,
Cup of instantaneous coffee,
Then, with fag-end torn from lip,
Sexy film and comic strip,
Nucleus of hydrogen,
Thousandth egg of battery hen,
Paint-brush used for marking wall,
Thoroughly compound them all.
This charm, once set and left to stand
Will cast a blight on any land.

Barbara Roe

MODERN WOMAN

She is supposed to be a cross between a saint and a drayhorse, a diplomat and an automatic washing machine, a psychiatrist and a bulldozer, a sanitary engineer and a mannequin.

Kenneth More

MODESTY

Einstein, having hit on his equation $E=mc^2$, came down stairs in his sweatshirt and bedroom slippers and said, "Mamma, I have a little new idea."

H. Harry Giles

False modesty has ruined more kidneys than drink.

Anon

MOLECULES

Molecules are made of atoms. Atoms are made of energy. Energy is made from Wheaties.

Anon, Jr.

MONEY

If a man's after money, he's moneymad; if he keeps it, he's a capitalist; if he spends it, he's a playboy! if he doesn't get it, he's a ne'er-do-well; if he doesn't try to get it, he lacks ambition. If he gets it without working for it, he's a parasite; and if he accumulates it after a lifetime of hard work, people call him a fool who never got anything out of life.

Anon

When you have money in your pocket, you are wise and you are handsome and you sing well, too.

Yiddish proverb

The rich need not beg a welcome.

French proverb

A full wallet is the best companion.

Anon

A heavy purse makes a light heart.

LLL

There is no dignity quite so impressive, and no independence quite so important as living within your means. . . . Any other course for me would be as the senseless imitation of a fowl which was attempting to light higher than its roost.

Calvin Coolidge

Money will say more in one moment than the most eloquent lover can in years.

Henry Fielding

They who are of the opinion that money will do everything, may very well be suspected to do everything for money.

Sir George Savile

There's nothing so comfortable as a small bank roll; a big one is always a danger.

Wilson Mizner

It saves a lot of trouble if, instead of having to earn money and save it, you can just go and borrow it.

Winston Churchill

Before borrowing money from a friend, decide which you need more.

Addison H. Hallock

If you would know the value of money, go and try to borrow some.

Franklin

'Tis better to give one shilling than to lend twenty.

Portuguese proverb

Riches are like muck, which stink in a heap, but spread abroad, make the earth fruitful.

Proverb

There are few sorrows, however poignant, in which a good income is of no avail.

Logan P. Smith

Money often costs too much.

Ralph Waldo Emerson

Money. The root of all good.

Minnesota Fats (Rudolf Walter Wanderone)

Money is the fruit of evil as often as the root.

Henry Fielding

Lack of money is the root of all evil.

Shaw

Making a lot of money is all right, provided you don't have to pay too much for it.

Albert Lasker

If you want to know what God thinks of money, just look at those he gave it to.

Anon (often attributed to Dorothy Parker)

A dollar may not go as far as it once did, but it makes up for it in speed.

Ned Preston

One says that money doesn't make happiness. Without doubt, one was speaking of the money of others.

Sacha Guitry

Money talks. It says "Goodbye!"

LLL

O, money, money, money, I am not necessarily one of those who
   think thee holy,
But I often stop to wonder how thou can'st go out so fast when
   thou comest in so slowly.

Ogden Nash

An empty purse and a new house make a man wise but too late.

English proverb

He that is without money might as well be buried in a rice tub with his mouth sewed up.

Chinese proverb

There are several ways in which to apportion the family income, all of them unsatisfactory.

Robert Benchley

I cannot afford to waste my time making money.

Louis Aggassiz

MONEY/HORSES

Anybody who finds it easy to make money on the horses is probably in the dog-food business.

Franklin P. Jones

MONOGAMY

Love has been in perpetual strife with monogamy.

Ellen Kay

MONOLOGUE

Talking to yourself is all right, as long as you listen.

LLL

THE MOON

People say the moon is made of green cheese which seems like spending a lot of money and going an awfully long way to get something I'm not too fond of in the first place.

Anon, Jr.

MONTHS/WEATHER

Spring being a tough act to follow, God created June.

Al Bernstein

MORALITY

We have two kinds of morality side by side: one which we preach but do not practice, and another which we practice but seldom preach.

Bertrand Russell

There are moral imbeciles just as there are mental imbeciles; but while the latter are recognized as having a congenital defect and are put away for their own good, the former often acquire great power and acclaim in the world—yet the man born with a deficient moral nerve is a thousand times more dangerous than the mental defective.

Sydney J. Harris

MORE/LESS

Everyone gives himself credit for more brains than he has and less money.

Italian proverb

MORNING

Lose an hour in the morning, and you will be all day hunting for it.

Richard Whately

MORTALITY

It's no use reminding yourself daily that you are mortal: it will be brought home to you soon enough.

Alfred Capus

MOSCOW

As if Los Angeles had no sun and no grass.

Lillian Hellman

MOTHER

An old-fashioned mother is one who washes the kid's mouth out with soap—without asking herself if the words he uttered had any "redeeming social significance."

Harold Emery

When yet was ever found a mother
Who'd give her booby for another.

John Gay

MOTHERHOOD

She never quite leaves her children at home, even when she doesn't take them along.

Margaret Culkin Banning

A group of recent mothers were discussing which month of pregnancy had been the most trying. One said the second, another said the ninth. At that moment a husband turned up and made the statement that he thought the tenth month was the most difficult. "Because," he said, "that's the month the father carries the baby."

Hal Price

MOTHER-IN-LAW

When mother-in-law comes in at the door, love flies out at the window.

Helen Rowland

The awe and dread with which the untutored savage contemplates his mother-in-law are amongst the most familiar facts of anthropology.

Sir James Fraser

I don't mind having my mother-in-law live with us, but I do wish she'd wait until we get married.

Anon

MOTIVES

Whenever a man does a thoroughly stupid thing, it is always from the noblest motives.

Wilde

MOTTO

The motto that should be engraved over the entrance of every institution of higher learning is the one proposed for scientists: Seek simplicity, and distrust it.

Alfred North Whitehead

And the motto that should be carved above every hospital entrance is: The best visitor is a short one.

Robert Wurgaft

Free hearts and warm hands.

On the coat of arms of the Glovers Company, London

If we were modest, we'd be perfect.

N.Y.C. ad agency

To suffer rather than die
That is the motto of mankind.

Jean de la Fontaine

Oh, what a tangled web we weave when first we practice to conceive.

Don Herold

Never let your schooling interfere with your education.

Mark Twain

A woman on time is one in nine.

Addison Mizner

None but the brave desert the fair.

Addison Mizner

God has given you one face, and you make yourself another.

Shakespeare

What on earth would a man do with himself if something did not stand in his way?

H. G. Wells

It would be a swell world if everybody was as pleasant as the fellow who's trying to skin you.

Kin Hubbard

When in doubt, tell the truth.

Mark Twain

MOUNTAINS

In the mountains we forget to count the days.

Japanese proverb

MOUSE IDEAS

We can never get rid of mouse ideas completely. They keep turning up again and again, and nibble, nibble—no matter how often we drive them off. The best way to keep them down is to have a few good strong cat ideas which will embrace them and ensure their not reappearing till they do so in another shape.

Samuel Butler (II)

MOUSE/CAT

Can a mouse fall in love with a cat?

English proverb

MOUSETRAP

If a man can write a better book, preach a better sermon, or make a better mousetrap than his neighbor, though he builds his house in the woods, the world will make a beaten path to his door.

Emerson

If a man write a better book, or make a better mousetrap than his neighbor, though he build his house in the woods, the world will make a beaten path to his door to steal it from him.

LLL

In baiting a mouse trap with cheese, always leave room for the mouse.

Saki

MOUTH

He that hath a mouth of his own should not say to another, blow.

Old English proverb

MOVEMENT/ENTERPRISE

When a mass movement begins to attract people who are interested in their individual careers, it is a sign that it has passed its vigorous stage, that it is no longer engaged in molding a new world but in possessing and preserving the present. It ceases then to be a movement and becomes an enterprise.

Eric Hoffer

MOVIES

Once held a mirror up to life—now it holds up a keyhole.

Arnold H. Glasgow

You may not remember that far back, but once upon a time movies were rated on how good they were, not on who was allowed to see them.

Changing Times

We had clean sex on the screen in my day. My sarong was thought very daring. But it seems like long underwear now.

Dorothy Lamour

All movies used to be "colossal." Now they're all "frank." I think I liked "colossal" better.

Beryl Pfizer

I like television better—it's not so far to the bathroom.

Anon, Jr.

Cecil B. De Mille,
Rather against his will,
Was persuaded to leave Moses
Out of *The Wars of the Roses.*

E. C. Bentley

MOVING

Three removes are as bad as a fire.

Benjamin Franklin

MUGWUMP

A mugwump is a person educated beyond his intellect.

Horace Porter

There are persons, not belonging to the highest intellectual zone, nor yet to the lowest, to whom perfect clearness of exposition suggests want of depth. They find comfort and edification in abstract and learned phraseology.

John Tyndall

MUM

Today there are all kinds of voice improvement and public speaking courses available. They give one the impression that the only way to communicate is by word of mouth. But in Ben Franklin's view, "None preaches better than the ant, and she says nothing." Often, when we visit a sick friend or someone in an institution, we are at a loss for words, and that may be all to the good. Our very silence can itself communicate comfort, concern, and compassion. Too much talk can be upsetting to the patient or prisoner. Sympathy, sensitivity, and sincerity are sometimes conveyed more easily and effectively with a simple smile or handshake.

Russell J. Fornwalt

MURDER

Murder is always a mistake; one should never do anything that one cannot talk about after dinner.

Wilde

MUSEUM

In Asiatic eyes, no more than an absurd concert in which contradictory themes are mingled and convulsed in an endless succession.

André Malraux

THE MUSHROOM AND THE SLUG

He nibbled the edges (of the mushroom) and ate the stalk
Devoured the umbrella and all in a walk,
The slug, gorged, sluggish and gormed
Back to its barky crevice wormed.
The Sun came up and the slug's silvery trail
Was all that was left to tell the tale.

Capt. Scarritt Adams

MUSIC

Music is much more enjoyable if you listen to it with your eyes shut. It is also more enjoyable if the people sitting near you listen to it with their mouths shut.

Anon

A nation creates music—the composer only arranges it.

Mikhail Glinka

Wagner's music is better than it sounds.

Bill Nye

The music teacher came twice each week to bridge the awful gap between Dorothy and Chopin.

George Ade

Beethoven's Fifth Symphony is the most divine noise that has ever penetrated into the ear of man.

E. M. Forster

Of all noises, I think music is the least disagreeable.

Samuel Johnson

In opera everything is based upon the not-true.

Tchaikovsky

In music as in love, pleasure is the waste product of creation.

Igor Stravinsky

MUSIC—WORSHIP

I don't object to having music. But it's an accessory, not an object, in life. . . . To make an object of it is sensuality. It is on all-fours with worshipping the wallpaper.

H. G. Wells

MUSICAL COMEDY

A good musical comedy consists largely of disorderly conduct occasionally interrupted by talk.

George Ade

MUTTERING

He that talks to himself, talks to a fool.

English proverb

MYTHS

The great enemy of the truth is very often not the lie—deliberate, contrived, and dishonest—but the myth—persistent, persuasive, and unrealistic. . . .

John F. Kennedy

NAPLES

Naples is a city that combines the vice of Paris, the misery of Dublin, and the vulgarity of New York.

John Ruskin

NAPOLEON

This is the very definition of the bourgeoisie and he was the biggest bourgeois of them all.

Jean Dutourd

NATIONALISM

Nationalism is an infantile disease. It is the measles of mankind.

Albert Einstein

NATIONS

England is an empire, Germany is a country, a race, France is a person.

Jules Michelet

Swedes are fake Norwegians.

Greg d'Alessio

In matters of commerce, the fault of the Dutch
Is offering too little and asking too much.

George Canning

In settling an island, the first building erected by a Spaniard would be a church; by a Frenchman, a fort; by a Dutchman, a warehouse; and by an Englishman, an alehouse.

Proverb

NATURAL RESOURCES

Only a few inches of topsoil separate us from death. Those few miraculous inches give us most of our food, our clothes, our houses, our cocktails and silverware and radios, and the books we read and the shoes we wear and the cool water we drink. Without topsoil and trees on the hillside there could not long be factories in the valley. Without the dogwood and the shade-bush that blossom here tonight there could not long be lights in the windows of the city.

Edwin L. Peterson

NATURE

Why did Nature create man? Was it to show that she is big enough to make mistakes, or was it pure ignorance?

Holbrook Jackson

The whole of nature is a conjunction of the verb to eat, in the active and passive.

William Ralph Inge

Grass is the forgiveness of nature—her constant benediction.
. . . Forests decay, harvests perish, flowers vanish, but grass is
immortal.

Ingalls

Especially crabgrass.

LLL

How beautifully everything is arranged by Nature; as soon as a
child enters the world, it finds a mother ready to take care of it.

Jules Michelet

We listen too much to the telephone and we listen too little to
nature.

André Kostelanetz

Moths can't grow big because they eat only holes.

Anon, Jr.

NAVAL ORDER

All echelons of the staff will coordinate the configuration of
plans with the requisite tailoring of the overview in order to
expedite the functional objective.

Reported by Capt. Scarrett Adams, USN, Ret.

NAVIGATION

The good seaman is better in bad weather.

Anon

NECESSARY

What is necessary is never a risk.

Cardinal de Retz

NECESSITY

Is a hard nurse, but she raises strong children.

Anon

Invention is the mother of necessity.

Samuel Butler (II)

"Necessity is the mother of invention" is a silly proverb. "Necessity is the mother of futile dodges" is much nearer the truth.

Alfred North Whitehead

Necessity knows no law.

St. Augustine

NECKING

A spot of necking does the youngsters good. The brain can
become overworked with too much study and that sort of relaxation helps a lot.

Town Alderman Arthur Bissell, Wednesbury, England

NEEDLEWORK

Whatsoever a man seweth, that shall he also rip.

LLL

NEGLECT

A little neglect may breed great mischief.

English proverb

THE NETHERLANDS

Whenever I go to Holland, I feel at once that I have reached the apotheosis of bourgeois society. The food, the comfort, the cleanliness, the kindliness, the sense of age and stability, the curious mixture of beauty and bad taste, the orderliness of everything including even nature and the sea—all makes one realize that here on the shore of the dyke-controlled Zuider Zee one has found the highest manifestation of the complacent civilization of the middle classes.

Leonard Woolf

NEUROSES

The neuroses are without exception disturbances of the sexual function.

Freud

Neurotic means: "He's not as sensible as I am."
Psychotic is: "He's even worse than my brother-in-law."

Dr. Karl Menninger

THE NEW

Novelty always appears handsome.

Proverb

The man with a new idea is a Crank, until the idea succeeds.

Mark Twain

NEW PROVERB

You are given a nose to breathe through so you can keep your mouth shut.

Miss Pat O'Haire

NEW SAWS

God help those who help themselves!

LLL

Faint heart ne'er won fur, lady.

Anon

Mud is thicker than water.

LLL

Beggars are never losers.

LLL

All work and no play makes Jack's wife a wealthy widow.

T. McDermott

A house divided makes many apartments.

Anon

You can't make a silk purse out of a spoiled child.

LLL

Know thyself—but don't tell anyone.

H. F. Henrichs

A bird in the hand is bad table manners.

Anon

One good turn, and you have most of the bed covers.

Elaine C. Moore

Work all the week long, rust on Sunday.

LLL

Too many crooks spoil the percentage.

H. Chandler

That which was sweet to endure may be bitter to remember.

LLL

If you can't be good, belittle.

Mrs. D. V. Cubberley

Many Hans make Volkswagens.

K. G. Hull

Two is company. Three is the result.

Anon

The Early Bird Gets The Worm—Special Shoppers Luncheon before 11:00 a.m.

Ad, Montreal restaurant

Nothing succeeds like excess.

Wilde

If at first you don't succeed, try a little ardour.

Anon

People who live in glass houses make interesting neighbors.

Anon

Youth is stranger than fiction.

Mrs. J.D. Fenna

It is bad when things are too good.

Harry Golden's mother

If at first you don't succeed, you're doing about average.

LLL

Every dogma has its day.

LLL

Out of the mouths of babes—usually when you've got your best suit on.

Mrs. G. Baxter

Now is the time for all good men to come to the aid of their planet.

Anon

NEW YEAR

The object of a New Year is not that we should have a new year. It is that we should have a new soul and a new nose, new feet, a new backbone, new ears, and new eyes. Unless a man starts on the strange assumption that he has never existed before, it is quite certain that he will never exist afterward.

G. K. Chesterton

NEW YORK CITY

In New York I get scared of talking to a telephone operator. People bark at each other. The word "please" is like some form of advanced voodoo. I heard of an experiment that was done once: they put three guinea pigs in a cage with bread and water. Fine. Then it was 12 pigs, and they began nipping. With 24, the whole place went crazy. An old Greek once said that a city with over 300,000 people wasn't worth living in. It's still true.

Walter Matthau

Most of the people living in New York have come here from the farm to try to make enough money to go back to the farm.

Don Marquis

There is more sophistication and less sense in New York than anywhere else on the globe.

Don Herold

A city of 7,000,000, so decadent that when I leave it I never dare look back lest I turn into salt and the conductor throw me over his left shoulder for good luck.

Frank Sullivan

New York City is a place where everyone will stop watching a championship fight to look at an usher giving a drunk the bum's rush.

Damon Runyon

NEWSPAPERS

If some great catastrophe is not announced every morning, we feel a certain void. "Nothing in the paper today," we sigh.

Paul Valery

I am unable to understand how a man of honor could take a newspaper in his hands without a shudder of disgust.

Baudelaire

An irresponsible reporter in front of a typewriter can do more damage than a drunken surgeon swinging a knife in the operating room.

Damon Runyon

There is nothing much wrong with American newspapers today except us publishers.

John Cowles

Today the news of this country is so filled with insanity and violence that the newspapers, from which I derive many of my ideas, have scant room for the sort of thing that turns me on— the bizarre, the unusual, the eccentric. In Britain they still have the taste for eccentricity.

S. J. Perelman, who moved to London

If words were invented to conceal thought, newspapers are a great improvement on a bad invention.

Thoreau

Perhaps an editor might . . . divide his paper into four chapters, heading the first, Truths; 2nd, Probabilities; 3rd, Possibilities; 4, Lies.

Thomas Jefferson

What you *see* is news, what you *know* is background, what you *feel* is opinion.

Lester Markel, N. Y. Times

The New York Times is a large, fourteen-floor fact factory on 43rd Street, off Broadway.

Gay Talese

The man who never looks into a newspaper is better informed than he who reads them, inasmuch as he who knows nothing is nearer the truth than he whose mind is filled with falsehoods and errors.

Thomas Jefferson

If St. Paul were to come back to our world in the flesh, he would become a newspaperman.

Abbe Michonneau

For what paper, dear God? For what paper?

Malcolm Muggeridge

He had been kicked in the head by a mule when young, and believed everything he read in the Sunday papers.

George Ade

NEWSPAPER WRITERS

Most newspaper writers regard truth as their most valuable possession, and therefore are most economical in its use.

LLL

NICOTINE

Nicotine is great for killing garden bugs.*

LLL

* People, too.

NIGHT

Shows stars and women in a better light.

Lord Byron

But in my age, as in my youth, night brings me many a deep remorse. I realize that from the cradle up I have been like the rest of the race—never quite sane in the night.

Mark Twain

RICHARD M. NIXON

A Main Street Machiavelli.

Patrick Anderson

All that stands between the U.S. and a Greek dictatorship.

LLL

NO

No is the worst merchandise.

Yiddish proverb

NOBILITY

We, my lords, may thank Heaven that we have something better than our brains to depend on.

Lord Chesterfield

Its creation has long been a convenient substitute for adequate pay.

Patrick O'Donovan

A nod from a lord is a breakfast for a fool.

English proverb

NOISE POLLUTION

If the general noisy conditions of everyday life continue . . . we shall become a race of shouting maniacs.

Sir Walter Fergusson Hannay, British Noise Abatement Society

It might be a good thing if people's ears would bleed. Then people might get aroused.

Anon environmental psychologist during symposium on noise pollution

NONENTITY

Rattle his bones over the stones;
He's only a pauper, whom nobody owns.

Thomas Noel

NONCONFORMITY

How glorious it is—and also how painful—to be an exception.

Alfred de Musset

NONSENSE

No one is exempt from talking nonsense; the misfortune is to do it solemnly.

Montaigne

A little nonsense now and then
Is relished by the best of men.

Anon

A little nonsense, be it human,
Ain't understood by any woman.

LLL

Slowly it wanders—pauses—creeps—
Anon it sparkles—flashes and leaps;
And ever as onward it gleaming goes
A light on the Bong-tree stem it throws:
And those who watch at that midnight hour
From Hell or Terrace or lofty Tower,
Cry as the wild light passes along,—
"The Dong!—The Dong!
The wandering Dong through the forest goes!
The Dong!—The Dong!
The Dong with the luminous Nose!"

Edward Lear

He thought he saw an Albatross
That fluttered round the lamp:
He looked again, and found it was
A penny postage stamp.
"You'd best be getting home," he said
"The nights are very damp."

Lewis Carroll

NORTH vs. SOUTH AMERICA

At home we work between meals; here you eat between working.

Chilean exchange student

NORTH CAROLINA

An oasis of humility between two mounts of conceit.

Anon

NOSINESS

It seems like one of the hardest lessons to be learned in this life is where your business ends and somebody else's begins.

Kin Hubbard

NOSTALGIA

When a man falls into his anecdotage, it is a sign for him to retire.

Benjamin Disraeli

Alas, Nostalgia isn't what it used to be.

Anon

NOVELS

One should not be too severe on English novels; they are the only relaxation of the intellectually unemployed.

Oscar Wilde

The premise of novel writing is that the city is a bad place . . . that's what makes it interesting.

Jeremy Larner

Many men have written well, but Dickens has written Weller.

Thomas Hood

The best part of the fiction in many novels is the notice that the characters are all purely imaginary.

F. P. Adams

NOW

Catch, then, O catch the transient hour;
Improve each moment as it flies;
Life's a short summer—man a flower—
He dies—alas! how soon he dies!

Samuel Johnson

Gather ye rose-buds while ye may,
Old Time is still a-flying
And this same flower, that smiles to-day,
To-morrow will be dying.

Robert Herrick

NOW AND THEN

Past and to come seem best; things present, worst.

Proverb

NUDITY

If it was the fashion to go naked, the face would be hardly observed.

Mary Montagu

The naked man never mislays his wallet.

Japanese proverb

If God had meant for people to go nude they would have been born that way.

Ad in The Village Voice

OATH OF LOVE

The sentimental version of check without funds.

Georges-Armand Masson

OATHS

The judge pounded his gavel for the court to come to order, then turned to the woman in the witness box. "The witness will please state her age," he ordered, "after which she will be sworn in."

Anon

OBITUARIES

I am alive and well and concerned about the rumors of my death. But if I *were* dead, I would be the last to know.

Paul McCartney, Beatle

A man was killed by a circular saw, and in his obituary it was stated that he was "a good citizen, an upright man, and an ardent patriot, but of limited information regarding circular saws."

Anon

OBESITY

About the only time overweight will make a man feel better is when he sees it on a girl he nearly married.

O. A. Battista

OBJECTIVE

An aim in life is the only fortune worth finding.

Robert Louis Stevenson

OBSCENITY

Obscenity can be found in every book except the telephone directory.

Shaw

OBSEQUIES

If you don't attend other people's funerals, you certainly can't expect them to come to yours.

Clarence Day's mother

OCEAN

There is sorrow on the sea; it cannot be quiet.

Jeremiah

OCCUPATION

The ugliest of trades have their moments of pleasure. Now, if I were a grave digger, or even a hangman, there are some people I could work for with a great deal of enjoyment.

Douglas Jerrold

OFFENSIVE

He that strikes with the sword shall be beaten with the scabbard.

English proverb

OFFICE HOLDERS

Presumptuousness is one of the greatest vices in a man in a place of public responsibility, and though a political leader need not necessarily be humble, he must absolutely be modest.

Cardinal Richelieu

OH, YEAH?

No king ever wielded a scepter more powerful than a five-cent pencil in the hands of an American citizen when he writes his senator or congressman.

Sen. Norris Cotton

OLD

Is not old wine wholesomest, old pippins toothsomest, old wood burn brightest, old linen wash whitest? Old soldiers, sweetheart, are surest, and old lovers are soundest.

John Webster

OLD/NEW

Nothing is so new as what has long been forgotten.

German proverb

Let our object be, our country, our whole country, and nothing but our country.

Daniel Webster, 1825

Let us object to our country, our whole country, and nothing but our country.

Hippie today

OLD AGE

Is when you're more interested in pension than passion.

Anon

Is it not strange that desire should so many years outlive performances.

Shakespeare

Is the time when, if you ever knew anything, you've forgotten it.

Mr. Dooley

I smoke almost constantly, sometimes in the middle of the night. And I drink anything I can get my hands on.

Joe Smart, on his one-hundredth birthday

OLD VERSION

He that hath a head made of glass must not throw stones at another.

English proverb

OPERA

How wonderful opera would be if there were no singers.

Rossini

OPINION

There are men who would even be afraid to commit themselves on the doctrine that castor oil is a laxative.

Camille Flammarion

Nothing is more unjust or capricious than public opinion.

Hazlitt

He never chooses an opinion; he just wears whatever happens to be in style.

Tolstoi

Wind puffs up empty bladders; opinion, fools.

Socrates

OPPORTUNITY

Is what makes the thief.

Proverb

A man may have less material resources than his neighbor and be able to do little about it. He may have the voice of a crow and the grace of a cow and be unable to do much to develop either, but until death calls, every man has as much time as the next one, and his management of this priceless resource is his own responsibility.

Robert W. McIntyre

Nowadays some people expect the door of opportunity to be opened with an electric eye.

Anon

I was seldom able to see an opportunity until it had ceased to be one.

Mark Twain

No great man ever complains of want of opportunity.

Emerson

OPPORTUNITY/ADVANTAGE

Next to knowing when to seize an opportunity, the most important thing in life is to know when to forgo an advantage.

Benjamin Disraeli

OPPOSITION

Kites rise highest against the wind—not with it.

Winston Churchill

OPTIMISM

The place where optimism most flourishes is the lunatic asylum.

Havelock Ellis

Sick people are invariably optimistic. Optimism itself may be a sickness.

Remy de Gourmont

In the long run the pessimist may be proved to be right, but the optimist has a better time on the trip.

Daniel L. Reardon

ORATIONS

Nothing is truer in a sense than a funeral oration: it tells precisely what the dead man should have been.

Louis Gustave Vapereau

ORATOR

He multiplieth words without knowledge.

Book of Job

Cicero said loud-bawling orators were driven by their weakness to noise, as lame men to take horse.

Plutarch

Love, knavery, and necessity make men good orators.

Old proverb

ORGASM

The little death.

Spanish saying

OVER 50

When a comfortable bed is the best night spot.

Arnold H. Glasgow

OVERPOPULATION

Population, when unchecked, increases in a geometric ratio . . .

subsistence only increases in an arithmetical ratio. . . . The power of population is indefinitely greater than the power in the earth to produce subsistence for man.

Thomas Robert Malthus, 1798

OVERWORK

I have so much to do that I am going to bed.

Savoyard proverb

PAMPHLETS

All printed matter contains poison, more or less diluted according to the size of the work, more or less harmful, more or less deadly. . . . One grain in a vat has no effect at all, in a tea cup it causes vomiting, in a spoonful it kills—and there you have the pamphlet.

Paul-Louis Courier

PARADISE

When man tries to imagine Paradise on earth, the immediate result is a very respectable Hell.

Paul Claudel

PARADOX

If love be good, from whence cometh my woe?

Chaucer

PARENTHOOD

To understand a parent's love: have a child.

Japanese proverb

The ability to say no is perhaps the greatest gift a parent has.

Sam Levenson

We get our parents when they are so old it is hard to change their habits.

Anon, Jr.

Few parents nowadays pay any regard to what their children say to them; the old-fashioned respect for the young is fast dying out.

Wilde

There may be some doubt as to who are the best people to have charge of children, but there can be no doubt that parents are the worst.

Shaw

Oh, to be only half as wonderful as my child thought I was when he was small, and only half as stupid as my teen-ager now thinks I am.

Rebecca Richards

PARIS

That monstrous growth on the Seine, the factory of greed and gaiety, of vice and art.

Thomas Craven

PARKING

The more parking spaces you provide, the more cars will come to fill them. It is like feeding pigeons.

Sir Hugh Casson

Now that women are jockeys, baseball umpires, atomic scientists, and business executives, maybe some day they can master parallel parking.

Bill Vaughan

PARKING/INFLATION

Parking meters, looking cold and penniless.

LeRoy J. Herbert, 1963

Today a parking meter takes a dime and not any less.

LLL, 1971

MRS. PARKINSON'S LAW

Heat produced by pressure expands to fill the mind available, from which it can pass only to a cooler mind.

PARTICIPATION

The tree is no sooner down but everyone runs for his hatchet.

American proverb

PASSING FANCIES

Woman's beauty, the forest echo, and rainbows soon pass away.

Anon

PASSION

Variety is the one simply and absolutely foolproof aphrodisiac.

Norman Douglas

PAST

We all live in the past, because there is nothing else to live in. To live in the present is like proposing to sit on a pin. It is too minute, it is too slight a support, it is too uncomfortable a posture, and it is of necessity followed immediately by totally different experiences, analogous to those of jumping up with a yell. To live in the future is a contradiction in terms. The future is dead, in the perfectly definite sense that it is not alive.

G. K. Chesterton

No man is rich enough to buy back his past.

Wilde

Even God cannot change the past.

Agathon

Take the proverb to thine heart,
   Take and hold it fast—
"The mill cannot grind
   With the water that is past."

Sara Doudney

Always forget the past. No man ever backed into prosperity.

Anon

The "good old times"—all times, when old, are good.

Lord Byron

PAST IMPERFECT

Neither beg of him who has been a beggar, nor serve him who has been a servant.

Proverb

PASTIMES

Baseball may be the national pastime, but surely dieting is a close second.

Oscar Homolka

PATIENCE

Be patient; in time even an egg will walk.

African proverb

A wife never ceases to wonder why a husband can't show as much patience waiting for dinner as he does when he's waiting for a fish to bite.

Anon

PATRIOTISM

Patriotism is the egg from which wars are hatched.

Guy de Maupassant

It seems like the less a statesman amounts to, the more he loves the flag.

Kin Hubbard

PAYMENT

The money paid, the work delayed.

Anon

He that pays last never pays twice.

English proverb

PAYOFF

The race is not always to the swift, nor the battle to the strong
—but that's the way to bet.

Damon Runyon

PEACE

I am unable to find any warrant for the belief that any period
has offered men the kind of peace and certainty that the modern age is clamoring for. The Middle Ages was a period of
fearful maladministration. The Greeks led the most chaotic,
passionate, and disorderly life conceivable. They preached
serenity, but calm composure and discipline were with them,
as they are with us, an individual achievement.

Jacques Barzun

In proportion as the antagonism between the classes vanishes,
the hostility of one nation to another will come to an end.

Marx and Engels

Peace has its victories no less than war, but it doesn't have as
many monuments to unveil.

Kin Hubbard

What a beautiful fix we are in now; peace has been declared.

Napoleon Bonaparte, 1802

Is when frogs sleep on water lilies.

Anon, Jr., New Delhi

PEACEMAKERS

Those who in quarrels interpose
Must often wipe a bloody nose.

John Gay

PEAKS

The higher the plum tree, the riper the plum; the richer the
cobbler, the blacker his thumb.

Proverb

PENTAGON

I have always believed that the civilian control of the military
is one of the strongest foundations of our system of free government. Many of our people are descended from men and

214

women who fled their native countries to escape the oppression of militarism. . . . One reason that we have been so careful to keep the military within its own preserve is that the very nature of the service hierarchy gives military commanders little if any opportunity to learn the humility that is needed for public service.

Harry S Truman

A Pentagon committee is a group of the unwilling, chosen from the unfit, to do the unnecessary.

David Brinkley

PEOPLE

The people are in their nature so gentle, that there never was a government yet in which thousands of mistakes were not overlooked. The most sensible and jealous people are so little attentive to government, that there are no instances of resistance, until repeated, multiplied oppressions have placed it beyond a doubt, that their rulers had formed settled plans to deprive them of their liberties.

John Adams

There is little chance for people to get together as long as most of us want to be in the front of the bus, the back of the church and the middle of the road.

Anon

Snowflakes, like people, are all different and beautiful, but they can be a nuisance when they lose their identity in a mob.

Bill Vaughan

Everybody is interested in what everybody else is doing that's wrong.

"Mr. Dooley," Finley Peter Dunne

I wish I loved the Human Race;
I wish I loved its silly face;
I wish I liked the way it walks;
I wish I liked the way it talks;
And when I'm introduced to one
I wish I thought What Jolly Fun!

Sir Walter Alexander Raleigh

Don't put no constrictions on de people. Leave 'em ta hell alone.

Jimmy Durante

PEP TALK

Gentlemen, we don't need good losers. What we want are gracious winners.

James C. Hund

PERFECT SPEECH

The shortest distance between two jokes makes a perfect speech.

O. A. Battista

PERFECTION

Nothing is perfect—are there not spots on the sun?

Anon

PERSISTENCE

Nothing in the world can take the place of persistence. Talent will not; nothing is more common than unsuccessful men of talent. Genius will not; unrewarded genius is almost a proverb. Education will not; the world is full of educated derelicts. Persistence and determination alone are omnipotent.

Calvin Coolidge

Consider the postage stamp: its usefulness consists in the ability to stick to one thing till it gets there.

Josh Billings

He that is thrown would ever wrestle.

English proverb

PERSONNEL

Twice as many people are engaged in clerical work as in 1940. Maybe we are no more mixed up than ever, but we are getting it all down on paper.

Anon

PERSONALITY

Never destroy any aspect of personality, for what you think is the wild branch may be the heart of the tree.

Mrs. Henry George

PERSPECTIVE

Never measure the height of a mountain until you have reached the top. Then you will see how low it is.

Dag Hammarskjold

PERSUASION

By persuading others, we convince ourselves.

Junius

PESSIMISM/OPTIMISM/PHILOSOPHY

A pessimist sees only the dark side of the clouds, and mopes;

a philosopher sees both sides and shrugs; an optimist doesn't see the clouds at all—he's walking on them.

D. O. Flynn

PETITION

He that asketh faintly beggeth a denial.

English proverb

PETITIONS

The story is told of a newspaper reporter who was sent out to get signers for a petition. Of the hundred and two people whom he induced to read his paper, many called it "dangerous and subversive" and only one person would sign it. The petition was a portion of the Declaration of Independence.

Edward E. Loveless

PHILADELPHIA

To be raised in Philadelphia is like being born with a big nose —you never get over it.

Anon

I spent a year in that town, one Sunday.

Warwick Deeping

PHILOSOPHERS

One cannot conceive anything so strange and so implausible that it has not already been said by one philosopher or another.

René Descartes, after Cicero

No one would be angry with a man for unintentionally making a mistake about a matter of fact; but if he perversely insists on spoiling your story in the telling of it, you want to kick him; and this is the reason why every philosopher and theologian is justly vexed with every other.

George Santayana

If I wished to punish a province, I would have it governed by philosophers.

Frederick the Great

PHILOSOPHY

The fruits of philosophy are the important thing, not the philosophy itself. When we ask the time, we don't want to know how watches are constructed.

Lichtenberg

I have tried, too, in my time to be a philosopher; but, I don't know how; cheerfulness was always breaking in.

Oliver Edwards

PICNICS

There are several reasons why a picnic is something at which I am apt to look askance.
　Not the least of them is ance.

Xico

PIGGY-BACK

A dwarf on a giant's shoulders sees further of the two.

George Herbert

PINCHED

George Moore unexpectedly pinched my behind; I felt rather honored that my behind should have drawn the attention of the great master of English prose.

Ilka Chase

PIONEERS

If you think there are no new frontiers, watch a boy ring the front doorbell on his first date.

Olin Miller

PIONEERS IN SCIENCE

In science the credit goes to the man who convinces the world, not to the man to whom the idea first occurs.

Sir William Osler

PIRATES

In a moment the pirates were all around us, rolling their eyes, gnashing their teeth, and filing their nails.

Stephen Leacock

PITY

He that pitieth another remembereth himself.

English proverb

Pity costs nothing, and ain't worth nothing.

Josh Billings

PIXIE PROVERBS

The wages of gin is breath.

LLL

Virtue is its own reward, alas!

LLL

A stitch in time saves embarrassment.

LLL

PLATONIC FRIENDSHIP

Is the short interval between introduction and seduction.

Anon

PLATONIC LOVE

Is like being invited down into the cellar for a glass of ginger ale.

Anon

Platonic love is a volcano without eruption.

André Prevot

PLAY-ACTING

Performers are only tools of the playwright. If they try to do more than give life to the script, they and the play die.

Edwige Feulliere

PLAYBOY MAGAZINE

In place of the citizen with a vote to cast or a job to do or a book to study or a god to worship, the editors of *Playboy* offer a vision of the whole man reduced to his private parts.

Benjamin De Mott

PLEASING

The whole art of pleasing lies in never speaking of oneself, always persuading others to speak of themselves. Everyone knows this and everyone forgets it.

Edmond and Jules de Goncourt

PLEASURE

The greatest pleasure I know is to do a good action by stealth and have it found out by accident.

Charles Lamb

There is no pleasure in having nothing to do; the fun is in having lots to do and not doing it.

Mary Little

The great pleasure in life is doing what people say you cannot do.

Walter Bagehot

PLEASURE/DESPAIR

To get an idea of our fellow countrymen's miseries, we have only to take a look at their pleasures.

George Eliot

219

PLEASURE/PAIN

Pain past is pleasure.

Anon

PLUMBER

A plumber is an adventurer who traces leaks to their source.

Arthur "Bugs" Baer

POET ON MARRIAGE

It's a funny thing that when a man hasn't anything on earth to worry about, he goes off and gets married.

Robert Frost

POETIC JUSTICE

A lawyer with his tongue cut out.

LLL

POETRY

Is the language in which man explores his own amazement.

Christopher Fry

A sonnet is a moment's monument . . . to one dead, deathless hour.

Dante Gabriel Rossetti

Children and lunatics cut the Gordian knot which the poet spends his life patiently trying to untie.

Jean Cocteau

It is easier to write a mediocre poem than to understand a good one.

Michel de Montaigne

There is a great deal of prose license in Walt Whitman's poetry.

Mary Little

Among our literary scenes,
Saddest this sight to me,
The graves of little magazines
That died to make verse free.

Keith Preston

POETRY-ORATORY

A poet puts the world into a nutshell; the orator, out of a nutshell, brings a world.

James Hurnand

POETS

Are born, not paid.

Addison Mizner

While pensive poets painful vigils keep
Sleepless themselves to give their readers sleep.

Alexander Pope

Some ladies now make pretty songs,
    And some make pretty nurses;
Some men are good for righting wrongs,
    And some for writing verses.

F. Locker-Lampson

Without a bit of madness
One gives up rhyming at thirty.

Grosset

Poets utter great and wise things which they do not themselves
understand.

Plato

A poet is one who feels the world as a gift.

James Dickey

We are all poets, at odd moments.

Matthew Arnold

Modern poets are bells of lead. They should tinkle melodiously
but usually they just klunk.

Lord Dunsany

A poem is a noise on paper. . . .

Dylan Thomas

POLITENESS

The highest perfection of politeness is only a beautiful edifice,
built, from the base to the dome, of graceful and gilded forms
of charitable and unselfish lying.

Mark Twain

POLITICAL ECONOMY

It's called political economy because it has nothing to do with
either politics or economy.

Stephen Leacock

POLITICAL PHILOSOPHY

A radical is a man with both feet firmly planted in the air. A
conservative is a man with two perfectly good legs who, however, has never learned to walk forward. A reactionary is a
somnambulist walking backwards. A liberal is a man who uses
his legs and his hands at the behest of his head.

F. D. Roosevelt

POLITICS

Is war without bloodshed, and war is politics with blood.

Mao Tse-tung

Public office is the last refuge of a scoundrel.

Senator Boise Penrose

Cease being the slave of a political party and you become its deserter.

Jules Simon

No party is as bad as its leaders.

Will Rogers

Has got so expensive that it takes lots of money to even get beat with.

Will Rogers

All political parties die at last of swallowing their own lies.

John Arbuthnot

He was a power politically for years, but he never got prominent enough t' have his speeches garbled.

Kin Hubbard

The necessary and wise subordination of the military to the civil power will be best sustained when life-long professional soldiers abstain from seeking high political office.

Dwight D. Eisenhower

If you can't stand the heat, get out of the kitchen.

Harry S Truman

Has it ever occurred to you that in our social system the politician is enabled to reach a position of responsibility without having any training? He serves no apprenticeship. He masters no course of study. He need pass no examination as to his ability. He receives neither a diploma nor a license to practice. The veterinary who doctors our dogs and cats is required to show more careful preparation for his calling than is the politician who seeks to assume the right to direct not only our industrial but much of our personal life.

Anon

There is no more independence in politics than there is in jail.

Will Rogers

In political discussion heat is in inverse proportion to knowledge.

J. G. C. Minchin

A man is a fool to put anything in writing if he knows how to talk, and he shouldn't talk if he is able to nod or shake his head.

Martin Lomasney

Now that politicians have opinion polls to find out what the voters think, some method should be developed to give the voters some idea of what the politicians think.

Burton Hillis

When politicians appeal to all intelligent voters, they mean everyone who is going to vote for them.

Franklin P. Adams

If nominated I will not accept; if elected I will not serve.

William Tecumseh Sherman

An ounce of convention is worth a pound of primaries.

Arnold H. Glasgow

In politics, nothing is contemptible.

Benjamin Disraeli

I take politics only medicinally, as a cure for occasional attacks of insomnia.

Kenneth Hare

Unleash Stassen!

perennial Republican slogan

You never know how dirty your hands are until you peel a hardboiled egg or go into politics.

LLL

The trouble with most of these elected politicians is that they think what they got from the public last November was not a mandate but a charge-a-plate.

Richard Mayer

A lot of politicians make the mistake of forgetting that they've been appointed instead of anointed.

Anon

A politician will do anything to keep his job—even become a patriot.

William Randolph Hearst

Whenever a politician in office humbly refers to himself as a "public servant," I reach for my wallet to see if it's still in my pocket.

Sydney J. Harris

I am not a politician and my other habits are good.

Artemus Ward

A politician is an arse upon which everyone has sat except a man.

e. e. cummings

POLLUTED PROVERBS

Two heads are better than none.

LLL

A closed ear catcheth no lies.

LLL

Bear poverty; wealth will bore itself.

LLL

It's no use crying over split atoms.

LLL

A shirt has a tail but cannot bark.

Douglas Hawson

Don't let the cat out of the bag after the barn door is locked.

Honey Flexer

Too many cooks spoil the broth of a boy.

LLL

No man goes before his time—unless the boss has left early.

Anon

A man can only die once—but usually that's enough.

LLL

He should not boast of his family tree who comes from the shady side.

LLL

Promise much; do little.

LLL

No leg's too short to reach the ground.

Lyndon Irving

It's a weak plaice that can't swim.

Rhoda Tuck Pook

Great oaths from little aching corns do grow.

Anon

A warm heart and a cold hand gather no moss.

LLL

What is sauce for the goose is better with oranges.

LLL

POLLUTION

The beautiful Tiber is one of the world's worst open sewers.

Anon Italian

I asked a coughing friend of mine why he doesn't stop smoking. "In this town it wouldn't do any good," he explained. "I happen to be a chain breather."

Bob Sylvester

PORNOGRAPHY

A taste for dirty stories may be said to be inherent in the human animal.

George Moore

PORTRAITS

The statue of the Duke of Kent
Is neither large nor prominent.
It occupies a modest space
On land adjoining Portland Place
And—quite against the normal course—
Is not provided with a horse.
So there he stands with books and scroll,
A dignified but kindly soul
Who—clothes apart—might also be
A relative of you and me.
(The Legend briefly states that he's
Remembered for his Charities.)
So very few who see him there
Can know that one who has the air
Of no one in particular
Was Queen Victoria's Papa.

H. J. R.

A portrait is a painting with something wrong with the mouth.
John S. Sargent

There are only two styles of portrait painting: the serious and the smirk.
Dickens

PORTRAITS, PERSONAL

Spiro Agnew is the Abbie Hoffman of the extreme right-wingers.
Nelsie Thompson

Matthew Arnold. An English saint in sidewhiskers.
Wilde

W. H. Auden. A face like a wedding cake left out in the rain.
Anon

Johann Sebastian Bach. A divine sewing machine.
Colette

William Blake was the purest romantic of all.
Esme Wingfield-Stratford

Henry Brougham. He was one of those characters in real life who would appear incredible in fiction. He was so marvellously ill-favored as to possess some of the attractiveness of a gargoyle. He had neither dignity, nor what a Roman would have called gravity. As Lord Chancellor, he distinguished himself by belching from the Woolsack. He once put about a story of his own death, in order to get a free advertisement in the obituary columns. . . .
Esme Wingfield-Stratford

Most Gracious Queen, we thee implore
To go away and sin no more,
But if that effort be too great,
To go away at any rate.

Epigram on Queen Caroline

Winston Churchill. Fifty percent genius, fifty percent bloody fool.

Clement Atlee

Dangeau was despicably vain and at the same time obsequious —two things that often go together, however opposite they may seem to be.

Claud Henri Saint-Simon

Madame de Castries was a quarter of a woman, a kind of half-baked biscuit, extremely small, but well-turned, and you could have put her through a medium-sized ring: no behind, no bust, no chin, very ugly, with a perpetual expression of pained surprise, and yet withal a face bursting with wit.

Saint-Simon

What I like about Clive
Is that he is no longer alive.
There is a great deal to be said
For being dead.

Edmund Clerthew Bentley

The Prince de Conti, who was so considerate, so charming, so delightful, cared for nothing and no one. He had friends, choosing them as one chooses pieces of furniture for one's house.

Saint-Simon

DeQuincey had the face of a child, but of a child that had seen Hell.

Carlyle

She is such a good friend that she would throw all her acquaintances into the water for the pleasure of fishing them out.

Talleyrand (of Mme. de Staël)

Norman Douglas. A mixture of Roman emperor and Roman cab driver.

Reginald Turner

Edward the Confessor
Slept under the dresser.
When that began to pall,
He slept in the hall.

E. C. Bentley

The other day, by a little lake,
Jean Fréron was bit by a snake.
What was the sequel? Needless to say,
The snake, not Fréron, passed away.

Voltaire

An hour with Buckminster Fuller is as unforgettable as a first parachute jump, the birth of a first baby, or being under fire.

Anon

Allen Ginsberg. That beard in search of a poet.

Caesar Bottom

Gladstone . . . and his capacity for saying nothing whatever with the noblest eloquence that ever stirred the great heart of a people.

Esme Wingfield-Stratford

I don't mind Gladstone's concealing an ace in his sleeve, but I object to his pretending, when exposed, that God Almighty had put it there.

George Labouchere

Johann Wolfgang von Goethe liked pretty girls all his life. . . . In his Italian journey, he left no petticoat unturned.

Luigi Barzini

Byron. Mad, bad and dangerous to know.

Lady Caroline Lamb

Harlay was a scrawny little man with a lozenge-shaped face, a big acquiline nose, and eyes like a vulture's which always seemed to be devouring things and seeing through walls.

Saint-Simon

Homer has taught all other poets the art of telling lies skillfully.

Aristotle

Oliver Herford. An embarrassed field mouse.

Frank Crowninshield

So far from writing *A Shropshire Lad,* I shouldn't have thought A. E. Housman capable of reading it.

Anon

He (Lafayette) has a canine appetite for popularity and fame.

Thomas Jefferson

T. E. Lawrence. An adventurer with a genius for backing into the limelight.

Lowell Thomas

Lowell Thomas. A man who has dined with practicing cannibals without becoming part of the dinner.

Russel Crouse

Don Marquis was a careful blend of Falstaff and Napoleon III.

Christopher Morley

Shelley, trying to lasso the Golden Calf.

Benjamin de Casseres

227

Margaret Mead. A short (5 feet 2 inches), sturdy woman of sixty-nine, she could pass for a midwestern housewife who had possibly taken a few judo lessons late in life.

David Dempsey

H. L. Mencken. A comedian playing Hamlet.

Irving Howe

Don Quixote. He is a muddled fool, full of lucid intervals.

Sancho Panza

The way Bernard Shaw believes in himself is very refreshing in these atheistic days when so many believe in no God at all.

Israel Zangwill

Harold Stassen. A political nymphomaniac.

Relman Morin

Robert Louis Stevenson. A Presbyterian pirate.

Doris N. Dalgleish

Tennyson could not think up to the height of his own towering style.

G. K. Chesterton

Thoreau. Unperfect, unfinished, inartistic, worse than provincial—parochial.

Henry James

Toulouse-Lautrec. A tiny Vulcan with pince-nez, a little twin-pouched bag in which he stuck his poor legs.

Jules Renard

Percy A. Tucker, who built one of the country's largest pen businesses from scratch. . . .

Richmond Times-Dispatch

Oscar Wilde. A fatuous cad.

Henry James

Sir Christopher Wren. An architect who treated Gothic as though it were a cantankerous old aunt; with affection and disrespect.

Ian Nairn

William Zeckendorf is the most imaginative man in the real estate field, but not the richest. Why? Because Bill learned only how to multiply, and never how to add.

Billy Rose

PORTRAITS, SELF

He slept beneath the moon,
He basked beneath the sun;
He lived a life of going-to-do,
And died with nothing done.

J. Albery, epitaph written for himself

If I had not been Alexander, I would have liked to have been
Diogenes.

Alexander the Great

Beethoven can write music, thank God—but he can do nothing
else on earth.

Ludwig von Beethoven

I am too old. . . . I remain the primitive of the path I opened up.

Paul Cezanne

My life is one dem'd horrid grind!

Charles Dickens

Within the oftentimes bombastic and truculent appearance
that I present to the world, trembles a heart shy as a wren
in the hedgerow or a mouse along the wainscoting.

George Moore

William Morris. The idle singer of an empty day.

William Morris

I do not know what I may appear to the world, but to myself
I seem to have been only like a boy playing on the sea-shore,
and diverting myself in now and then finding a smoother pebble, or a prettier shell than ordinary, whilst the great ocean
of truth lay all undiscovered before me.

Sir Isaac Newton

Damon Runyon. A day-coach boy in a parlor car seat.

Damon Runyon

I have never been the academic sort, for I never was able to
get out of the habit of writing fast.

Saint-Simon

Twenty-four years ago, I was strangely handsome; in San
Francisco in the rainy season I was often mistaken for fair
weather.

Mark Twain

PORTRAITS, MEN

He is old enough to know worse.

Wilde

He's a pumpkin plus eyes and nose.

Japanese proverb

No butter will stick to his bread.

Saying

A little, round, fat oily man of God.

James Thomson

A wit with dunces, and a dunce with wits.

Alexander Pope

He doesn't act on the stage—he behaves.

Wilde

He is every other inch a gentleman.

Rebecca West

He had no principles and was delightful company.

Mark Twain

He was not made for climbing the tree of knowledge.

Sigrid Undset

He mouths a sentence as a cur mouths a bone.

Charles Churchill

The years have spread his nose across his face.

LLL

He was like a cock who thought the sun had risen to hear him crow.

George Eliot

He was the flower—or should we say, the fungus?—of nobility.

Alain Lesage

He blows his horn so loudly, he hasn't any wind left for the climb.

Miss Pat O'Haire

While he was not dumber than an ox, he was not any smarter.

James Thurber

He didn't utter a word, but he exuded mute blasphemy from every pore.

Mark Twain

Musically, he was so ignorant that he didn't know his brass from his oboe.

Anon

He will do almost anything for the poor, except get off their backs.

Tolstoi

Shake a bridle over a Yorkshireman's grave, and he'll rise and steal a horse.

Lancashire proverb

He is useless on top of the ground; he ought to be under it, inspiring the cabbages.

Mark Twain

Shake a Leicestershire man by the collar, and you shall hear the beans rattle in his belly.

English proverb

Nature designed thee for a hero's mould
But ere she cast thee, let the stuff grow cold.

George Moore

Seemed washing his hands with invisible soap
In imperceptible water.

Thomas Hood

As a youth, he once ran away with a circus—but they caught
him and made him give it back.

Anon

He fell down a great deal during his boyhood because of a trick
he had of walking into himself.

James Thurber

He needs a wife because sooner or later something is going
to happen that he can't blame on the government.

Anon

He was good-natured, obliging, and immensely ignorant, and
was endowed with a stupidity which by the least little stretch
would go around the globe four times and tie.

Mark Twain

A man so various, that he seem'd to be
Not one, but all mankind's epitome;
Stiff in opinions, always in the wrong,
Was everything by starts, and nothing long.
But in the course of one revolving moon,
Was chymist, fiddler, statesman, and buffoon.

John Dryden

PORTRAITS, WOMEN

In came Mrs. Fezziwig, one vast substantial smile.

Charles Dickens

Fate wrote her a most tremendous tragedy, and she played it
in tights.

Max Beerbohm

She was a large woman, who seemed not so much dressed as
upholstered.

Sir James Barrie

She invariably was first over the fence in the mad pursuit of
culture.

George Ade

She was a soprano of the kind often used for augmenting the
grief at a funeral.

George Ade

She is an excellent creature, but she never can remember
which came first, the Greeks or the Romans.

Benjamin Disraeli

She looks like the deluxe edition of a wicked French novel
meant especially for the English market.

Oscar Wilde

She ought never to have been a mother, but she'll make a rare mother-in-law.

Samuel Butler (II)

Though her mien carries much more invitation than command, to behold her is an immediate check to loose behavior; to love her was a liberal education.

Sir Richard Steele

Matilda told such Dreadful Lies
It made one Gasp and Stretch one's Eyes;
Her Aunt, who, from her Earliest Youth,
Had kept a strict Regard for Truth,
Attempted to Believe Matilda:
The effort very nearly Killed her.

Hilaire Belloc

POSITIVE

Conviction is strongest
When knowledge is least.

Anon

POSSESSION

Mine is better than ours.

Franklin

The gown is hers that wears it; and the world is his who enjoys it.

Flemish proverb

The master's eye makes the horse fat.

Proverb

POSSIBILITIES

A likely impossibility is always preferable to an unconvincing possibility.

Aristotle

POST OFFICE DEPT.

The Post Office boys, if I had my way,
Would reverse their current stunts
Of picking up mail ten times a day
And delivering only once.

LLL

POSTMEN'S PRIDE

Our rural carriers are often bitten by jaguars.

Angelico Loureiso, Rio de Janeiro Postmaster

POULTRY

The chicken craves the capon.

Dutch proverb

No good chicken cackles in your house and lays in another's.

Proverb

POVERTY

A poor man's debt makes a great noise.

English proverb

We shall soon with the help of God be in sight of the day when poverty will be banished from this nation.

Herbert C. Hoover, 1920

We in America today are nearer to the final triumph over poverty than ever before in the history of any land.

Herbert C. Hoover, 1928

I am a poor man, but I have this consolation: I am poor by accident, not by design.

Joseph Billings

An empty purse fills the face with wrinkles.

English proverb

The poor man is not he who is without a cent, but he who is without a dream.

Harry Kemp

Dreading that climax of all human ills
The inflammation of his weekly bills.

Lord Byron

Honest poverty is a gem that even a king might be proud to call his own, but I wish to sell out.

Mark Twain

It is easier to praise poverty than bear it.

Proverb

He who knows how to be poor, knows everything.

Jules Michelet

Poverty is feeling poor.

Emerson

POWER

A man is the prisoner of his power, and any excess of power in one part is usually paid for by some defect in a contiguous part.

Emerson

Power is not revealed by striking hard or often but by striking true.

Balzac

PRAISE

The love of praise, howe'er concealed by art,
Reigns more or less, and glows in ev'ry heart.

Edward Young

None ever gives the lie to him that praiseth him.

Proverb

To refuse praise is to seek praise twice.

La Rochefoucauld

The praise of fools is censure in disguise.

Italian proverb

It is safer to commend the dead than the living.

Proverb

Among the smaller duties of life I hardly know any one more important than that of not praising where praise is not due.

Sydney Smith

PRAISE/BLAME

It is more difficult to praise rightly than to blame.

Proverb

PRAYER

The day returns and brings us the petty round of irritating concerns and duties. Help us to play the man, help us to perform them with laughter and kind faces, let cheerfulness abound with industry. Give us to go blithely on our business this day, bring us to our resting beds weary and content and undishonored, and grant us in the end the gift of sleep.

Robert Louis Stevenson

I kneel not now to pray that Thou
Make white one single sin,
I only kneel to thank Thee, Lord
For what I have not been.

Harry Kemp

My prayer to God is a very short one: "O Lord, make my enemies most ridiculous!" God has granted it.

Voltaire

Lord, make me to know mine end, and the measure of my days, what it is; that I may know how frail I am.

Psalms

Teach me to feel another's woe,
To hide the fault I see;
That mercy I to others show,
That mercy show to me.

Alexander Pope

What men usually ask of God when they pray is that two and two not make four.

Anon

He that would learn to pray, let him go to sea.

English proverb

Great Spirit, help me never to judge another until I have walked two weeks in his moccasins.

Sioux Indian

I pray each day that I may be made strong enough not to hurt anybody.

Acharya

When the gods wish to punish us they answer our prayers.

Wilde

PREACHERS

It's my feeling that when people go to sleep in church, somebody should wake up the preacher.

Burton Hillis

PRECAUTION

It's good to be merry and wise.
It's good to be honest and true.
It's best to be off with the old love
Before you are on with the new.

Songs of England and Scotland

PRECEDENTS

To follow foolish precedents, and wink with both our eyes, is easier than to think.

William Cowper

PRECEPT

Be ever vigilant, but never suspicious.

Anon

Hope for the best, get set for the worst,
And take to the hills when the dam has burst.

LLL

Do wisely from Expensive Sins refrain
And never break the Sabbath, but for gain.

John Dryden

PREDICTIONS

Of all the horrid, hideous notes of woe,
Sadder than owl songs on the midnight blast
Is that portentious phrase, "I told you so."

Lord Byron

235

Any astronomer can predict with absolute accuracy just where every star in the heavens will be at half-past eleven tonight. He can make no such prediction about his young daughter.

James Truslow Adams

PREJUDICE

The world is full of people who have never, since childhood, met an open doorway with an open mind.

E. B. White

The difference between a prejudice and a conviction is that you can explain a conviction without getting mad.

Anon

Prejudice is a great time-saver. You can form opinions without having to get the facts.

Anon

If we were to wake up some morning and find that everyone was the same race, creed, and color, we would find some other causes for prejudice by noon.

Senator George Aiken

PRESERVING

It is not everyone that can pickle well.

English proverb

THE PRESIDENCY

My movements to the chair of government will be accompanied by feelings not unlike those of a culprit, who is going to the place of his execution; so unwilling am I, in the evening of a life nearly consumed in public cares, to quit a peaceful abode for an ocean of difficulties, without that competency of political skill, abilities, and inclination, which are necessary to manage the helm.

George Washington

No man who ever held the office of President would congratulate a friend on obtaining it. He will make one man ungrateful, and a hundred men his enemies, for every office he can bestow.

John Adams

No man will ever bring out of the Presidency the reputation which carried him into it.

Thomas Jefferson

The Presidency is a distinction far more glorious than the crown of any hereditary monarch in Christendom; but yet it is a crown of thorns.

James Buchanan

If you are as happy, Mr. Lincoln, on entering this house as I am in leaving it and returning home, you are the happiest man in this country.

James Buchanan, 1861

What is the Presidency worth to me if I have no country?

Abraham Lincoln

Nobody ever left the Presidency with less regret, less disappointment, fewer heart-burnings, or more general content with the result of his term (in his own heart, I mean) than I do.

Rutherford B. Hayes

I look upon the four years next to come as a self-inflicted penance for the good of my country. I see no pleasure in it.

Grover Cleveland

The presidential office is not a rosewater affair. This is an office in which a man must put on his war paint.

Woodrow Wilson

My God, this is a hell of a job! I have no trouble with my enemies. I can take care of them all right. By my damn friends, my Goddamn friends, they're the ones that keep me walking the floors nights.

Warren G. Harding

I think the American public wants a solemn ass as a President and I think I'll go along with them.

Calvin Coolidge

A few hair shirts are part of the mental wardrobe of every man. The President differs only from other men in that he has a more extensive wardrobe.

Herbert Hoover

The first twelve years are the hardest.

F. D. Roosevelt

Being a President is like riding a tiger. A man has to keep on riding or be swallowed.

Harry S Truman

If forced to choose between the penitentiary and the White House for four years, I would say the penitentiary, thank you.

William Tecumseh Sherman

The best reason for not being President is that you have to shave twice a day.

Adlai Stevenson

PRESIDENTIAL BEEF

During the Depression, soon after President Hoover initiated a number of "major recovery programs" he told former President Coolidge that he could not understand why the results were as yet disappointing and his critics so vociferous.

"You can't expect to see calves running in the field," said Coolidge, "the day after you put the bull to the cows."

"No," replied Hoover, "But I *would* expect to see contented cows."

Arthur Krock

THE PRESS

I would have been ruined long ago if it had not been for the sustained malignancy of the press. The best thing that can happen to a public man is to be depicted as a villain. Then, when he does make an appearance, he is so much different than they expected that the public says, Why, he is an angel. I am very grateful for the many years of misrepresentation.

Aneurin Bevan

PRETENDING

The only good in pretending is the fun we get out of fooling ourselves that we fool somebody.

Booth Tarkington

PRETENSE

Pretend not to that of which thou art ignorant, lest thine actual knowledge be discredited.

Arabic proverb

PRETENSION

Every stink that fights the ventilator thinks it is Don Quixote.

Lec

PREVARICATION

Old men and far travelers may lie by authority.

Proverb

PRIDE

Of all the causes which conspire to blind
Man's erring judgment, and misguide the mind,
What the weak head with strongest bias rules
Is pride, the never-failing vice of fools.

Alexander Pope

Other sins find their vent in the accomplishment of evil deeds, whereas pride lies in wait for good deeds, to destroy them.

Saint Augustine

A proud look makes foul work in a fine face.

English proverb

PRIDE/SHAME

Pride goes before, and shame follows after.

Proverb

PRIMROSE PATH

Once a hidden lane, now a roaring thruway.

Anon

PRINCIPLE

When a fellow says, "It ain't the money but the principle of the thing," it's the money.

Kin Hubbard

PRINTING

In a certain sense, printing proved a drawback to letters. It . . . cast contempt on books that failed to find a publisher.

Remy de Gourmont

PRIVACY

Love thy neighbour, but pull not down thy hedge.

Proverb

PROBLEM/SOLUTION

If you're not part of the solution—you're part of the problem.

Anon

PROBLEMS OF WRITING

An ocean is likely to be a troublesome collaborator for a writer. Writing at its side is like writing in a temple surrounded by statues of heroes. I am inclined to sit and ponder the mighty problems of evolution in a set of unwieldy phrases.

Ben Hecht

PROCRASTINATION

Do not put off till tomorrow what can be enjoyed today.

Josh Billings

Going along the street of mañana, bye and bye one arrives at the house of never.

Cervantes

Tomorrow comes never.

Proverb

PROCREATION

One fool makes many.

Proverb

PROFITS

It is a socialist idea that making profits is a vice; I consider the real vice is making losses.

Winston Churchill

PROGRESS

At every crossway on the road that leads to the future, each progressive spirit is opposed by a thousand men appointed to guard the past.

Anon

The reasonable man adapts himself to the world; the unreasonable one persists in trying to adapt the world to himself. Therefore all progress depends on the unreasonable man.

Shaw

There is no adequate defense, except stupidity, against the impact of a new idea.

Percy W. Bridgman

Every great advance in natural knowledge has involved the absolute rejection of authority.

Thomas H. Huxley

The march of the human mind is slow.

Edmund Burke

Men are called fools in one age for not knowing what they were called fools for averring in the age before.

Henry Ward Beecher

All progress grows out of discontent with things as they are: discomfort, disgust, displeasure, dissatisfaction, disease.

D. Kenneth Winebrenner

Is it progress when a cannibal uses knife and fork?

Lec

Every reform is only a mask under cover of which a more terrible reform, which dares not yet name itself, advances.

Emerson

Man is in danger of being made obsolete by his own progress.

Burton Hillis

We've made great progress in the last twenty-five years but all I can notice we're doing better is eating.

Country Parson

PROGRESSION

The first, the Retort Courteous; the second, the Quip Modest; the third, the Reply Churlish; the fourth, the Reproof Valiant; the fifth, the Countercheck Quarrelsome; the sixth, the Lie with Circumstance; the seventh, the Lie Direct.

Shakespeare

PROMISCUITY

Make love to every woman you meet; if you get 5 percent on
your outlay, it's a good investment.

Arnold Bennett

PROMISES

Promises and piecrust are made to be broken.

Jonathan Swift

Vows made in storms are forgotten in calm.

Proverb

Some persons make promises for the pleasure of breaking
them.

William Hazlitt

The newly elected mayor said that during his year in office he
would lay aside all his political prepositions and be "like Caesar's wife, all things to all men."

Anon

PROMISES/GIFTS

We obtain more services by means of promises than by means
of gifts; for people make an effort to deserve what they hope
to get from us, but credit only themselves for what they
receive.

Saint-Evremond

PROMPTNESS

Be early which, if you are not, you will, when it is too late,
wish you had been.

Lord Chesterfield

A friend of mine goes by her own time. She keeps her watch
set at ten minutes to nine, no matter what time it is, because
she says it's not too early, not too late, and she has ten minutes to get there.

George Fuermann

PROPHECY

Our present addiction to pollsters and forecasters is a symptom of our chronic uncertainty about the future. Even when
the forecasts prove wrong, we still go on asking for them. We
watch our experts read the entrails of statistical tables and
graphs the way the ancients watched their soothsayers read
the entrails of a chicken.

Eric Hoffer

I shall always consider the best guesser the best prophet.

Cicero

PROPHETS

Hence it comes about that all armed Prophets have been victorious and all unarmed Prophets have been destroyed.

Machiavelli

The wisest prophets make sure of the event first.

Horace Walpole

The best qualification of a prophet is to have a good memory.

Halifax

Among people who haven't.

LLL

PROPOSAL

Come live with me and be my love
And we'll defy the storms above.
We'll lack for food, we'll lack for gold,
No lack of tales when we are old.

Christopher Marlow

PROSPERITY

Prosperity is the surest breeder of insolence I know.

Mark Twain

It requires a strong constitution to withstand repeated attacks of prosperity.

J. L. Basford

PROVERBS

Get out of the forest while you still have daylight.

Japanese proverb

Don't keep your coals in a volcano.

Publius Syrus

It is a bad well into which one must put water.

Anon

Better go back than go wrong.

Anon

Little wit in the head makes much work for the feet.

Anon

A little oil may save a deal of friction.

Anon

What costs nothing is worth nothing.

Anon

He who knows nothing is confident of everything.

Anon

A thing lost is a thing known.

Anon

If you don't touch the rope, you won't ring the bell.

Anon

Learn as if you were to live forever; live as if you were to die tomorrow.

Anon

PROVIDENCE

I believe in the Providence of the most men, the largest purse, and the longest cannon.

Abraham Lincoln

PRUDERY

The peculiarity of prudery is to multiply sentinels in proportion as the fortress is less threatened.

Victor Hugo

There are those who so dislike the nude that they find something indecent in the naked truth.

F. H. Bradley

PSYCHIATRY

No man is a hero to his wife's psychiatrist.

Dr. Eric Berne

PSYCHOANALYSIS

Who looks after the psychoanalyst's wife while the psychoanalyst is away being psychoanalyzed?

Scarritt Adams

No doubt fate would find it easier than I do to relieve you of your illness. But you will be able to convince yourself that much will be gained if we succeed in transforming your hysterical misery into common unhappiness.

Freud

The relation between psychiatrists and other kinds of lunatics is more or less the relation of a convex folly to a concave one.

Karl Kraus

Is spending $40 an hour to squeal on your mother.

Mike Connolly

PSYCHOLOGIST

An animal psychologist is a man who pulls habits out of rats.

Anon

PUBLIC OPINION

Is the last refuge of a politician without any opinion of his own.

Mark Bonham-Carter

PUBLICITY

There were brave men before Agamemnon; but, all unwept and unknown, they are lost in the distant night, being without a divine poet.

Horace

The more you are talked about, the less powerful you are.

Benjamin Disraeli

The problem of attracting the whole world's attention without incurring the ridicule of anyone has never yet been solved.

Anon

PUBLISHERS

As repressed sadists are supposed to become policemen or butchers, so those with irrational fear of life become publishers.

Cyril Connolly

PUBLISHING

I settled my temporal business. It is now about eighteen years since I began writing and printing books, and how much in that time have I gained by printing? Why, on summing up my accounts, I found that on March 1, 1756 . . . I had gained by printing and preaching together, a debt of twelve hundred and thirty-six pounds.

John Wesley

PUNCTUALITY

I have always been a quarter of an hour before my time, and it has made a man of me.

Horatio Nelson

Also, a superb admiral.

LLL

The trouble with being punctual is that nobody's there to appreciate it.

Lettice Philpots

The trouble with being punctual is that people think you have nothing more important to do.

Anon

The only meeting that ever started on time was held up for an hour while things were explained to people who came in late and didn't know what was going on.

Doug Larson

I am a believer in punctuality though it makes me very lonely.

E. V. Lucas

If you're there before it's over, you're on time.

James J. Walker

Unfaithfulness in the keeping of an appointment is an act of clear dishonesty. You may as well borrow a person's money as his time.

Horace Mann

Better to steal his money—that can be replaced.

LLL

PUNS

Punning is a talent which no man affects to despise but he that is without it.

Jonathan Swift

Of puns it has been said that those most dislike who are least able to utter them.

Poe

I never knew an enemy to puns who was not an ill-natured man.

Charles Lamb

PUNISHMENT

He that eats the king's geese shall be choked with the feathers, but he who gooses the king shall be tickled to death.

LLL

PURCHASING

He that buys land buys many stones,
He that buys flesh buys many bones.
He that buys eggs buys many shells,
But he that buys good ale buys nothing else.

Proverb

PURITANS

The Puritan hated bear-bating not because it gave pain to the bear but because it gave pleasure to the spectators.

Thomas Macaulay

PUT-DOWNS

God made him, and therefore let him pass for a man.

Shakespeare

QUACKING

Where there are women and geese, there wants no noise.

Proverb

QUACKS

The rashness of Quacks, with the dismal accidents occasion'd by it, makes the Physician and his Art in vogue; If the physician lets you die, the Quacks kill you.

La Bruyère

QUADRUPEDS

A horse is an animal dangerous at both ends and uncomfortable in the middle.

Anon

QUAKERS

A gentle Quaker, hearing a strange noise in his house one night, got up and discovered a burglar busily at work. So he went and got his gun, then came back and stood quietly in the doorway. "Friend," he said, "I would do thee no harm for the world, but thou standest where I am about to shoot."

James Hines

QUALITY

Of wine the middle, of oil the top, and of honey the bottom is best.

Proverb

QUALITY/QUANTITY

In the physical world, one cannot increase the size or quantity of anything without changing its quality.

Paul Valery

QUARK

n. any one of three types of elementary particles that are believed by some physicists to form the basis of all matter in the universe (applied by M. Gell-Mann after a coinage in *Finnegans Wake* by James Joyce)

The Random House Dictionary of the English Language

On reading of scientists in search of the quark in bits and pieces of just about everything, especially oysters:

O newly titled Quark how
    dark
The perilous place wherein
    men seek

One little spark-like clue of
    you
From oyster stew to Finne-
    gan's
Wake for God's sake show
Before we make a mess of it
By grinding to particular
    dust your out-
Size images and this entire
    effete
Earth we hippily happily
    plunder o
Let us see you plain ere we
    expire
In a realm of High Energy
    Subatomic Theoretical
    Particle Physical Circuitry
    wherein no longer
Once and miserable matter-
    ful Man
But a one-eyed Quark
Is King.

Gladys J. Carr

QUARREL

The quarrel is a very pretty quarrel as it stands; we should
only spoil it by trying to explain it.

Richard Sheridan

Nobody ever forgets where he buried the hatchet.

Kin Hubbard

QUEEN VICTORIA

An amiable fieldmouse.

James Pope-Hennessy

A mixture of national landlady and actress.

V. S. Pritchett

QUESTIONING

Questioning is not the mode of conversation among gentlemen.

Samuel Johnson

It is not every question that deserves an answer.

Syrus

QUESTION

Why should a worm turn? It is probably the same on the other
side.

Irvin S. Cobb

Who's there, besides foul weather?

Shakespeare

QUIET

Anything for a quiet life, as the man said when he took the situation at the lighthouse.

Charles Dickens

Truth and honesty have no need of loud protestations.

Dutch proverb

RABBITS

If music be the food of love, why don't rabbits sing?

D. J. Hurst

RADIO

Is the manly art of shouting brave words into a defenseless microphone.

Peter Lind Hayes

Every time we hear a disc jockey play the top 40 tunes, we get the shakes thinking what the bottom 40 must sound like.

Anon

RADIUM

Radium was discovered by Madman Curry.

A Child's Garden of Misinformation.

RAGE

A wise man cannot evade pain or rage, but when they come to him he treats them as visitors and not as permanent relatives. A man who suffers too long or remains too long angry is not at grips with an enemy but coddling a disease.

Ben Hecht

RAILROADS

A railroad! It would frighten horses, put the owners of public vehicles out of business, break up inns and taverns, and be a monopoly generally.

Andrew Johnson

RAIMENT

We are all Adam's children, but silk makes the difference.

French saying

No fine clothes can hide the clown.

Proverb

It is not the cowl that makes the friar.

Proverb

RAIN

Into each life some rain must fall—
Unless you never leave Las Vegas at all.

LLL

RASCALITY

Has limits; stupidity has not.

Napoleon Bonaparte

READING

When you reread a classic, you do not see more in the book than you did before; you see more in you than there was before.

Clifton Fadiman

I took a course in speed reading, learning to read straight down the middle of the page, and I was able to go through *War and Peace* in twenty minutes. It's about Russia.

Woody Allen

REALITY

If this were play'd upon a stage now, I could condemn it as an improbable fiction.

Shakespeare (Twelfth Night)

The map appears to us more real than the land.

D. H. Lawrence

REASON

It is useless for us to attempt to reason a man out of a thing he has never been reasoned into.

Jonathan Swift

The man who listens to reason is lost: reason enslaves all whose minds are not strong enough to master her.

Shaw

Nothing has an uglier look to us than reason, when it is not of our side.

Halifax

Every why hath a wherefore.

Shakespeare

REBUTTAL

If you can't answer a man's arguments, all is not lost; you can still call him vile names.

Elbert Hubbard

RECOMMENDATION

The hardest thing is writing a recommendation for someone you know.

Kin Hubbard

RECOGNITION

Just as those who practice the same profession recognize each other instinctively, so do those who practice the same vice.

Proust

RECONCILIATION

Many promising reconciliations have broken down because, while both parties came prepared to forgive, neither party came prepared to be forgiven.

Charles Williams

RECORDING INDUSTRY

The record business is a cross between the theatre and the garment center; the best of both—which is the worst.

Dustin Hoffman

RE-DOING

Were things done twice, then all were wise.

English proverb

REFORM

There is no lantern by which the crank can be distinguished from the reformer when the night is dark. Just as every conviction begins as a whim, so does every emancipator serve his apprenticeship as a crank. A fanatic is a great leader who is just entering the room.

Heywood Broun

Reform comes from below. No man with four aces asks for a new deal.

Anon Irishman

Nothing so needs reforming as other people's habits.

Mark Twain

It is a stupidity second to none, to want to busy oneself with the correction of the world.

Molière

REGIMEN

So live and hope as if thou would'st die immediately.

Pliny

REGRET

Too many people ruin what could be a happy today by dwelling on a lost yesterday and in this way jeopardize tomorrow.

Ursula Bloom

There's no use crying over spilt milk; it only makes it salty for the cat.

Anon

REINCARNATION

Ann Kennard, personnel chief for the N.Y.C. Health Dept., when asked if she believed in reincarnation:
"Indeed, yes. I witness a demonstration every day at five o'clock when dead employees come to life in time to go home."

RELATIONS

Since the advent of jet transportation, "distant relative" has become an obsolete term.

LLL

If a man's character is to be abused, there's nobody like a relative to do the business.

Thackeray

To whom God gave no sons, the devil gives nephews.

Anon

RELAXATION

A tailor once gave this advice: "To keep your clothes in good condition, empty your pockets every night." This is good advice for all of us, in a figurative sense. In preparing for sleep, we should always remember to empty our minds of fear, worry, bitterness, and enmity, even as we empty our pockets.

Eric Butterworth

Oh, Lord, teach me when to let go.

W. G. Carleton

The very fact that I'm relaxed,
To worry quite impervious,
When everybody else is taut,
Is just what makes me nervous!

S. Omar Barker

RELIGION

Is by no means a proper subject of conversation in mixed company.

Lord Chesterfield

Is the belief in the subnormal.

LLL

One day, St. Dunstan, an Irishman by nationality and a saint by profession . . .

Voltaire

The first step is the hardest.

Comment by Mme. du Deffand on the legend of St. Denis who, after his beheading in Montmartre, took his head and walked with it to the town that bears his name

A young saint, an old devil.

English proverb

The atheist who seriously studies religion in order to attack it is closer to the spirit of God than the bovine believer who supports religion because it is comfortable, respectable, and offers consolation without thought. If God's greatest gift to men is reason, then refusing to exercise reason is the greatest impiety.

Sydney J. Harris

God help the poor, for the rich can help themselves.

Scottish proverb

God help the rich, the poor can beg.

English proverb

The whole religious complexion of the modern world is due to the absence from Jerusalem of a lunatic asylum.

Havelock Ellis

It was fear that first made gods in the world.

Statius

If you become a nun, dear
A friar I will be;
In any cell you run, dear,
Pray look behind for me.

Leigh Hunt

A monastery is a home for unwed fathers.

Anon

As the French say, there are three sexes, men, women, and clergymen.

Sydney Smith

A man who could not seduce men cannot save them either.

Sören Kierkegaard

There is not the least use preaching to anyone unless you chance to catch them ill.

Sydney Smith

'Tis a strange thing that among us people can't agree the whole week because they go different ways upon Sundays.

George Farquhar

What religion is he of? Why, he is an Anythingerian.

Jonathan Swift

There has never been a kingdom given to so many civil wars as that of Christ.

Montesquieu

Men will wrangle for religion; write for it; fight for it; die for it; anything but live for it.

Charles Colton

Most men's anger about religion is as if two men should quarrel for a lady they neither of them care for.

Halifax

We have just enough religion to make us hate, but not enough to make us love one another.

Jonathan Swift

Many people think they have religion when they are merely troubled with dyspepsia.

Robert Ingersoll

Leave the matter of religion to the family altar, the church, and the private school, supported entirely by private contributions. Keep the church and the State forever separate.

Ulysses S. Grant

The absurdity of a religious practice may be clearly demonstrated without lessening the number of persons who indulge in it.

Anatole France

Scratch the Christian and you find the pagan spoiled.

Israel Zangwill

Perhaps no one can be really a good, appreciating pagan who has not once been a bad puritan.

Bourne

Leopards break into the temple and drink the sacrificial chalices dry; this occurs repeatedly, again and again: finally it can be reckoned upon beforehand and becomes part of the ceremony.

Franz Kafka

Where it is a duty to worship the sun it is pretty sure to be a crime to examine the laws of heat.

Christopher Morley

An apology for the devil: it must be remembered that we have heard only one side of the case; God has written all the books.

Samuel Butler (II)

It always strikes me, and it is very peculiar, that whenever we see the image of indescribable and unutterable desolation—of loneliness, poverty, and misery, the end and extreme of things—the thought of God comes into one's mind.

Vincent Van Gogh

By night an atheist half believes a God.

Edward Young

And in storm, believes completely.

LLL

Danger past, God is forgotten.

English proverb

If God made us in his own image, we have more than reciprocated.

Voltaire

Some movie stars wear their sunglasses even in church; they're afraid God might recognize them and ask for autographs.

Fred Allen

In a small house God has His corner; in a big house He has to stand in the hall.

Swedish proverb

A man who believes that he eats his God we do not call mad; a man who says he is Jesus Christ, we call mad.

Claude Adrien Helvétius

If God lived on earth, people would break his windows.

Yiddish proverb

Who does God pray to?

LLL

REMAINING

Too late I stayed,—forgive the crime,—
Unheeded flew the hours;
How noiseless falls the foot of time
That only treads on flowers.

William Robert Spencer

REMEDY

The heart which grief hath cankered
Hath one unfailing remedy—the Tankard.

Charles Calverley

REPENTANCE

Repentance is not so much remorse for what we have done as the fear of consequences.

La Rochefoucauld

REPUBLICANS

The trouble with the Republican party is that it has not had a new idea for thirty years. I am not speaking as a politician. I am speaking as an historian.

Woodrow Wilson

REPUTATION

Reputation, reputation, reputation. O, I have lost my reputation. I have lost the immortal part, sir, of myself, and what remains is bestial.

Shakespeare

The only time you realize you have a reputation is when you're not living up to it.

José Iturbi

Many a man's reputation would not know his character if they met on the street.

Elbert Hubbard

To enjoy a good reputation, give publicly and steal privately.

Josh Billings

RESEARCH

What is research but a blind date with knowledge?

Will Henry

RESOLUTIONS

Father Time is something that goes in one year and out the other.

LLL

RESPONSIBILITY

A decision is what man makes when he can't get anybody to serve on a committee.

Fletcher Knebel

No snowflake in an avalanche ever feels responsible.

Lec

RESTAURANTS

Most bus-boys must figure that they are being paid by the decibel.

LLL

255

Are you positive you're the same waiter I gave my order to?
Somehow I thought you'd be a much older man.

Anon

RESULT

I scrimped and saved all these years so that my son could burn
down the college of his choice.

Anon parent

RETREAT

One pair of heels is often worth two pair of hands.

Proverb

REVENGE

Wait time and place to get thy revenge, for it is never well
done in a hurry.

Spanish proverb

The only people you should want to get even with are those who
have helped you.

Anon

REVIEWING

Though by whim, envy, or resentment led,
They damn those authors whom they never read.

Charles Churchill

REVISED PROVERB

Poverty makes strange bedfellows.

LLL

Hell hath no fury like a woman's corns.

LLL

A dollar saved is a penny earned.

LLL

There's many a sip 'twixt the cup and the lip.

LLL

One man's meat is another man's poisson.

Anon

REVISED QUOTATIONS

Salome, darling, not in the fridge!

New Statesman

Joan, are you smoking more and enjoying it less?

Anon

Vincent, lend an ear.

LLL

When lovely woman stoops to folly
The evening can be very jolly.

Anon Englishman

Don't clasp the asp, Cleo!

Anon

REVISED RHYME

Candy is dandy,
But depravities won't give you cavities.

LLL

REVOLUTION

Be not deceived. Revolutions do not go backward.

Abraham Lincoln

The purity of a revolution can last a fortnight.

Jean Cocteau

RHYMES

Little snax,
Bigger slax.

Ruth S. Schenley

I like the winter's icy might,
The blackened trees with ruffs of white,
The way a snowflake swoops and soars,
Unless of course—I'm out of doors.

Elinor K. Rose

Angels who guard you when you drive
Usually retire at 65.

Burma Shave

RICHES

Are the result of fear of poverty.

Anon

He is truly rich, who desires nothing; and he is truly poor, who covets all.

Solon

If Heaven had looked upon riches to be a valuable thing, it would not have given them to such a scoundrel.

Jonathan Swift

Wealth is not his who gets it, but his who enjoys it.

Dorset proverb

He is rich that is satisfied.

Proverb

There is no one so rich that he does not still want something.

German proverb

Poor and content is rich, and rich enough.

Shakespeare

Poverty is an anomaly to rich people. It is very difficult to make out why people who want dinner do not ring the bell.

Walter Bagehot

The wretchedness of being rich is that you live with rich people.

Logan P. Smith

It is in spending oneself that one becomes rich.

Sarah Bernhardt

RIDICULE

Cervantes smiled Spain's chivalry away.

Lord Byron

RIGHT AND WRONG

Two wrongs should never make a riot.

LLL

When everyone is wrong, everyone is right.

Nivelle de La Chaussee

We are not satisfied to be right, unless we can prove others to be quite wrong.

Hazlitt

RIGHTEOUSNESS

A healthy appetite for righteousness, kept in due control by good manners, is an excellent thing; but to "hunger and thirst" after it is often merely a symptom of spiritual diabetes.

C. D. Broad

Protest long enough that you are right, and you will be wrong.

Yiddish proverb

RIGOR MENTIS

Is the inability to change in the face of change.

Walter Pitkin

RIGOR MORTIS

Is the next step after cool.

Anon

RIPE AGE

In Paris, that which in the past one called maturity is tending to disappear. One remains young a very long time and then one becomes senile.

Alfred Capus

ON RISING

Who has once the fame to be an early riser may sleep till noon.

W. D. Howells

ROLES

I much prefer playing kings to beggars. I'm treated so much more royally in the studio commissary.

Peter Ustinov

ROMANCE

Nothing spoils a romance so much as a sense of humor in the woman.

Wilde

RONALD REAGAN

The consummate electronic candidate of our time.

Max Lerner

ROOM SIGN

Is forbidden to steal hotel towels, please. If you are not person to do such is please not to read notice.

in Tokyo hotel

ROPE DANCE

Three merry boys, and three merry boys
And three merry boys are we,
As ever did sing in a hempen string
Under the gallows-tree.

John Fletcher

ROUTE

The best way out is always thru.

Robert Frost

ROYALTY

And everybody will roundly vow
She's fair as the flowers in May,
And say "How clever!"
At whatsoever
She condescends to say!
O, 'tis a glorious thing, I ween,
To be a regular Royal Queen.

Sir William Gilbert

If all the world went naked, how could we tell the kings?

Anon

Life at court does not satisfy a man, but it keeps him from being satisfied with anything else.

La Bruyere

They say princes learn no art truly, but the art of horsemanship. The reason is, the brave beast is no flatterer. He will throw a prince as soon as his groom.

Jonson

Kings are not born; they are made by universal hallucination.

Shaw

I almost had to wait.

Louis XIV

RUDENESS

Is the weak man's imitation of strength.

Eric Hoffer

RULING

It is impossible to reign and be innocent.

Louis-Antoine de Saint-Just

RUNNING

The typical Frenchman is likely to advise: "Never run after a bus, a woman, or an educational theory; there will be another one along very soon."

M. Pevre

RURAL LIVING

To live happily in the country one must have the soul of a poet, the mind of a philosopher, the simple tastes of a hermit—and a good station wagon.

Anon

RUSH

No man who is in a hurry is quite civilized.

Will Durant

RUSSIA

Oh Lord, how wretched our Russia is!

Alexander Pushkin

RUSSIAN VIEW

The French are either sad optimists or jolly pessimists.

Ilya Ehrenburg

SAFE DRIVING

Always try to drive so that your license will expire before you do.

Anon

SAFETY

Distrust is the mother of safety, but must keep out of sight.

English saying

SAILING

I'm on the sea! I'm on the sea!
I am where I would ever be,
With the blue above and the blue below,
And silence whereso'er I go.

Bryan Procter

A life on the ocean wave!
A home on the rolling deep—
Where the scattered waters rave,
And the winds their revels keep!

Epes Sargent

Worse things happen at sea.

Proverb

SAINTS

An open door may tempt a saint.

English proverb

We had been discussing, of all things, saints. We were calling favorites among them. "Which saint would you like best to be?" we asked her (Patsy), expecting the usual platitudes about the vivacious Theresa or the modest Clare. But our child had a mind of her own.
"Oh," she said firmly, "I'd choose to be a martyr."
We evidently gaped unbelieving, but she had her reasons marshalled.
"You see, you only have to be a martyr once."

Phyllis McGinley

SAINTS/SINNERS

Remember—there is no saint without a past—no sinner without a future.

Excerpt from ancient Persian mass

SALESMANSHIP

Consists of transferring a conviction by a seller to a buyer.

Arnold H. Glasgow

Who will sell a blind horse praises the feet.

German proverb

SALVATION

I remember a newspaper cutting about a prophet who, when he baptized converts, at night, in a deep river, also drowned them, so that, being cleansed of sin, and having no time to sin again, they went straight to Paradise.

Joyce Cary

SAN FRANCISCO

Anyone who's ever climbed the streets of San Francisco will appreciate the native's observation: "The wonderful thing about this city is that when you get tired, you can always lean against it."

Anon

SANITY

Every man has a sane spot somewhere.

Robert Louis Stevenson

The way it is now, the asylums can hold the sane people, but if we tried to shut up the insane we should run out of building materials.

Mark Twain

SARSAPARILLA

Is a hygienic drink, something like a cross between beer and a mouthwash.

Prince André Poniatowsky

SATIRE

A sort of glass wherein beholders do generally discover everybody's face but their own.

Johnathan Swift

SAUNA

The sauna is a Finnish bath and a great deal more. It is a sacred rite, a form of human sacrifice in which the victim is boiled like a missionary, than baked to a turn, then beaten with sticks until he flees to the icy sea, then lathered and honed and kneaded and pummeled by the high priestess of this purgatorial pit.

Rex Smith

SAVING

Better keep now than seek anon.

Anon

SAVING/HOARDING

Keep a thing seven years and you will find a use for it.

Proverb

SAVOIR FAIRE

Is to know how to make oneself be asked as a favor what one is dying to offer.

Daniel Dare

SCHOOL

The modern child, when asked what he learned today, replies, "Nothing, but I gained some meaningful insights."

Bill Vaughan

SCHOOL BOARDS

In the first place God made idiots; this was for practice; then he made school boards.

Mark Twain

SCHOOL TEACHER

A disillusioned girl who used to think she liked children.

Anna Herbert

SCIENCE

Lives of scientists oft remind us
We can make our own sublime—
If they don't blow up Creation,
Leaving naught but Space and Time.

Bob Stannard

The great tragedy of science—the slaying of a beautiful hypothesis by an ugly fact.

Thomas H. Huxley

Basic research is when I'm doing what I don't know I'm doing.

Werner Von Braun

Science gives us knowledge, but only philosophy can give us wisdom.

Will Durant

Fleabotamy is the study of fleas' bottoms. There are not many men doing this work.

Anon, Jr.

SCORN

As for the calumnies, the insults, the angry cries outside, let them go on building up—no matter what height they reach, it will still fall short of my contempt.

François Guizot

263

SCOTLAND

Had Cain been Scot, God would have changed his doom
Nor forced him wander, but confined him home.

John Cleveland

SCREWED-UP SAYING

You never miss the well till the water runs dry.

LLL

THE SEA

That wilderness of glass.

Edgar Allen Poe

SEA MONSTERS

A mermaid is a virgin from the waist up and a sturgeon from
there down.

Anon

SEAMANSHIP

It is the ordinary way of the world, to keep folly at the helm,
and wisdom under the hatches.

Proverb

THE SEASONS

January snowy; February flowy; March blowy; April show'ry;
May flow'ry; June bow'ry; July moppy; August croppy; Sep-
tember poppy; October breezy; November wheezy; December
freezy.

R. B. Sheridan

Spring is a virgin; Summer a mother; Autumn a widow;
Winter a stepmother.

Russian proverb

Winter is a beastly time, when the sun, himself, has a red nose.

Henry Murger

SEAT BELTS

You may think that seat belts are uncomfortable—but have
you ever tried a stretcher?

Anon

SECOND MARRIAGE

He loves his bonds, who, when the first are broke,
Submits his neck into a second yoke.

Robert Herrick

SECRET OF LIFE

Digestion is the great secret of life.

Sydney Smith

SECRETS

The reason we are so pleased to find out other people's secrets is that it distracts public attention from our own.

Wilde

To whom you betray your secret, you give your liberty.

Proverb

Thy secret is thy prisoner; if thou let it go, thou art a prisoner to it.

Spanish proverb

If the bed could tell all it knows, it would put many to the blush.

Proverb

In the springs, a young man's fancy.

LLL

No one ever keeps a secret so well as a child.

Victor Hugo

Three may keep a secret, if two of them are dead—and the third is an illiterate mute.

LLL

SECURITY

The psychic task which a person can and must do for himself is not to feel secure but to be able to tolerate insecurity.

Erich Fromm

SEDUCTION

The main problem with honest women is not how to seduce them, but how to take them to a private place. Their virtue hinges on half-open doors.

Jean Giradoux

SEEING

Lord of the far horizons,
  Give us the eyes to see
Over the verge of the sundown
  The beauty that is to be.

Bliss Carman

There is a time to wink as well as to see.

Benjamin Franklin

To the jaundiced all things seem yellow.

Anon

SELF-ADVERTISING

Don't speak either too well or too bad of yourself. If well, men will not believe you; if bad, they will believe a great deal more than you say.

Anon

SELF-DESTRUCTION

I hold it as certain that no man was ever written out of reputation but by himself.

Richard Bentley, 1662–1724

No man is demolished but by himself.

Thomas Bentley, 1693–1742

SELF-ESTEEM

Every potter praises his own pot, and more if it be broken.

English saying

Perhaps the only true dignity of man is his capacity to despise himself.

George Santayana

People will always take you at your own valuation—if you downgrade yourself.

LLL

You have no idea what a poor opinion I have of myself, and how little I deserve it.

William Gilbert

SELF-INTEREST

If we were not all so excessively interested in ourselves, life would be so uninteresting that none of us would be able to endure it.

Schopenhauer

SELF-KNOWLEDGE

I know merit; those praising me are right.

Pierre Corneille

He who knows himself best esteems himself least.

Proverb

SELF-LOVE

People fall in love with themselves almost immediately after birth. This is invariably the beginning of a life-long romance. There is no record of infidelity, separation, or divorce between humans and their egos.

Harry Singer

SELF-REALIZATION

"Know thyself?" If I knew myself, I'd run away.

Goethe

SELFISHNESS

We must especially beware of that small group of selfish men who would clip the wings of the American eagle in order to feather their own nests.

F. D. Roosevelt

SENATE

About all I can say for the United States Senate is that it opens with prayer, and closes with an investigation.

Will Rogers

SENSATIONS

Wonder lasts but nine nights in a town.

Proverb

SENSE

Of all things, good sense is the most fairly distributed; everyone thinks he is so well supplied with it that even those who are the hardest to satisfy in every other respect never desire more of it than they already have.

René Descartes

Good sense is the concierge of the mind: its business is not to let suspicious-looking ideas enter or leave.

Daniel Stern

We are all very proud of our reason, and yet we guess at full one-half we know.

Anon guesser

Some folks get credit for having horse sense that hain't ever had enough money to make fools of themselves.

Kin Hubbard

THE SENSES

We hear, we see, we taste, we feel, we "scent" and the brain interprets. We hear danger, we see pleasure, we taste cacaphony or music, we respond to textures, we smell enmity or friendship—and the mind collects, sorts, stores! As our civilization builds a protective wall around living, and makes it seem unnecessary for the senses to be vigilant, we use them less. We let them sleep. They wake for a little while when love, which causes us to be creators, occurs. Then we let them sleep again. Sometimes the ear is so much asleep that we are killed, even though death made a noise to warn us. With our eyes it is the same. The other senses, except when in pain, human beings rarely use at all.

Virginia Brasier

Sight has to do with the understanding; hearing with reason; smell with memory. Touch and taste are realistic and depend on contact; they have no ideal side.

Schopenhauer

The man who cannot believe his senses, and the man who cannot believe anything else, are both insane.

G. K. Chesterton

SERIOUSNESS

Unmitigated seriousness is always out of place in human affairs. Let not the unwary reader think me flippant for saying so; it was Plato, in his solemn old age, who said it.

George Santayana

SERMON

The average man's idea of a good sermon is one that goes over his head and hits a neighbor.

Anon

SERVANTS

If you pay not a servant his wages, he will pay himself.

Proverb

A servant is known by his master's absence.

English proverb

SEX

America has a greater obsession with sex than Rome ever had.

Billy Graham

The preservation of the species was a point of such necessity that nature has secured it at all hazards by immensely overloading the passion, at the risk of perpetual crime and disorder.

Emerson

I could be content that we might procreate like trees, without conjunction, or that there were any way to perpetuate the world without this trivial and vulgar way of coition.

Sir Thomas Brown

Lord, deliver me from myself.

Sir Thomas Brown

Civilization has immensely elaborated the opportunities, the fruitfulness, and the significance of sex, and it has also increased the difficulties of achieving its ends.

Dr. Karl A. Menninger

What cures Morris makes Martha sick indeed nine months after.

Anon

A quarter hour's physical intimacy between two persons of different sexes who feel for each other, I won't say love, but liking, creates a trust, a tender interest that the most devoted friendship does not inspire even when it has lasted ten years.

Senac de Meilhan

The oddest of all the animals is man; in him, as in other animals, the sexual interest is the strongest, yet the desire is inveterate in him to reject it.

George Moore, c. 1900

Why do we fear to speak without shame of the act of generation, so natural, so necessary and so just; why do we exclude it from our serious and regular discourses? We pronounce boldly, to rob, to murder, to betray, and this we dare not but between our teeth.

Montaigne

All this talk about sex, all this worry about sex—big deal. The sun makes me happy. I eat a good fish, he makes me happy. I sleep with a good man, he makes me happy.

Melina Mercouri

There are no unseductable women—only inept men.

LLL

Sex is the ersatz, or substitute, religion of the 20th century.

Malcolm Muggeridge

Rare are those who prefer virtue to the pleasures of sex.

Confucius

SEX/AGE

God forbid that I should be taken as urging loose sex activity. There is a brief time for sex, and a long time when sex is out of place. But when it is out of place as an activity there still should be the large and quiet space in the consciouness, where it lives quiescent. Old people can have a lovely quiescent sort of sex, like apples, leaving the young free for their sort.

D. H. Lawrence

SEX AND SLEEP

Man cannot live by bed alone.

Anon playwright

THE SEXES

A great many of our troubles are man-maid.

Anon

A woman worries about the future until she has a husband, but a man never worries about the future until he has a wife.

Liselotte Pulver

The only thing a man finds harder to resist than woman's wiles are her wails.

Imogene Fey

Woman was made of a rib out of the side of Adam, not out of his feet to be trampled upon by him, but out of his side to be equal with him, under his arm to be protected, and near his heart to be loved.

Matthew Henry

SHARING

He who shareth honey with the bear, hath the least part of it.

English proverb

SHAW

Harold Hobson once observed that Shaw knew all the answers, but none of the questions. Nonsense. Shaw knew the questions, but asked them a generation too soon.

John Barkham

I often quote myself; it adds spice to my conversation.

Shaw

THE SHOCK TECHNIQUE

My secret in gaining attention was to turn the obvious into the scandalous by stating it plainly.

H. L. Mencken

SHOES/FEET

There is a big variation in shoe sizes throughout the country. For instance, in the southwest feet tend to be short and narrow. They are wider in the northeast, long and narrow in Minnesota, and short and wide in Southern California.

Lionel M. Levey, president Shoe-Towns

SHOPPING

What this country needs is a supermarket cart with four wheels that point in the same direction.

Ray Fine

SHUNNING

I do desire we may be better strangers.

Shakespeare

SIGN IN ALASKA ARMY BARRACKS

Shut the door, Stupid! Not you, Sir.

SIGN IN ALLEY

These cans are for our tenants' rubbish only. Throw your trash where you pay your rent.

North Hollywood, California

SIGN APPROACHING PENFIELD, PA.

Home of 500 Happy People; Only a Few Grouches.

SIGN IN BRITISH RAILWAY CARS

A gentleman raises the seat in the toilet.

SIGN IN CAFETERIA

Courteous Self-Service.

Greenwich Village

SIGN AT CHICAGO MARRIAGE LICENSE BUREAU

Out to lunch. Sit down and think it over.

SIGN IN DELICATESSEN

Delicious Ice Cubes.

Greenwich Village

SIGN IN DRY CLEANER'S

Clothes Made Repellant while You Wait.

SIGN IN EMPLOYEE'S ROOM

Warning—Customer's Are Perishable.

Seattle store

SIGN IN AUTO REPAIR SHOP

We Stand In Front of Our Brake Jobs.

M. W. Martin

SIGN IN JAIL CELL

I wouldn't be here except for night law school.

SIGN IN MENTAL INSTITUTION

We are here because we are not all here.

SIGN ON MILK TRUCK
From moo to you in an hour or two.

SIGN ON MOVIE MARQUEE
Suggestive for Mature Audiences Only.

SIGN IN NUDIST COLONY
Gentlemen playing leap frog, please complete your jump.

SIGN ON PEDIATRICIAN'S DOOR
Out to wunch—will weturn at twee o'clock.

SIGN IN PET SHOP
Sun glasses for dogs.

SIGN IN LIQUOR STORE WINDOW
Going out of Boozeness.

REAL ESTATE SIGN
We have lots to be thankful for.

SIGN OF REDUCING SALON
Come in and shoo the fat.

Los Angeles

STORE SIGN
If you don't see what you want, Japan hasn't copied it yet.

SIGNS
On one side of a Massachusetts signboard is the inscription: "Road closed—do not enter!" The other side reads: "Welcome back, Stupid!"

Ollie M. James

If You Can't be Virtuous, You Can at Least be Discreet.

Bob Levinson

If Doctor is out on a call, please make date with my wife.

Support your Girl Scouts—today's Brownie is tomorrow's cookie.

James Dent

SILENCE
In New York City you now have to pay for silence. If you want

272

to eat a placid luncheon you must go to some expensive restaurant where there is a built-in hush, otherwise your plate is swimming in clatter and chatter. If you want to have quiet while you ride along, you can't find it in subway, bus, or taxi—you must get a chauffered limousine with closed windows. If you want undisturbed rest at night you need thick, insulated walls—and these are the most expensive of all.

LLL

A man is known by the silence he keeps.

Oliver Herford

Keep quiet and people will think you a philosopher.

Latin proverb

I have noticed that nothing I never said ever did me any harm.

Calvin Coolidge

When you are climbing a mountain, don't talk; silence gives ascent.

Robert J. Burdette

An inability to stay quiet is one of the most conspicuous failings of mankind.

Walter Bagehot

Men fear silence as they fear solitude, because both give them a glimpse of the terror of life's nothingness.

André Maurois

Most of us know how to say nothing. Few of us know when.

Anon

Silence is what you don't hear when you listen.

Anon, Jr.

SILENT MAJORITY

The term "silent majority" is far from new. It was used more than a century ago. It meant those who were dead. And after, a fashion, it still does.

Tom Anderson

SIMPLICITY

Give me a look, give me a face,
That makes simplicity a grace.
Robes loosely flowing, hair as free;
Such sweet neglect more taketh me,
Than all th' adulteries of art;
They strike mine eyes, but not my heart.

Jonson

SIN

That which we call sin in others is experiment for us.

Emerson

It is a sin to believe evil of others, but it is seldom a mistake.

H. L. Mencken

I am one of those who believe that a man may sin and do wrong, and after that may do right. If all of us who have sinned were put to death . . . there would not be many of us left.

Andrew Johnson

The fallen man again can soar
But Woman falls to rise no more.

John Held, Jr.

SINCERITY

People are always sincere. They change sincerities, that's all.

Tristan Bernard

A little sincerity is a dangerous thing, and a great deal of it is absolutely fatal.

Wilde

I am not sincere, even when I am saying that I am not sincere.

Jules Renard

SINGERS

The singing man keeps his shop in his throat.

Italian proverb

SINGING

Once men sang together round a table in chorus; now one man sings alone for the absurd reason that he can sing better.

G. K. Chesterton

SIREN

A siren is a signal used by the police to warn burglars that they are approaching.

LLL

SITTING

Our language is full of suggestions that it is a privilege to work sitting down. We respect our chairman, we honor the throne, we speak of a professor's chair, a seat in Parliament. The lawyer looks to the judge's bench, and the Turks speak of their divan, and the Hebrews of the Sanhedrin, all in the same sense. Even the word "president" means the man in the best seat. All this betokens a habit of mind, respecting the man who does his work sitting down.

Professor David L. Thompson

SKELETONS

Not only is there a skeleton in every closet, but there is a screw loose in every skeleton.

Samuel Butler (II)

There is something about a closet that makes a skeleton terribly restless.

John Barrymore

SLANDER

Is like a hornet; if you can't kill it dead the first blow, better not strike at it.

H. W. Shaw

The more implausible a slander is, the better fools remember it.

Casimir Delavigne

He who repeats the ill he hears of another is the true slanderer.

Proverb

If you can't speak ill of the absent, then whom?

LLL

SLANDER/GOSSIP

It takes your enemy and your friend, working together, to hurt you to the heart: the one to slander you and the other to get the news to you.

Mark Twain

SLANG

Slang, which used to be the toy or tool of the immature and the less educated, now salts—and sometimes sours—the speech of the better educated as well.

Theodore M. Bernstein

The essential feature of slang is words misapplied.

H. G. Wells

SLAVERY

I can only say that there is not a man living who wishes more sincerely than I do to see a plan adopted for the abolition of slavery.

George Washington

In this world of ours all humans are slaves; their chains, however, differ with their rank; some wear them of gold and some of iron.

Mathurin Regnier

Serving one's own passions is the greatest slavery.

Proverb

SLEEP

Blessings on him who invented sleep, the mantle that covers all human thoughts, the food that appeases hunger, the drink that quenches thirst, the fire that warms cold, the cold that moderates heat, and lastly, the general coin that purchases all things, the balance and weight that equals the shepherd with the king, and simple with the wise.

Miguel de Cervantes

Twin beds are becoming more popular because sleep incompatibles can wreck a marriage that is happy otherwise. The snorers, the cover-snatchers, and bed-hogs are undoubtedly responsible for the rise of the single bed.

Stanley Lukes, Pres., British Bedding Federation

A good contriver is better than an early riser.

English proverb

Thou hast been called, O sleep! the friend of woe;
But 'tis the happy that have called thee so.

Robert Southey

No small art it is to sleep: it is necessary to keep awake all day for that purpose.

Nietzsche

In sleep, what difference is there between Solomon and a fool?

Proverb

The amount of sleep required by the average person is just five minutes more.

Anon

Is sleep a mating with oneself?

Baron Fredrich von Hardenberg

Sweet pillows, sweetest bed;
A chamber deaf to noise, and blind to light;
A rosy garland, and a weary head.

Aldernon Sidney

Sleep faster, we need the pillows.

Yiddish proverb

There will be sleeping enough in the grave.

Irish proverb

SLUMS

The overcrowding is caused by too many people being in them.

Vice President Spiro Agnew

SMALL TOWN

You know you're in a small town if you pinch a girl and everybody squeals.

Anon

SMART HUSBAND

A clever man is one who complains to his wife that his secretary doesn't understand him.

LLL

SMART KIDS

How is it that although little children are so intelligent, most adults are so stupid? Education must have something to do with it!

Alexandre Dumas, fils

SMASH TRASH

The Friends of Central Park will meet at 2:30 P.M. on Sunday, July 25, at the Boy's Gate, Central Park West and 100th Street, to fight park litter. Bring a shopping bag and an old glove.

Village Voice Greenwich

SMOKING

A custom loathsome to the eye, hateful to the nose, harmful to the brain, dangerous to the lungs, and in the black stinking fume thereof nearest resembling the horrible Stygian smoke of the pit that it bottomless.

King James I, "A Counterblast to Tobacco"

The best cigaret filter is the cellophane on an unwrapped package.

Anon

Much smoking kills live men and cures dead swine.

George D. Prentice

I've been smoking for sixty-five years and my doctor says it would be dangerous to stop.

Man Ray

SMUGGLING

I once undertook on behalf of a friend to smuggle a small dog through the customs. I was of ample proportions, and managed to conceal the little dog upon my person. All went well until my bosom barked.

Mrs. Patrick Campbell

SNEEZING

The autocrat of Russia possesses more power than any other man in the earth; but he cannot stop a sneeze.

Mark Twain

277

SNOB

Godolphin Horne was nobly born;
He held the human race in scorn.

Belloc

SNOBBERY

Snobbery is the religion of England.

Frank Harris

A fine imitation of self-esteem for those who can't afford the real thing.

Frederic Morton

SNOW

A man shovels snow for the same reason he climbs a mountain —because it's there.

Nathan Nielsen

SOCIAL CLIMBING

Is the art of stepping on the right people.

reported by Earl Wilson

How convenient it would be to many of our great families of doubtful origin could they have the privilege of the heroes of yore who, whenever their origin was involved in obscurity, modestly announced themselves descended from a god.

Washington Irving

SOCIALISM

When I was young I thought Socialism was the mathematics of justice. Now I realize it is only the arithmetic of envy.

Martin Collins

It is the common error of Socialists to overlook the natural indolence of mankind.

John Stuart Mill

SOCIETY

Society is now one polished horde,
Form'd of two mighty tribes,
The Bores and Bored.

Lord Byron

If you wish to appear agreeable in society, you must consent to be taught many things you know already.

Charles Talleygrand-Perigord

SOCIETY ITEM

No one has more fun planning a party than the Kenilworth Committee of Planned Parenthood.

Chicago Tribune

SOCIETY/SEX

Man is constrained to be more or less social by his mode of propagation.

Santayana

SODA WATER

Heaven sent us soda water as a torment for our crimes.

G. K. Chesterton

SOFT WORDS

Hurt not the mouth.

French proverb

SOLAR SYSTEM

The sun, with all those planets revolving around it and dependent upon it, can still ripen a bunch of grapes as if it had nothing else in the universe to do.

Galileo

SOLEMNITY

How many people become abstract as a way of appearing profound!

Joseph Joubert

SOLLILOQUY UPDATED

To be, or the contrary? Whether the former or the latter be preferable would seem to admit of some difference of opinion; the answer in the present case being of an affirmative or of a negative character according to whether one elects on the one hand to mentally suffer the disfavour of fortune, albeit in an extreme degree, or on the other to boldly envisage adverse conditions in the prospect of eventually bringing them to a conclusion. The condition of sleep is similar to, if not indistinguishable from, that of death; and with the addition of finality the former might be considered identical with the latter; so that in this connection it might be argued with regard to sleep that, could the addition be effected, a termination would be put to the endurance of a multiplicity of inconveniences, not to mention a number of downright evils incidental to our fallen humanity, and thus a consummation achieved of a most gratifying nature.

Sir Arthur Thomas Quiller-Couch

SOLUTIONS/DRAMATIC

I don't know of any major problem in living that can be settled in two hours.

Alec Guinness

SONG

The most despairing songs are the loveliest of all,
I know immortal ones composed of one long sigh.

Alfred de Musset

What I want to write is songs without words—or music.

Samuel Butler (II)

Swans sing before they die—
'Twere no bad thing
Should certain persons die
Before they sing.

Coleridge

SOUR GRAPES

The girl who can't dance says the band can't play.

Yiddish proverb

SOVIET JUSTICE

A man may be caught quite by chance in the wheels of the
huge bureaucratic machine. He may think that only a fold of
his jacket has got caught and that everything is all right except
a certain discomfort under the armpits. But all the time the
slow movements of the machinery gradually pulls him in and
mangles him.

Andrei Amalrik

SOWING AND REAPING

Sow an act and you reap a habit. Sow a habit and you reap a
character. Sow a character and you reap a destiny.

Charles Reade

SPACE TRAVEL

Is even more hazardous than it looks. The way population is
increasing, you could come back and find your place taken.

Anon

SPEECH

If you your lips would keep from slips,
Five things observe with care;
To whom you speak, of whom you speak,
And how, and when, and where.

W. E. Norris

Deep rivers move in silence, shallow brooks are noisy.

English proverb

Every man has a right to utter what he thinks truth, and every
other man has a right to knock him down for it.

Samuel Johnson

The right to be heard does not include the right to be taken seriously. The latter depends on what is being said.

Hubert Humphrey

A man of words and not of deeds,
Is like a garden full of weeds.

English proverb

When a sparrow has said "Peep!" it thinks it has said everything there is to say.

Jules Renard

According to your purse, govern your mouth.

Italian proverb

When people talk to me about the weather, I always feel they mean something else.

Wilde

If you want to get rid of somebody just tell 'em something for their own good.

Kin Hubbard

The secret of the demagogue is to make himself as stupid as his audience so that they believe they are as clever as he.

Karl Kraus

The hardest part of a lecture is waking up the audience after the man who introduces me has concluded his remarks.

Anon speaker

It usually takes me more than three weeks to prepare a good impromptu speech.

Mark Twain

Speak clearly if you speak at all;
Carve every word before you let it fall.

O. W. Holmes

Speak fair, and think what you will.

Proverb

Choose a wife rather by ear than by eye.

Anon

But what am I?
An infant crying in the night;
An infant crying for the light;
And with no language but a cry.

Tennyson

Most men cry better than they speak. You get more nature out of them by pinching than addressing them.

Thoreau

Language most shews a man; Speak, that I may see thee.

Jonson

Talk is cheap, but you can't buy it back.

William Blatt

To air is human.

LLL

SPEECH/ART

We should talk less and draw more. Personally, I would like to renounce speech altogether and, like organic nature, communicate everything I have to say in sketches.

Goethe

SPEECH/GABBLE

Gratiano speaks an infinite deal of nothing, more than any man in all Venice. His reasons are as two grains of wheat hid in two bushels of chaff: you shall seek all day ere you find them; and when you have them, they are not worth the search.

Shakespeare

Every ass loves to hear himself bray.

Anon

Great talkers are like leaky pitchers, everything runs out of them.

English proverb

As a vessel is known by the sound, whether it be cracked or not; so men are proved by their speeches, whether they be wise or foolish.

Demosthenese

Once uttered, words run faster than horses.

Japanese proverb

Don't let your will roar when your power only whispers.

Dr. Thomas Fuller

Most men make little use of their speech than to give evidence against their own understanding.

Halifax

A flow of words is no proof of wisdom.

Anon

But that's what pays off these days.

LLL

SPEECH IMPEDIMENT

She had palpitation of the tongue.

LLL

SPEECH/KNOWLEDGE

He who knows talks not;
He who talks knows not.

Japanese proverb

SPEECH-MAKING

An audience is always feminine, even when composed of men, and a successful speech is always a seduction—if not a rape.

Frenchman quoted by James Laver

If you don't strike oil in twenty minutes, stop boring.

Andrew Carnegie

SPEECH AND SILENCE

Drawing on my fine command of language, I said nothing.

Robert Benchley

Talk does not cook rice.

Chinese proverb

There are few wild beasts more to be dreaded than a talking man having nothing to say.

Jonathan Swift

There is nothing can't be made worse by telling.

Terence

A fool's tongue is long enough to cut his own throat.

English proverb

Remember that your tongue is in a wet place and likely to slip.

Margaret Blair Johnstone

It is difficult to keep quiet if you have nothing to do.

Schopenhauer

Or to say.

LLL

Look wise; say nothing, and grunt. Speech was given to conceal thought.

Sir William Osler

SPEECH/THOUGHT

How can I tell what I think till I see what I say?

Forster

SPELLING

It is a pity that Chawcer, who had geneyus, was so unedicated; he's the wuss speller I know of.

Artemus Ward

I don't give a damn for a man that can spell a word only one way.

Mark Twain

SPENDTHRIFTS

He that has but four and spends five, has no need for a purse.

Proverb

SPINSTERS

When there is an old maid in the house, a watchdog is unnecessary.

Balzac

SPORT

You base foot-ball player.

Shakespeare

To play billiards well is a sign of an ill-spent youth.

Herbert Spencer

Baseball has the great advantage over cricket of being sooner ended.

Shaw

SPRING

Every April God rewrites the Book of Genesis.

Anon

Spring has set in with its usual severity.

Horace Walpole

Spring hasn't really reached the suburbs until you are awakened by the first lawn-mower.

Dan Kidney

The way things are going, spring poets probably will have to rhapsodize over the tender freshness of parking lots.

Anon

In the spring a young man's fancy
Lightly turns to love, they say.
And some, who otherwise are smart,
Get hooked for life that way!

Anon

SPYING

Espionage is a nasty practice of foreign countries designed to ruin our counterespionage.

Gene Raskin

SQUATTING

I wish that low-slung cars and chairs
Would leave for outer space.
Till then I sit, dejectedly,
With knees about my face.

Helen Thompson

THE STAGE

By increasing the size of the keyhole, today's playwrights are in danger of doing away with the door.

Peter Ustinov

Farce is tragedy removed one step over the border into burlesque.

Tom Walls

STAGECRAFT

Make 'em laugh; make 'em cry; make 'em wait.

Charles Reade

STAGES

A man is young if a woman can make him happy or unhappy. He is middle-aged when she can make him happy but can no longer make him unhappy. He's old when a woman can make him neither happy nor unhappy.

Anon

STANCE

Why stand on the shoulders of titans when we have two fine feet of clay of our own?

Clifton Fadiman

STANDARDIZATION

You can go from airport to airport all around the world and wonder where you are. They all look exactly alike. This standardizing tendency in our modern industrial system makes one all the more eager to cling to any sense of separate personality, culture, or tradition.

Barbara Ward

STARDOM

Rome is the place to break in, if you've got your own little stock of money, a wardrobe that makes you look like a million dollars, and a cast-iron bottom.

Ann Collin

STARTS

He who commences many things, finishes but few.

English proverb

STATESMAN

A stateman is a man who plays both ends against the muddle.

Raymond J. Cvikots

STATESMANSHIP

You can always get the truth from an American statesman after he has turned seventy, or given up all hope of the Presidency.

Wendell Phillips

STATURE

Men are not to be measured by inches.

Napoleonic proverb

STATUS

We laugh at the savages who take a tribal pride in the size of their totem poles, but we ourselves judge the status of a citizen by the number and length of the cars in his driveway.

Sydney J. Harris

STAYING YOUNG

You will always stay young if you live honestly, eat slowly, sleep sufficiently, work industriously, worship faithfully and lie about your age.

Anon

STEALING

It is criminal to steal a purse, daring to steal a fortune, a mark of greatness to steal a crown. The blame diminishes as the guilt increases.

Schiller

STERN/SWEET

Severities should be dealt out all at once, that by their suddenness they may give less offense; benefits should be handed out drop by drop, that they may be relished the more.

Niccolo Machiavelli

STOCK MARKET

There is no more mean, stupid, pitiful, selfish, envious, ungrateful animal than the stock-speculating public. It is the greatest of cowards, for it is afraid of itself.

Hazlitt

STONED

Let he who was never stoned cast the first sin.

Eek, via Howie Schneider

STRATEGY

It is good to strike the serpent's head with your enemy's hand.

Proverb

If you have an important point to make, don't try to be subtle
or clever. Use a pile-driver. Hit the point once. Then come
back and hit it again. Then hit it a third time—a tremendous
whack.

Winston Churchill

The weak who know how to play on their weaknesses are
strong. This is the secret of women, and of the developing
countries.

Maurice Couve de Murville

In telephoning for a taxicab to meet a specific engagement,
such as a train or a dinner, it is better to ask that the cab call
at 6:55, rather than 7 P.M. An even hour is vague, but an odd
hour is specific.

William Feather

STRAW

He that maketh a fire of straw hath much smoke, but little
warmth.

English proverb

STRENGTH

What does not destroy me, makes me stronger.

Nietzsche

STRUTTING

A man who struts in my presence hopes to find in my eyes an
importance missing in his own.

Ben Hecht

STUPIDITY

No one can fully appreciate the fatuity of human nature until
he has spent some time in a theatre box-office.

St. John Ervine

STYLE

One who uses many periods is a philosopher; many interroga-
tions, a student; many exclamations, a fanatic.

J. L. Basford

An hourglass was a lady's figure popular in Olden Days. As the
lady grew older, she gradually sank to the bottom.

Anon, Jr.

SUBCONSCIOUS

He was a simple soul who had not been introduced to his own
subconscious.

Warwick Deeping

SUBLIME/RIDICULOUS

The sublime and the ridiculous are often so nearly related, that it is difficult to call them separately. One step above the sublime makes the ridiculous, and one step above the ridiculous makes the sublime again.

Thomas Paine

SUBTLETY

His hand seemed to be in everything—but not his fingerprints.

Gay Talese

SUBTOPIA

A middle state, neither town nor country, an even spread of abandoned aerodromes and fake rusticity, wire fences, traffic roundabouts, gratuitous notice boards, car parks, and Things in Fields. It is a morbid condition which spreads both ways from suburbia out and back into the devitalized hearts of towns so that the most sublime backgrounds, English or foreign, are now to be seen only over a foreground of casual and unconsidered equipment, litter and lettered abominations— Subtopia is the world of universal low-density mess.

Ian Nairn

SUBURBIA

Country club country is a hotbed of social rest.

Shana Alexander

SUBURBS

Are affluent slums.

Joseph Wood Krutch

SUCCEEDING

A man must have a certain amount of intelligent ignorance to get anywhere.

Charles F. Kettering

SUCCESS

If at first you don't succeed, you're fired.

Miss Jean Graman

There are moments when everything goes as you wish; don't be frightened—it won't last.

Jules Renard

To succeed in life, you need two things: ignorance and confidence.

Mark Twain

Success generally depends upon knowing how long it takes to succeed.

Montesquieu

The road to success is filled with women pushing their husbands along.

Thomas Dewar

Every man has a right to be conceited until he is successful.

Benjamin Disraeli

Nothing makes a man so cross as success.

Trollope

It never fails: everybody who really makes it does it by busting his ass.

Alan Arkin

There's always something about your success that displeases even your best friends.

Mark Twain

The penalty of success is to be bored by the attentions of people who formerly snubbed you.

Mary Little

The successful people are the ones who think up things for the rest of the world to keep busy at.

Don Marquis

Success may go to one's head, but the stomach is where it gets in its worst work.

Kin Hubbard

SUCCESS/FAILURE

The common idea that success spoils people by making them vain, egotistic, and self-complacent is erroneous; on the contrary, it makes them, for the most part, humble, tolerant, and kind. Failure makes people cruel and bitter.

W. Somerset Maugham

SUFFICIENT

More than enough is too much.

Proverb

SUICIDE

If you wish to drown, do not torture yourself with shallow water.

Bulgarian proverb

The relatives of a suicide always take it in bad part that he did not remain alive out of consideration for the family dignity.

Nietzsche

SUICIDE/CIVILIZATION

The prevalence of suicide, without doubt, is a test of height of civilization; it means that the population is winding up its nervous and intellectual system to the utmost point of tension and that sometimes it snaps.

Havelock Ellis

SUICIDE/CONSOLATION

The thought of suicide is a great consolation: with the help of it one has got through many a bad night.

Nietzsche

SULTAN'S VERSION

A loaf of bread, a jug of wine and Eenie, Meenie, Minie, Mo.

Howard Bell

SUN

It is all sunshine that makes a desert.

Arabian proverb

Thank heavens, the sun has gone in, and I don't have to go out and enjoy it.

Logan P. Smith

Keep your face to the sunshine and you cannot see the shadow.

Helen Keller

SUNDAY CLOSING

No Sunday Blue-Law advocate ever objected to money working seven days a week.

Anon

SUNSET

A sunset has no intention of pleasing our eye; it is the result of precise forces.

Man Ray

SUPERSTITION

Superstition, idolatry, and hypocrisy have ample wages, but truth goes abegging.

Martin Luther

He that would have good luck in horses, must kiss the parson's wife.

English proverb

SURF-RIDER

A surfer is an American lemming.

Dr. Jacob Bronowski

SURRENDER

Yielding is sometimes the best way of succeeding.

Proverb

SURTAX

Is a tax on a tax—which is a case of adding insult to penury.

Robert Orben

SUSPICION

There is no rule more invariable than that we are paid for our suspicions by finding what we suspected.

Thoreau

SWEETNESS

Make yourself all honey, and the flies will devour you.

Proverb

SWITCHED SAYINGS

Take things as you find them, but be sure no one sees you.

LLL

If a man deceives me once, shame on him; if he deceives me twice, he's got nothing to be ashamed of.

LLL

Confession is good for the soul but bad for the reputation.

Anon

TACT

This week's Tact and Diplomacy award goes to a Boston society lady who spotted an uninvited gate-crasher at her debutante daughter's exclusive coming-out party. Approaching the culprit, she extended her hand graciously, and said in a pleasant voice, "I heard you were looking for me—because you wanted to say good night."

Joe McCarthy

TACTICS

He who findeth fault meaneth to buy.

English proverb

If you have a loitering servant, place his dinner before him, and send him on an errand.

Spanish proverb

The best way of answering a bad argument is to let it go on.

Sydney Smith

TALENT

Use what talents you have; the woods would have little music if no birds sang their song except those who sang best.

Rev. Oliver G. Wilson

An educator fears that we are suppressing outstanding talent, although casual conversations with parents indicate that genius these days must be just about universal.

Senator Soaper

TALENT/LUCK

The luck of having talent is not enough; one must also have a talent for luck.

Berlioz

TALK

Some persons talk simply because they think sound is more manageable than silence.

Margaret Halsey

In much of your talking, thinking is half murdered.

Kahlil Gibran

Let not your tongue run away with your brains.

French proverb

TARDINESS

People count up the faults of those who are keeping them waiting.

French proverb

TASTE

There's no accounting for tastes, as the woman said when somebody told her her son was wanted by the police.

F. P. Adams

TATTLE-TALE

The informer is the worst rogue of the two.

Proverb

A fool is his own informer.

Yiddish proverb

TAXES

Taxes are the way the government has of artificially inducing the rainy day everybody has been saving for.

Anon

There's no smoke without taxes.

Mrs. R. Linshaw

TEA

Love and scandal are the best sweeteners of tea.

Henry Fielding

TEACH-ESE

To clarify the conversation for those who, willingly or not, listen to the shop talk of pedagogues, a partial glossary:
Enrichment: Extra work for somebody.
Group Dynamics: Everybody talking at once.
Motivation: A student's drive to learn how to acquire a car.
Sibling Rivalry: Brotherly love, as with Cain and Abel.
Vacation: Changing jobs temporarily.

Anon

TEACHING

You cannot teach a man anything; you can only help him to find it within himself.

Galileo

A schoolmaster should have an atmosphere of awe, and walk wonderingly, as if he was amazed at being himself.

Walter Bagehot

Smart parents know better than to teach their children the value of a dollar. Why fill their heads with a lot of useless information?

Daisy Brown

To teach your offspring to steal, make them beg hard for all that you give them.

Josh Billings

TEAMSTERS

There is no racketeering like there was years ago. It is all make-believe.

Barney Baker, Teamsters' organizer

TEARS

I loved the very tears I made her shed.

Jean Racine

TEEN-AGERS

Are girls who have not yet realized that their weaknesses are their strengths.

Brigitte Bardot

TEETOTALER

I'm only a beer teetotaler, not a champagne teetotaler; I don't like beer.

Shaw

TELEPHONES

In heaven when the blessed use the telephone they will say what they have to say and not a word besides.

Somerset Maugham

There is something about saying "OK" and hanging up the receiver with a bang that kids a man into feeling that he has just pulled off a big deal, even if he has only called up central to find out the correct time.

Robert Benchley

I don't mind being put on "hold," but I think they've got me on "ignore."

Troy Gordon

TELEPHONE CRISIS

At times it was like dialing M for Murder and getting C for Chicken Delight.

William A. McWhirter

TELEVISION

Is dope for the eyes.

Stanley Levinson

Is an animated comic strip—art for people who don't even read the newspapers.

Harry Golden

Is educational. If it weren't for the old movies, today's kids might not know that there was a time when the Russians were the good guys and the Germans were the bad guys.

Bill Vaughan

When the Roman Empire was falling apart, the people were distracted and kept happy with circuses. Now we have television.

Benjamin Spock, M.D.

Another change television has made in a number of homes is that there are now more cockroaches in the living room than in the kitchen.

Anon

Poor reception is about the only way you can improve some television programs.

Franklin P. Jones

On days when it is cold or wet
The children watch the TV set
In just the way the darlings do
When it is warm and skies are blue.

Tom Pease

No matter what the critics say, it's hard to believe that a television program which keeps four children quiet for an hour can be all bad.

Beryl Pfizer

Just think of all the commercials, old movies, Westerns, politicians, comedians, quiz shows, soap operas, and other intrusions we can keep out of our homes just by turning off one little knob.

Fred Randall

No wonder the audiences for the late-night talk shows are growing. Who can get to sleep after hearing the 11 P.M. news?

Terence O'Flaherty

They say TV really is still in its infancy, which helps explain why you have to get up so much and change it.

Anon

TEMPER

When you are in the right you can afford to keep your temper, and when you are in the wrong, you cannot afford to lose it.

Sign on wall of Ghandi's room

He who blows his stack adds to the world's pollution.

Will Henry

TEMPERAMENT

We boil at different degrees.

Emerson

TEMPO

Deliberate slowly, execute promptly.

English saying

TEMPTATION

Nothing makes temptation as easy to resist as being broke.

Mac Benoff

Temptation is an irresistible force at work on a movable body.

H. L. Mencken

There are terrible temptations which it requires strength and courage to yield to.

Wilde

Why resist temptation—there will always be more.

Don Herold

Get thee behind, me Satan.

LLL

TEXAS

If I owned Texas and Hell, I'd rent out Texas and live in Hell.

General Phil Sheridan

THANKS

When every bone in your body aches, you can thank the Lord that you're not a herring.

Quin Ryan

THE THEATER

Acting consists of the ability to keep an audience from coughing.

Jean-Louis Barrault

Except when you're in a flop play. Then you're grateful to hear a cough in the theater. It proves you're not alone.

Sir Cedric Hardwicke

Trying to anticipate any theatrical season is like wiping off the lipstick before you've kissed the girl.

Anon

The public has had enough of the nudity in productions like *Oh, Calcutta* and *Hair*. More Bibles are sold than copies of *Playboy*.

Guy Lombardo

THEFT

Thieves respect property; they merely wish the property to become their property that they may more perfectly respect it.

G. K. Chesteron

He who steals my purse steals cash.

Sam Shakespeare

THESE DAYS

The hand that rocks the cradle raids the refrigerator.

Franklin P. Jones

"THEY SAY"

The biggest liar in the world.

Paul Harvey

THINKING

One must learn to think well before learning to think; afterward it proves too difficult.

Anatole France

A man may dwell so long upon a thought that it may take him prisoner.

Halifax

Thinking is like loving and dying. Each of us must do it for himself.

Josiah Royce

I have thought too much to stoop to action.

Philippe Auguste Villiers de L'Isle-Adam

THINKING/COMPREHENSION

We hear and apprehend only what we already half know.

Thoreau

THOROUGHNESS

Don't do anything halfway, else you find yourself dropping more than can be picked up.

Louis Armstrong

THOUGHT

If you make people think they're thinking, they'll love you; but if you really make them think, they'll hate you.

Don Marquis

A great many people think they are thinking when they are merely rearranging their prejudices.

William James

Few people think more than two or three times a year; I have made an international reputation for myself by thinking once or twice a week.

Shaw

THOUGHTS

Like fleas jump from man to man, but they don't bite everybody.

Lec

My thoughts are my trollops.

Denis Diderot

THRIFT

It's very well to be thrifty, but don't amass a hoard of regrets.

Charles d'Orleans

TIGHT TALK

Anyone who says something when he's drinking that he wouldn't say when he wasn't drinking shouldn't be drinking.

Toots Shor

TIME

There isn't any "now." By the time you've said the word your "now" is "then."

Anon

Now is the time for all good men to come to.

Anon

I wish I could stand on a busy street corner, hat in hand, and beg people to throw me all their wasted hours.

Bernard Berenson

You do not waste time; time wastes you.

Gene Fowler

We talk of killing time, as if, alas, it weren't time that kills us.

Alphonse Allais

Time is the principal ingredient in the development of a chronic disease.

E. Cheraskin, M.D.

What greater crime than loss of time?

Anon

Time stoops to no man's lure.

Swinburne

The years skip along easily, it is the days that are tough.

Harry Golden thinks Ring Lardner said it

Time is a great legalizer, even in the field of morals.

H. L. Mencken

Time is money and many people pay their debts with it.

Josh Billings

In the city, time becomes visible.

Lewis Mumford

Wouldn't it be nice if two weeks on vacation seemed to last as long as two weeks on a diet?

Earl Wilson

Time is a dressmaker specializing in alterations.

Faith Baldwin

A man who does nothing never has time to do anything.

Anon

The afternoon knows what the morning never suspected.

Swedish proverb

Just when you think tomorrow will never come, it's yesterday.

Earl Wilson's column

TIMING

Good that comes too late, is good as nothing.

English proverb

TIP

A tip is a small sum of money you give to someone because you are afraid he wouldn't like not being paid for something you haven't asked him to do.

Ann B. Caesar

TOAST

May all your labors be in vein.

Yorkshire miners' toast

TOBACCO

I kissed my first woman and smoked my first cigarette on the same day; I have never had time for tobacco since.

Arturo Toscanini

Perfection is such a nuisance that I often regret having cured myself of using tobacco.

Émile Zola

When you smoke cigarets, you're likely to burn yourself to death; with chewing tobacco the worst thing you can do is drown a midget.

Fred Allen

TODAY

Ours is an age which is proud of machines that think, and suspicious of any man who tries to.

Howard Mumford Jones

Today is the tomorrow you worried about yesterday. Now you know why.

Anon

TODAY'S MOTTO

In Got We Trust.

LLL

TOLERANCE

An open mind is all very well in its way, but it ought not to be so open that there is no keeping anything in or out of it. It should be capable of shutting its doors sometimes, or it may be found a little drafty.

Samuel Butler (II)

299

TOLERANCE/EMPATHY

When my friends are one-eyed, I try to see them in profile.

Joseph Joubert

TOMORROW

Is often the busiest day of the year.

Spanish proverb

TOO MUCH

When a dog is drowning, everyone offers him water.

English proverb

TOOTHACHE

The tongue ever turns to the aching tooth.

Proverb

TOURIST

A tourist is a fellow who climbs a 7,000-foot mountain to put a dime in a telescope so he can see where he came from.

Austin Miles

TOYS

Behold the child, by Nature's kindly law,
Pleas'd with a rattle, tickled with a straw:
Some livelier plaything gives his youth delight,
A little louder, but as empty quite;
Scarfs, garters, gold, amuse his riper stage,
And beads and prayer-books are the toys of age,
Pleas'd with this bauble still, as that before,
Till tir'd he sleeps, and life's poor play is o'er.

Alexander Pope

TRADE SECRET

The laundress washeth her own smock first.

Proverb

TRAFFIC

The two greatest highway menaces are drivers under 25 going 65 and drivers over 65 going 25.

Anon

TRAGEDY/COMEDY

All tragedies are finish'd by a death,
All comedies are ended by a marriage.

Lord Byron

TRAINING

Training is everything; the peach was once a bitter almond; cauliflower is nothing but cabbage with a college education.

Mark Twain

One of the hardest things to teach a child is that the truth is more important than the consequences.

O. A. Battista

TRANQUILITY

Anythin' for a quiet life, as the man said wen he took the sitivation at the lighthouse.

Charles Dickens

TRANSLATING

Is like trying to pour yourself into an invisible glass so that you take the shape of your vessel and transmit the author's light and flavor.

Nevill Coghill, translator of Chaucer

TRANSPLANTED PROVERBS

Idleness is the root of all evil.

TRAPPING

Let not the mouse-trap smell of blood.

Proverb

TRAVEL

I always like to begin a journey on Sundays because I shall have the prayers of the church to preserve all that travel by land or by water.

Jonathan Swift

Nothing makes a man or woman look so saintly as seasickness.

Samuel Butler (II)

And let him go where he will, he can only find so much beauty or worth as he carries.

Emerson

Every year it takes less time to fly across the Atlantic and more time to drive to the office.

Anon

To travel safely through the world, a man must have a falcon's eye, an ass's ears, an ape's face, a merchant's words, a camel's back, a hog's mouth, and a hart's legs.

Proverb

Russia is the only country in the world you can be homesick for while you're still in it.

John Updike

In America there are two classes of travel—first class and with children.

Robert Benchley

If an ass goes a'traveling, he'll not come home a horse.

Spanish proverb

It is a pity that people travel in foreign countries; it narrows their minds so much.

G. K. Chesterton

Better shelter under an old hedge, than a young furzebush.

Old English saying

A bad bush is better than the open field.

Old English Saying

Go soothingly on the greasy mud, for therein lurks the skid demon.

Chinese road sign

He who is carried doesn't realize how far the town is.

African proverb

We are all pretty much alike when we get out of town.

Kin Hubbard

Who knows but that hereafter some traveler like myself will sit down upon the banks of the Seine, the Thames, or the Zuyder Zee, where now, in the tumult of enjoyment, the heart and eyes are too slow to take in the multitude of sensations. Who knows but he will sit down solitary amid silent ruins, and weep for a people immured and their greatness changed into an empty name?

Constantin de Volney

Thanks to the miles of superhighways under construction, America will soon be a wonderful place to drive—if you don't want to stop.

Fletcher Knebel

TRAVELESE

"Old World Charm" means "no bathroom."

LLL

TRAVELING

Drive carefully! Remember, it's not only a car that can be recalled by its maker.

Anon

302

TREASON

Treason doth never prosper, what's the reason?
For if it prosper, none dare call it Treason.

Sir John Harington

TRIVIA

Trivial matters take up more time for discussion because some of us know more about them than we do about important matters.

Theodore S. Weiss

TRIVIALITIES

It is the little bits of things that fret and worry us; we can dodge an elephant, but we can't a fly.

Josh Billings

TROUBLE

Woes cluster; rare are solitary woes; they love a train, they tread each other's heel.

Edward Young

Why hoard your troubles? They have no market value, so just throw them away.

Ann Schade

He that seeks trouble, it were a pity he should miss it.

English proverb

Only the dead have no troubles.

LLL

TRUE CONCENTRATION

Is the ability to do your child's homework while he is watching television.

Terry McCormick

TRUISMS

Covetousness is always filling a bottomless vessel.

English proverb

If it were necessary to tolerate from others all that one permits of oneself, life would be unbearable.

Georges Courteline

TRUNKS

The fact that people and trees and elephants and cars all have trunks just proves that there are more things than there are words.

Anon, Jr.

TRUST

We are inclined to believe those whom we do not know because they have never deceived us.

Samuel Johnson

TRUTH

Men occasionally stumble over the truth, but most of them pick themselves up and hurry off as if nothing had happened.

Winston Churchill

No human being is constituted to know the truth, the whole truth, and nothing but the truth; and even the best of men must be content with fragments, with partial glimpses, never the whole fruition.

Dr. William Osler

It is a terrible thing for a man to find out suddenly that all his life he has been speaking nothing but the truth.

Wilde

A man that should call everything by its right name would hardly pass the streets without being knocked down as a common enemy.

Halifax

It is always the best policy to speak the truth, unless, of course, you are an exceptionally good liar.

Jerome K. Jerome

If you tell the truth, you don't have to remember anything.

Mark Twain

Lest men suspect your tale untrue,
Keep probability in view.

John Gay

In quarreling, the truth is always lost.

Publilius Syrus

My way of joking is to tell the truth; it's the funniest joke in the world.

Shaw

When you have eliminated the impossible, whatever remains, however improbable, must be the truth.

Conan Doyle

The terrible thing about the quest for truth is that you find it.

Remy de Gourmont

Truth is the cry of all but the game of the few.

Bishop Berkeley

Pretty much all the honest truth-telling there is in the world is done by children.

Oliver Wendell Holmes

Truth is the safest lie.

Yiddish proverb

It is hard to believe that a man is telling the truth when you know that you would lie if you were in his place.

H. L. Mencken

Those who feel it is okay to tell white lies soon go color blind.

Anon

Tell no lies and you'll be asked a hell of a lot of questions.

LLL

Who lies for you will lie against you.

Bosnian proverb

It is one thing to show a man that he is in error, and another to put him in possession of the truth.

John Locke

He who has but a short time to live
No longer needs dissemble.

Philippe Quinault

TRUTH/BEAUTY

Only the true is beautiful, runs a much-revered line,
And I reply, with no fear of sacrilige:
Only the beautiful is true, nothing is true without beauty.

Alfred de Musset

TRUTH/ERROR

In the immense spaces of error, truth is but a point. Who has grasped this point?

Jean Francois Marmontel

TRUTH/LIE

Truth needs not many words; but a false tale a long preamble.

Proverb

It's the deaf people that create the lies.

Irish proverb

TWENTIETH CENTURY

The natural role of twentieth-century man is anxiety.

Norman Mailer

This age will serve to make a very pretty farce for the next.

Samuel Butler (II)

TWINS

The same kid twice.

Dennis the Menace

TYPICAL AMERICAN

The typical American today is a graduate of a multiversity who lives in a condominium of a megalopolis, works for a conglomerate, and feels lonesome.

Bill Vaughan

TWISTED TRUTHS

If the shoe fits, ask for it in another color.

Beryl Pfizer

You can lead a horse to drink, but you can't make him water.

LLL

TWISTED PROVERBS

Where there's smoke, there's fire. Also danger of cancer, heart disease, and emphysemia.

• LLL

The first hundred years are the heartiest.

LLL

Familiarity breeds overpopulation.

LLL

Tell no truths and you'll be asked no questions.

LLL

Sin is its own reward.

LLL

TWO PARTY SYSTEM

The Democratic thunderbolts
Assail Republicans as dolts.
The G.O.P., in its conclaves,
Belabors Democrats as knaves.
It is my prayer, my hope, my song
That both the parties are dead wrong.
But sometimes I wake up at night
Chilled by the thought both might be right.

Bradley L. Morison

UGLINESS

Nobody's sweetheart is ugly.

Anon

Ugly men are the most seductive in the world. When young, I tried to look handsome, and couldn't get a job. Now that I capitalize on my funny looks, women adore me. I work steadily and have been awarded the Legion of Honor.

Fernandel

UNCOMFORT

Uncomfortable lies the head that wears a crown.

LLL

UNDERSTANDING

Disraeli, the great English statesman, had a very understanding wife. She arranged with one of Disraeli's associates in the government that she was to be notified, late each day, when her husband had had a difficult session in the Cabinet and was therefore weary and melancholy. On these occasions she would welcome her husband home at night with all lights in the great house turned on, for she knew how sparkling lights always revived his low spirits and dissipated his melancholia.

Leo Bennett

A man is capable of understanding how the aether vibrates, and what's going on in the sun—but how any other man can blow his nose differently from him, that he's incapable of understanding.

Aleksandr Turgenev

UNFORESEEN BENEFIT

Once a pupil got mad because I wouldn't criticize his work and threw a book at me. I picked up the book and found something very interesting in it—a low-starch diet I've been using ever since.

Man Ray

UNIMPORTANCE OF SEX

The discussion of the sexual problem is, of course, only the somewhat crude beginning of a far deeper question, namely, that of the psychic or human relationship between the sexes. Before this later question the sexual problem pales in significance.

Carl Jung

UNITED STATES

In the United States whenever you hear the word "Save," it is usually the beginning of an advertisement designed to make you spend money.

Renee Pierre-Gosset

Of course, America had often been discovered before Columbus, but it had always been hushed up.

Wilde

An asylum for the sane would be empty in America.

Shaw

In America, the President reigns for four years, and journalism governs forever and ever.

Wilde

As a nation we are wasting our air, our water and our soil. The only thing we seem to be encouraging is our concrete.

Bill Vaughan

By the aid of a few scientific discoveries, they have succeeded in establishing a society which mistakes comfort for civilization.

Benjamin Disraeli

USA/ENGLAND

H. L. Mencken liked to compare a sign in the British Museum washroom with one in a U.S. railroad station. The former said: "These Basins Are for Casual Ablutions Only"; the latter said: "Don't Spit, Remember the Johnstown Flood."

UNIVERSE

I have taken it into my head that every star may well be a world. I wouldn't swear, however, that this is true; but I hold it to be true because it is pleasant to believe it. . . . In my opinion, attractiveness is indispensable even where truths are concerned.

Bernard Le Bovier de Fontenelle

UNIVERSITIES

The use of a university is to make young gentlemen as unlike their fathers as possible.

Woodrow Wilson

UNSELFISHNESS

He that plants trees loves others besides himself.

Old English proverb

There's nothing in Christianity or Buddhism that quite matches the sympathetic unselfishness of an oyster.

Saki

UTILITIES

Con Edison is Tom Edison's delinquent brother.

Anon, Jr.

VACATIONS

Admit how many times you have sent a post card reading "Having a wonderful time" when you weren't.

Jimmy Cannon

VALUES

When one despairs of any form of life, the first solution which always occurs, as though by a mechanically dialectic impulse of the human mind, the most obvious, the simplest, is to turn all values inside out. If wealth does not give happiness, poverty will, if learning does not solve everything, then true wisdom will lie in ignorance.

Ortega y Gasset

VANITY

Vanity dies hard; in some obstinate cases it outlives the man.

Robert Louis Stevenson

VARIETY/MONOTONY

A variety of nothing is superior to a monotony of something.

Jean Paul Richter

VICE-PRESIDENT

Spiro Agnew is a medicine man whose remedies would put an end to the patient as well as the problem.

Tom Wicker

VICTIM

It is better to suffer wrong than to do it, and happier to be sometimes cheated than not to trust.

Samuel Johnson

VICTORIAN DAYS

Were the age of inspired office boys.

G. K. Chesterton

VIEWPOINT

The present is always considered to be "a catastrophical era" so that the grandchildren can be told about the good old days.

Anon Swiss

It is difficult to see the picture when you are inside the frame.

R. S. Trapp

The one infallible formula for getting the wrong slant is to look down your nose.

Damon Runyon

VIGILANCE

Though thy enemy seem a mouse, yet watch him like a lion.

Proverb

VIRGINITY

A virgin is a member of the army of the unenjoyed.

LLL

One of the superstitions of the human mind is to suppose that virginity could be a virtue.

Voltaire

VIRTUE

The resistance of a woman is not always a proof of her virtue but more frequently of her experience.

Ninon de Lenclos

Enforced monogamy is society's plan for perpetuating the commonplace.

Elbert Hubbard

Pygmies are pygmies still, though perched on Alps,
And pyramids are pyramids in vales.
Each man makes his own stature, builds himself:
Virtue alone outbuilds the Pyramids;
Her monuments shall last when Egypt's fall.

Edward Young

VIRTUES/ANIMALS

Brag's a good dog, but Holdfast is a better.

British saying

VISITORS

People are either born hosts or born guests.

Max Beerbohm

His shortcoming is his long staying.

LLL

Unbidden guests are welcomest when they are gone.

Scottish proverb

VOCABULARY

The difference between the right word and the almost right word is the difference between lightning and the lightning bug.

Mark Twain

VOWELS

A vowel is something two people take before they marry.

Anon, Jr.

310

WAGNER

Wagner has beautiful moments but awful quarter hours.

Rossini

WAITER

A waiter is a man who is paid to fuss with the silverware on the table until you are ready to order—at which time you discover he has disappeared for fifteen minutes.

LLL

WAITING

Everything comes to him who waits except a borrowed book.

Kin Hubbard

WALDEN

It is hard for the modern generation to understand Thoreau, who lived beside a pond but didn't own water skis or a snorkel.

Bill Vaughan

WALKING-STICK

An article that serves the purpose of an advertisement that the bearer's hands are employed otherwise than in useful effort, and it therefore has utility as an evidence of leisure.

Thornstein Veblen

WALLS

Hotel room walls are a problem,
  A problem that irks me a heap,
They're thick when you're trying to listen . . .
  And thin when you're trying to sleep!

F. G. Kernan

WANTS

A man never feels the want of what it never occurs to him to ask for.

Arthur Schopenhauer

WAR

In time of war the loudest patriots are the greatest profiteers.

August Bebel

Ben Battle was a soldier bold,
  And used to war's alarms;
But a cannon ball took off his legs,
  So he laid down his arms.

Thomas Hood

Children play at being soldiers. That is sensible. But why should soldiers play at being children?

Karl Kraus

Nothing except a battle lost can be half so melancholy as a battle won.

Duke of Wellington

Soldiers win battles and generals get the credit.

Napoleon Bonaparte

Napoleon's armies always used to march on their stomachs, shouting: *"Vive l'interieur!"*

Walter Seller

How good bad music and bad reasons sound when we march against an enemy.

Nietzsche

War hath no fury like a noncombatant.

Charles Montague

I have already given two cousins to the war and I stand ready to sacrifice my wife's brother.

Artemus Ward

War was once cruel and magnificent, but now cruel and squalid.

Winston Churchill

The tragedy of war is that it uses man's best to do man's worst.

Harry Emerson Fosdick

I hate war; it ruins conversation.

Bernard Le Bovier de Fontenelle

War is cannibalism while dieting.

LLL

WAR AND PEACE

War appears to be as old as mankind, but peace is a modern invention.

Sir Henry Maine

WARNING

Praise the sea, but keep on land.

Proverb

If we are bound to forgive an enemy, we are not bound to trust him.

Proverb

Beware when the great God lets loose a thinker on this planet.

Emerson

312

GEORGE WASHINGTON

Where the prevailing weakness of most public men is to slop over . . . he never slopt over!

Artemus Ward

WATER

'Tis a little thing
To give a cup of water; yet its draught
Of cool refreshment, drain'd by fever'd lips,
May give a shock of pleasure to the frame
More exquisite than when Nectarian juice
Renews the life of joy in happiest hours.

Sir Thomas Talfourd

The sea refuses no river.

Proverb

WE/THEM

We carry our neighbor's failings in sight; we throw our own crimes over our shoulders.

Proverb

WEALTH

As a general rule, nobody has money who ought to have it.

Benjamin Disraeli

Wealth is not his that has it, but his that enjoys it.

Anon

I haven't got as much money as some folks, but I've got as much impudence as any of them, and that's the next thing to money.

Josh Billings

WEATHER

In India "cold weather" is merely a conventional phrase and has come into use through the necessity of having some way to distinguish between weather which will melt a brass door-knob and weather which will only make it mushy.

Mark Twain

A Scotch mist may wet an Englishman to the skin.

English proverb

Bad weather always looks much worse through a window.

John Kieran

The rain it raineth on the just
And also on the unjust fella:
But chiefly on the just, because
The unjust steals the just's umbrella.

Charles Bowen

313

When two Englishmen meet, their first talk is of the weather.

Samuel Johnson

The frost hurts not weeds.

Book of Proverbs

When wind stops blowing, it is just air. When wind starts blowing again, it is March.

Anon, Jr.

The fellow who brags about how cheap he heats his home always sees the first robin.

Kin Hubbard

WEATHER FORECAST

Clear today except for early fog, followed by smog, followed by evening fog.

Pasadena Independent

WEATHER, NEW ENGLAND

If you don't like the weather in New England, just wait a few minutes.

Mark Twain

WEATHERMAN

A group of active young reformers who wish to improve the world by blowing it up and burning it down.

LLL

WELFARE

It usually happens, within certain limits, that to get a little help is to get a notion of being defrauded of more.

Dickens

WELL-TO-DO

The well-to-do
The sprucely dressed,
Are rarely "cleaned,"
And seldom "pressed"!

S. S. Biddle

THE WELSH

The older the Welshman, the more madman.

British proverb

THE WHEEL

What a lucky thing the wheel was invented before the automobile; otherwise, can you imagine the awful screeching?

Samuel Hoffenstein

WHEN IN ROME

It is hard to sit in Rome an' fight wi' the Pope.

Scottish proverb

WHISKEY

The guest who has to be drugged with alcohol to make him interesting is hardly worth inviting in the first place.

Dr. Roy L. Smith, Indiana Temperance League

Being moderatelie taken it sloweth age, it strengtheneth youth, it helpeth digestion, it cutteth flegme, it lighteneth the mind, it quickeneth the spirits, it cureth hydropsie, it pounceth the stone, it expelleth gravell, it puffeth away all ventositie, it keepeth the weason from stifling, the stomach from wambling, the heart from swelling, the bellie from writching, the guts from numbling, the hands from shivering and the sinews from shrinking, the veins from crumbling, the bones from aking, and the marrow from soaking.

Holinshed's Chronicle, 1577

JAMES ABBOTT McNEILL WHISTLER

Whistler, with all his faults, was never guilty of writing a line of poetry.

Wilde

THE WHITE HOUSE

The finest prison in the world.

Harry S Truman

WHORES

There are more secret whores than open ones.

Russian proverb

WIDOWHOOD

Is the financial remains of a love affair.

George Jean Nathan

WIDOWS

Are dangerous animals to be at large.

J. W. Stowe

My idea of walking into the jaws of death is to marry some woman who has lost three husbands.

Kin Hubbard

A buxom widow must be either married, buried, or shut up in a convent.

Spanish proverb

He had heard that one is permitted a certain latitude with widows, and went in for the whole 180 degrees.

George Ade

A widow and her money are soon courted.

Anon

The rich widow cries with one eye and rejoices with the other.

Miguel de Cervantes

The rich widow's tears soon dry.

Danish saying

The determination of life insurance salesmen to succeed has made life pretty soft for widows.

William Feather

The comfortable estate of widowhood is the only hope that keeps a wife's spirit up.

John Gay

Be very careful o' vidders all your life.

Dickens

WIFE

Think you, if Laura had been Petrarch's wife,
He would have written sonnets all his life?

Lord Byron

I won't say that a woman cannot have a fancy for her husband —after all, he is a man.

Gerard de Nerval

A wife is somebody who has turned a man-about-town into a mouse-around-the-house.

Anon

His wife is ten years older than he is, and she calls him "Father."

Ed Howe

THE WIND

Never run after your own hat—others will be delighted to do it; why spoil their fun.

Mark Twain

The speed limit for gales is 75 miles. After and above that they are called hurricanes and other names.

Anon, Jr.

WINE

Good wine ruins the purse, and bad wine ruins the stomach.

Anon

To praise, revere, establish and depend;
To welcome home mankind's mysterious friend
Wine, true begetter of all arts that be;
Wine, privilege of the completely free;
Wine, the foundation, wine the sagely strong;
Wine, bright avenger of sly-dealing wrong.

Hilaire Belloc

Wine makes a man better pleased with himself; I do not say that it makes him more pleasing to others.

Samuel Johnson

WINE-TASTING

Get a wineglass that exposes the wine to plenty of air. The more air you can expose wine to, the better you can taste it. And be sure you can get your nose in the glass. That's important because in wine-tasting, the nose does 75 percent of the work. A glass with a 3-inch brim is best for most wines. But if you have a larger than average nose, you'll need a larger than average glass.

Inglenook Winery

WINNERS/LOSERS

The difference between a good winner and a bad loser is about $20 a night.

Carmichael

WINNING

Anybody can win, unless there happens to be a second entry.

George Ade

WINTER

The English winter—ending in July, to recommence in August.

Lord Byron

'Tis a hard winter when one wolf eats another.

Norwegian proverb

WISDOM

Wisdom cries out in the streets, and no man regards it.

Shakespeare

The sublimity of wisdom is to do those things living which are to be desired when dying.

Jeremy Taylor

He swallowed a lot of wisdom, but it seemed as if all of it had gone down the wrong way.

Lichtenberg

Be not wise in thine own eyes!
Solomon the Wise

The wise know too well their weakness to assume infallibility;
and he who knows most, knows best how little he knows.
Thomas Jefferson

Nine-tenths of wisdom is being wise in time.
Theodore Roosevelt

Wisdom is ofttimes nearer when we stoop
Than when we soar.
Wordsworth

Wise men in the world are like timber trees in a hedge, here
and there one.
Proverb

Cunning craft is but the ape of wisdom.
English proverb

The farther he went west, the more convinced he felt that the
wise men came from the east.
Sydney Smith

If things were to be done twice, all would be wise.
Anon

WISE/FOOLS

The wise man knows he knows nothing, the fool thinks he
knows all.
Proverb

The wise man draws more advantage from his enemies than
a fool from his friends.
Proverb

A wise man may look ridiculous in the company of fools.
English proverb

The wise guy is the sucker after all.
Diamond Jim Brady

WISDOM/KNOWLEDGE

Knowledge is proud that he has learn'd so much;
Wisdom is humble that he knows no more.
William Cowper

Knowledge comes by taking things apart. But wisdom comes
by putting things together.
John A. Morrison

WISHES

Would that the Roman people had but one neck!
Caligula

She has buried all her female friends. I wish she would make friends with my wife.

Martial

WISHING

A man will sometimes devote all his life to the development of one part of his body—the wishbone.

Robert Frost

When I wish I was rich, then I know I am ill.

D. H. Lawrence

Many of us spend half our time wishing for things we could have if we didn't spend half our time wishing.

Alexander Woollcott

WIT

Is the power to say what everybody would like to have said, if they had happened to think of it.

Whistler

What a good thing Adam had—when he said a good thing, he knew nobody had said it before.

Mark Twain

Wit in conversation is, in the midwives' phrase, a quick conception and an easy delivery.

Jonathan Swift

Wit ought to be a glorious treat, like caviar; never spread it about like marmalade.

Noel Coward

His wit invites you by his looks to come.
But, when you knock, it never is at home.

William Cowper

Many get the name for being witty, only to lose the credit of being sensible.

Gracian

The greatest advantage I know of being thought a wit by the world is that it gives one the greater freedom of playing the fool.

Jonathan Swift

Nothing sharpens the wits like promiscuous flirtation.

George Moore

We grant, altho' he had much wit,
He was very shy of using it.

Samuel Butler (I)

319

WIVES

A lazy wife is one who thinks her work was done when she swept down the aisle.

Anon

All are good maids, but whence come the bad wives?

English proverb

A man is in general better pleased when he has a good dinner upon his table than when his wife talks Greek.

Samuel Johnson

One can always recognize women who trust their husbands; they look so thoroughly unhappy.

Wilde

You may beat the devil into your wife, but you'll never bang him out again.

Anon Scotsman

A dead wife under the table is the best goods in a man's house.

Jonathan Swift

WITCHES

What are these
So wither'd, and so wild in their attire,
That look not like th' inhabitants o' th' earth,
And yet are on't!

Shakespeare

WOE-BEGONE

The nature of bad news infects the teller.

Shakespeare

WOMAN

What is swifter than smoke
Unless it be the blazing flame?
What swifter than the flame? The wind;
Swifter than the wind? Woman;
What swifter? Nothing, she outruns
the wind, smoke, or flame.

Theodore Agrippa D'Augigne

Woman is a necessary evil, a natural temptation, adorable calamity, a domestic peril, a deadly fascination, and a painted ill.

Chrysostum

O woman! lovely woman! nature made thee
To temper man; we had been brutes with you.
Angels are painted fair, to look like you:

There's in you all that we believe of heaven;
Amazing brightness, purity, and truth,
Eternal joy, and everlasting love.

Thomas Otway

The great question that has never been answered, and which
I have not yet been able to answer despite my thirty years of
research into the feminine soul, is: What does a woman want?

Freud

The fundamental fault of the female character is that it has
no sense of justice.

Schopenhauer

When a woman becomes a scholar there is usually something
wrong with her sexual organs.

Nietzsche

Woman inspires us to great things, and prevents us from
achieving them.

Dumas

A very little wit is valued in a woman, as we are pleased with
a few words spoken plain by a parrot.

Jonathan Swift

A mill, a clock, and a woman always want mending.

English proverb

I expect that Woman will be the last thing civilised by Man.

George Meredith

Woman has no more been domesticated than the cat.

LLL

A woman, especially if she have the misfortune of knowing
anything, should conceal it as well as she can.

Jane Austen

But—oh! ye lords of ladies intellectual!
Inform us truly, have they not hen-pecked you all?

Lord Byron (Don Juan)

A woman's mind is like spring weather.

Japanese proverb

You can never trust a woman; she may be true to you.

Douglas Ainslee

There are no ugly women; there are only women who do not
know how to look pretty.

La Bruyère

An intelligent woman is a woman with whom we can be as
stupid as we like.

Paul Valery

A woman's strength is in her tongue.

English proverb

Silence is a fine jewel for a woman, but it's little worn.

Proverb

Time and tide wait for no man, but time always stands still for a woman of thirty.

Robert Frost

The years that a woman subtracts from her age are not lost. They are added to other women's.

Diane de Poitiers

A woman that loves to be at the window, is like a bunch of grapes on the highway.

English saying

In order to avoid being called a flirt, she always yielded easily.

Talleyrand

When a woman is speaking to you, listen to what she says with her eyes.

Victor Hugo

Every woman is wrong until she cries, and then she is right, instantly.

Thomas Halliburton

A little woman is a dangerous thing.

Anon

A woman is the only thing I am afraid of that I know will not hurt me.

Abraham Lincoln

With time and exposure to light, the skin loses its tensile strength—like an old worn girdle. No amount of massage has ever been shown to restore an old, old girdle.

Dr. Marjorie F. Bauer

There are some meannesses which are too mean even for man —woman, lovely woman alone, can venture to commit them.

Thackeray

A woman forgives only when she is in the wrong.

Arsene Houssaye

The great trick with a woman is to get rid of her while she thinks she's getting rid of you.

Sören Kierkegaard

Few virtuous women do not weary of being so.

La Rochefoucauld

Any woman in the world, even a nun, would rather lose her virtue than her reputation.

Lionel Strachey

I wish Adam had died with all his ribs in his body.

Dion Boucicault

You see, dear, it is not true that woman was made from man's rib; she was really made from his funny bone.

Sir James Barrie

There are moments when women would rather be treated a little roughly than with too much consideration; men are more often defeated because of their own clumsiness than because of a woman's virtue.

Ninon de Lenclos

A woman's place is in the wrong.

Mrs. E. Vanables

One woman's poise is another woman's poison.

Katharine Brush

Call your husband cuckold in jest, and he'll never suspect you.

Englishwoman's saying

He is a fool who thinks by force or skill
To turn the current of a woman's will.

Sir Samuel Tuke

The females of all species are most dangerous when they appear to retreat.

Don Marquis

Look at a woman at night, from afar, or under an umbrella.

Japanese proverb

The way to fight a woman is with your hat—grab it and run.

John Barrymore

Being a woman is a terribly difficult trade, since it consists principally of dealing with men.

Joseph Conrad

When a female says she won't be a minute, she's usually right.

Dan Bennett

When a woman is wearing shorts her charms are enlarged without being enhanced.

Beverley Nichols

WOMAN/BEAUTY

A beautiful woman should break her mirror early.

Gracian

WOMAN/MAN

Woman gives herself as a prize to the weak and as a prop to the strong, and no man ever has what he should.

Cesare Pavese

It's the woman who chooses the man who will choose her.
Paul Geraldy

'Tis strange what a man may do, and a woman yet think him an angel.
Thackeray

No self-made man ever did such a good job that some woman didn't want to make a few alterations.
Kin Hubbard

For a woman the first kiss is the end of the beginning, for a man it is the beginning of the end.
Helen Rowland

A clever, ugly man every now and then is successful with the ladies, but a handsome fool is irresistible.
Thackeray

If men knew all that women think, they'd be twenty times more daring.
Alphonse Karr

WOMEN

In days of yore, heaven protected the working girl. Nowadays it takes a union, a wage-hour law, unemployment compensation, social security, health insurance and a pension plan.
Anon

Women do not have friends—they only have rivals.
Edmond Gondinet

There is nothing which more disunites two women than to be obliged to make their devotions at the same altar.
Honoré de Balzac

Were kisses all the joy in bed, one woman would another wed.
Shakespeare

One assumes that the shrews, vixens, and harridans of the Age of Dickens represent the price man had to pay for the subjection of woman. Looking back over our history, one is astonished that the agitation for the emancipation and education of women was not led by angry manhood.
R. J. Cruikshank

I think a woman ought to be elected to public office. They have made a mess of things raising so many sorry men. Either they've got to raise better men or take over the government.
Jerry Carter

They are only children of a larger growth: they have an entertaining tattle and sometimes wit; but for solid reasoning good-sense, I never knew in my life one that had it, or who reasoned or acted consequentially for four and twenty hours together.

Lord Chesterfield

There is a tide in the affairs of women which, taken at the flood, leads—God knows where.

Lord Byron

Women have a wonderful sense of right and wrong, but little sense of right and left.

Don Herold

I will not say that women have no character; rather, they have a new one every day.

Heinrich Heine

For a man to pretend to understand women is bad manners; for him really to understand them is bad morals.

Henry James

The silliest woman can manage a clever man, but it needs a very clever woman to manage a fool.

Kipling

Women are a dime a dozen . . . but it's when you cut the number down to one that it starts costing.

John Steinbeck

Faithful women are all alike, they think only of their fidelity, never of their husbands.

Jean Giraudoux

Not all women give most of their waking thoughts to the problem of pleasing men. Some are married.

Emma Lee

Brigands demand your money or your life; women require both.

Samuel Butler (II)

Women in mischief are wiser than men.

English proverb

Of all the plagues with which the world is curst,
Of every ill, a woman is the worst.

George Granville

One tongue is enough for two women.

Arabic proverb

God created woman only to tame man.

Voltaire

Women are timid, and 'tis well they are—else there would be no dealing with them.

Laurence Sterne

I never knew but one woman who would not take gold—and she took diamonds.

Horace Walpole

Whether they give or refuse, women are glad to have been asked.

Ovid

About women's age, all I know is what my daddy told me: If she looks old, she's old; if she looks young, she's young; if she looks back, follow her.

Bob Hope

There are three classes of elderly women: first, that dear old soul; second, that old woman; third, that old witch.

Coleridge

The only things worse than a girl in a Mini/With toothpick shafts far too skinny/Are the ones all over town/With piano legs, put on upside down.

LLL

The great tactic of women is to make you believe they love when they don't love and when they love, to hide it.

Jean Cocteau

Women have less heat because they have more humidity.

Guillaume Bouchet

From the day on which she weighs 140, the chief excitement of a woman's life consists in spotting women who are fatter than she is.

Helen Rowland

I'm not denying that women are foolish; God Almighty made them to match the men.

George Eliot

WOMEN AND ART

A woman is fascinated not by art, but by the noise made by those who are in the art field.

Chekhov

WOMEN'S CLUBS

My advice to the women's clubs of America is to raise more hell and fewer dahlias.

William Allen White

WOMEN, BY DIOR

Women are most fascinating between the ages of thirty-five and forty, after they have won a few races and know how to

326

pace themselves. Since few women ever pass forty, maximum fascination can continue indefinitely.

Christian Dior

WOMEN DRIVERS

Women's girdles are a driving safety hazard. A well-encased woman driver tends to squirm, which takes her attention away from her driving, and fights back against the garter pull, pushing down with her accelerator foot.

Canadian survey

There is no foundation for these statements.

Girdle Manufacturers

WOMEN AND HELL

When a man takes a wife, he ceases to dread Hell.

Romanian proverb

WOMEN AND HORSES

In buying horses and in taking a wife,
Shut your eyes tight and commend yourself to God.

Tuscan proverb

WOMEN'S LIB

A lot of dame foolishness.

Anon male

Six loud ladies in New York yelling and getting on the cover of *Time* Magazine. The rest of the country simply isn't interested.

Joan Rivers

Equality of the sexes is a slogan invented by women to achieve the subjugation of men.

Anon man

Women do not find it difficult nowadays to behave like men, but they often find it extremely difficult to behave like gentlemen.

Compton Mackenzie

What is . . . responsible . . . for the vanishing of "old-fashioned love" and permanent marriage is the masculinization of women—and the accompanying effeminization of men. This Maleizing of women has been the most significant event to happen in my time, one that more than all our other "revolutions" has changed the vital qualities of our living. Yet it appears to have attracted hardly a commentator. It is somewhat as if the Japs had landed in California and captured the U.S.A. unnoticed.

Ben Hecht

I say no one should be denied equal rights because of the shape of their skin.

Pat Paulsen

Women are no longer satisfied with having the last word. Now they want to add Lib.

Lorraine Cowin

I never think of Hamlet as a man. I think of the character as a tortured, humiliated, agonized soul. A human being who plays every stop on the emotional pipe. I am being criticized for taking this role, but I don't care a damn about that. Why shouldn't a woman play it?

Dame Judith Anderson

WOMEN/MEN

There are two things a real man likes—danger and play; and he likes woman because she is the most dangerous of playthings.

Nietzsche

WOMAN'S VOICE

Her voice was ever soft,
Gentle, and low, an excellent thing in women.

Shakespeare

WOMEN, WINE, AND SONG

Who loves not women, wine, and song remains a fool his whole life long.

Martin Luther

WORDS

I am not yet so lost in lexicography as to forget that words are the daughters of earth, and that things are the sons of heaven.

Samuel Johnson

Words signify man's refusal to accept the world as it is.

Walter Kaufmann

Words are not crystal, transparent, and unchanged; they are the skin of living thoughts, and may vary greatly in color and content according to the circumstances and time in which they are used.

Oliver Wendell Holmes

It is a little hard to believe but the *Oxford Dictionary* carries 14,070 different definitions for the 500 most used words in English. This is an average of 28 separate definitions per word.

John O'Hayre

A cluster of buildings is a complex. A psychological fixation is likewise a complex. Thus an architect who insists on designing nothing but industrial complexes can be said to have a complex complex.

Complex also means complicated. So, if the architect's problem is complicated by other factors as well, he has a complex complex complex.

All of which proves that the more complex our civilization becomes, the more versatile each word must be.

Anon

Actions lie louder than words.

Carolyn Wells

WORK

Work is not a curse, it is the prerogative of intelligence, the only means to manhood, and the measure of civilization. Savages do not work.

Calvin Coolidge

Half a loaf is better than no free time at all.

J. D. Ward

It's always been and always will be the same in the world: The horse does the work and the coachman is tipped.

Anon

One chops the wood, the other does the grunting.

Yiddish proverb

I learned to work mornings, when I could skim off the cream of the day and use the rest for cheese-making.

Goethe

THE WORLD

In Hollywood, they bring you ice-cold Coke to show you're a regular guy. In England they bring you milky tea to show you're one of the chaps. In France, it's champagne if you're really *sympathique*. But in Italy they bring you nothing— they are too busy kissing your arms.

Gina Lollobrigida

Up until recent months I had always thought I'd fall to pieces before the world did, but it's beginning to look as if it may be a dead heat.

Anon

The price of an affluent society may be that by the time one is well enough off to turn the dirty work over to someone else, there will be no one willing to do it.

W. Willard Wirtz

It takes time to ruin a world, but time is all it takes.

Fontenelle

We treat this world of ours as if we had a spare in the trunk.

Al Bernstein

If I were running the world I would have it rain only between 2 and 5 A.M.—anyone who was out then ought to get wet.

William Phelps

The world is composed of takers and givers. The takers may eat better, but the givers sleep better.

Byron Frederick

The world is a net; the more we stir in it, the more we are entangled.

Anon

What is wicked is to shock the world; to sin in private is not to sin.

Molière

The trouble with the world is that the stupid are cocksure and the intelligent full of doubt.

Bertrand Russell

Half the world is composed of people who have something to say and can't, and the other half who have nothing to say and keep on saying it.

Robert Frost

Don't believe the world owes you a living; the world owes you nothing—it was here first.

Robert J. Burdette

The course of true anything never does run smooth.

Samuel Butler (II)

Men who pass most comfortably through the world are those who possess good digestions and hard hearts.

Harriet Martineau

When we are born, we cry that we are come
To this great stage of fools.

Shakespeare

The world is a stage, but the play is badly cast.

Wilde

All the world's a stage and most of us are desperately under-rehearsed.

Sean O'Casey

The world is moving so fast these days that the man who says it can't be done is generally interrupted by someone doing it.

Elbert Hubbard, c. 1900

330

When there is more pleasure than pain the world perversely begins to ignore the pleasure and seek the lost pain.

LLL

THE WORLD AND LITERATURE

There are books in which the footnotes, or the comments scrawled by some reader's hand in the margin, are more interesting than the text. The world is one of these books.

Santayana

WORLD RELATIONS

The world situation is so mixed up because the wolves continue to ask for guarantees against attacks by the lambs.

Celal Nasri

WORLD THREAT

Two dangers constantly threaten the world: order and disorder.

Paul Valery

WORRY

Worry affects circulation, the heart and the glands, the whole nervous system, and profoundly affects the heart. I have never known a man who died from overwork, but many who died from doubt.

Dr. Charles Mayo

The reason why worry kills more people than work is that more people worry than work.

Robert Frost

If you want to test your memory, try to remember what you were worrying about a year ago today.

Leonard Thomas

Wear your worries like a loose garment.

Anon

If you must worry, don't worry out loud. It wastes the time of others as well as your own.

Arnold H. Glasow

Comedian Jerry Lewis was advised by his doctor, "Don't worry." Jerry countered, "How do you don't?"

Bob Hansen

WRESTLING

He must have iron nails that scratcheth with a bear.

WRINKLES

Wrinkles should merely indicate where smiles have been.

Mark Twain

An old wrinkle never wears out.

English proverb

WRITERS

A writer is a person who can't resist raping an innocent piece of paper.

Anon

Many a writer seems to think he is never profound except when he can't understand his own meaning.

George D. Prentice

How these authors magnify their office! One dishonest plumber does more harm than a hundred poetasters.

Augustine Birrell

A man may write himself out of reputation when nobody else can do it.

Thomas Paine

A writer never has a vacation. For a writer life consists of either writing or thinking about writing.

Eugene Ionesco

He was an author whose works were so little known as to be almost confidential.

Stanley Walker

God deliver me from a man of one book.

English proverb

An author who speaks about his own books is almost as bad as a mother who talks about her own children.

Benjamin Disraeli

The author must keep his mouth shut when his work starts to speak.

Nietzsche

A writer is rarely so well inspired as when he talks about himself.

Anatole France

The *historian*, essentially, wants more documents than he can really use; the *dramatist* only wants more liberties than he can really take.

Henry James

A man sometimes does not recognize as his own what he has written as a poet.

Victor Hugo

Write sixteen pages, you are a pamphleteer, and may find yourself in prison. . . . Write sixteen hundred, and you will be presented to the king.

Paul-Louis Courier

If you give me six lines written by the most honest man, I will find something in them to hang him.

Duke of Richelieu

In Russia you can't get in the writers' guild until you turn in a manuscript—and two other writers.

Don Rickles' writers

Someone said: "The dead writers are remote from us because we *know* so much more than they did." Precisely, and they are that which we know.

T. S. Eliot

Only a mediocre writer is always at his best.

Somerset Maugham

If you want to get rich from writing, write the sort of thing that's read by persons who move their lips when they're reading to themselves.

Don Marquis

I'm a Hollywood writer; so I put on a sports jacket and take off my brain.

Ben Hecht

God have mercy on the sinner
Who must write without a dinner
  No gravy and no grub,
  No pewter and no pub,
  No belly and no bowels,
Only consonants and vowels.

J. C. Ransom

No man but a blockhead ever wrote except for money.

Samuel Johnson

WRITING

All writing is a form of prayer.

John Keats

Avoid clichés like the plague.

Anon

He who has a pen has war.

Voltaire

Writing is a coy game you play with your unconscious.

Thornton Wilder

What is written without effort is in general read without pleasure.

Samuel Johnson

I hate to hunt down a tired metaphor.

Lord Byron

Satire lies about literary men while they live, and eulogy lies about them when they die.

Voltaire

If you don't write it, you'll not have to retract it.

Anon

Do not on any account attempt to write on both sides of the paper at once.

Walter Seller

WRONG

I am not afraid of a knave. I am not afraid of a rascal. I am afraid of a strong man who is wrong, and whose wrong thinking can be impressed upon other persons by his own force of character and force of speech.

Woodrow Wilson

It takes less time to do a thing right than to explain why you did it wrong.

Longfellow

XANTHIPPE

Socrates' wife was the first hippe xant,
A scold given to rage and rave and rant.
Soc couldn't arrange the loss of her,
So he became a philosopher.

LLL

XERES

Is the former name of Jerez, which we pronounce "sherry,"
A wine which, if we drink enough of, makes us merry.

LLL

XEROX

To double your salary, Xerox your paycheck.

Pat O'Haire

XMAS

If Christmas is to be spelt that way, why not a gathering of Xians for a xening of a baby named Xopher at Xchurch in Xiana?

Robin Sokal

X RAY

A device which enables us to see how the bones in the back room are doing.

Don Quinn

XYLOPHONE

The xylophone is an instrument for transforming timber into timbre.

LLL

YEARS

The years, like great black oxen, tread the world,
And God, the herdsman, goads them on behind,
And I am broken by their passing feet

W. B. Yeats

YOUNG/OLD

All the world's a mass of folly,
Youth is gay, age melancholy:
Youth is spending, age is thrifty,
Mad at twenty, cold at fifty;
Man is nought but folly's slave,
From the cradle to the grave.

W. H. Ireland

YOUTH

My salad days,
When I was green in judgment.

Shakespeare

What is more enchanting than the voices of young people when you can't hear what they say?

Logan P. Smith

A youth with his first cigar makes himself sick; a youth with his first girl makes other people sick.

Mary Little

Impatience and not inexperience is the greatest handicap of youth.

Arnold H. Glasgow

Young people are always more given to admiring what is gigantic than what is reasonable.

Eugene Delacroix

Remember! we're none of us infallible—not even the youngest among us.

W. H. Thompson, Master of Trinity College, Cambridge

In his youth, everybody believes that the world began to exist only when he was born, and that everything really exists only for his sake.

Goethe

For God's sake give me the young man who has brains enough to make a fool of himself.

R. L. Stevenson

Overeducation is the curse of today's youth.

LLL

Have you noticed it's no longer necessary to encourage young people to set the world on fire?

Arnold H. Glasgow

If Booth Tarkington were to write *Seventeen* today, he'd have to call it *Twelve*.

Anon teacher

Ask the young: they know everything!

Joseph Joubert

Youth is wholly experimental.

Robert Louis Stevenson

Young people suffer less from their own mistakes than from older people's wisdom.

Denis Diderot

It is better to waste one's youth than to do nothing with it at all.

Georges Courteline

I gave my kid an ultimatum: Mow the lawn or cut your hair.

Robert Sylvester

You know, I'm starting to wonder what my folks were up to at my age that makes them so doggoned suspicious of me all the time!

Margaret Blair

Time is the rider that breaks youth.

Proverb

When I was a boy with never a crack in my heart....
William Butler Yeats

YOUTH/AGE

The young man is deliberately odd and prides himself on it; the old man is unintentionally so, and it mortifies him.
Jean Paul Richter

Youth thinks intelligence a good substitute for experience, and his elders think experience a substitute for intelligence.
Lyman Bryson

The young have aspirations that never come to pass, the old have reminiscences of what never happened.
Saki

In youth we run into difficulties, in old age difficulties run into us.
Josh Billings

The old forget. The young don't know.
Japanese proverb

We are ever young enough to sin; never old enough to repent.
Proverb

YOUTHFUL CONFIDENCE

Don't let young people confide in you their aspirations; when they drop them, they will drop you.
Logan P. Smith

ZEALOT

Zeal without knowledge is fire without light.
English proverb

ZEBRA

Is twenty-six sizes larger than an abra.
Louise Topping

ZOO

The camel's hump is an ugly lump
Which well you may see at the Zoo;
But uglier yet is the hump we get
From having too little to do.
Rudyard Kipling

Zoos are animal slums.

Desmond Morris

Wild animals can survive and even multiply in city zoos, but at the cost of losing the physical and behavioral splendor they possess in their natural habitat.

René Dubos

ZOOLOGY

The rabbit has a charming face;
Its private life is a disgrace.

Anon

The turtle lives 'twixt plated decks
Which practically conceals its sex.
I think it clever of the turtle
In such a fix to be so fertile.

Ogden Nash

THE END

Our revels now are ended. These our actors,
As I foretold you, were all spirits, and
Are melted into air, into thin air:
And, like the baseless fabric of this vision,
The cloud-capp'd towers, the gorgeous palaces,
The solemn temples, the great globe itself,
Yea, all which it inherit, shall dissolve
And, like this insubstantial pageant faded,
Leave not a rack behind. We are such stuff
As dreams are made on ; and our little life
Is rounded with a sleep.

Shakespeare

INDEX

Get a thorough insight into the Index, by which the whole book is governed and turned, like fishes by the tail. For to enter the palace of Learning at the great gate, requires an expense of time and forms; therefore men of much haste and little ceremony are content to get in by the back-door.

Jonathan Swift

As this book is arranged alphabetically, it has no index.

LLL